In Pursuit of the Public Good

In Pursuit of the Public Good

Essays in Honour of Allan J. MacEachen

Edited by

TOM KENT

McGill-Queen's University Press
Montreal & Kingston · London · Buffalo

© McGill-Queen's University Press 1997
ISBN 0-7735-1684-0

Legal deposit third quarter 1997
Bibliothèque nationale du Québec

Printed in Canada on acid-free paper

McGill-Queen's University Press is grateful to the
Canada Council for support of its publishing
program.

Canadian Cataloguing in Publication Data

Main entry under title:
    In pursuit of the public good: essays in honour of
    Allan J. MacEachen
    ISBN 0-7735-1684-0
    1. Canada – Politics and government – 1963-1984.
    2. Canada – Politics and government – 1984-1993.
    3. Canada – Politics and government – 1993-
    4. MacEachen, Allan J., 1921-   I. Kent, Tom, 1922-
    II. MacEachen, Allan J., 1921-
    H97.I5 1997   971.064   C97-900379-2

This book was typeset by Typo Litho Composition Inc.
in 10/12 Palatino.

Contents

Debating the Public Good, with
Afterthoughts / 156
TOM KENT

Foreword

"An intellectual conference that wrestles with some of the great challenges facing government and society today is a most fitting way to pay tribute to a man who has been so central to the pursuit of the public good in Canada for so many years." In these words Marc Lalonde, the conference chair, expressed the spirit of the gathering at St Francis Xavier University that, on 4–6 July 1996, marked the seventy-fifth birthday, and therewith the retirement from the Senate, of Allan J. MacEachen.

Most of the content of this book is derived from the conference papers and discussions. There are two supplements. In the opening chapter, Allan MacEachen provides his own reflections on practice and purpose in public affairs; and, in the "Afterthoughts" section of the final chapter, I offer some further comments.

The purpose throughout is to look forward. The contributors examine the experience of the past forty years as a context for policies needed now. To do so is to confront a paradox: we have lately been moving, in pursuit of the public good as many people see it, in a direction very different from that taken by Allan MacEachen and others of his generation. In a democracy, our agent for our public good is government; what, else, is democracy? But discussion of the public good today must begin with recognition that, for a decade and more, governments almost everywhere have been in retreat.

Not, of course, in all respects: complex technologies and the burgeoning of cities compel even the most laissez faire governments to intensify some forms of regulation and augment some services. But in the areas where the expansion of public responsibilities was the characteristic of the first twenty or more postwar years – economic management for full employment, social programs to enhance security and lessen inequalities, public enterprise where it seemed required for public goods – the more recent years have been ones of withdrawal, retrenchment, lowered ambitions, and weakening performance.

Retreat from full employment and social security? Many heroes turn in their graves, many survivors of past struggles shudder. But the central questions underlying this volume are whether retreat has been necessary; whether the public good will be enhanced by continuing to retreat. Or whether, on the contrary, that trend is not destiny but is the consequence of policy mistakes that were and are avoidable; whether the future public good will be best served by measures that, while responding to changing circumstances, have the same objectives as those of the early postwar years.

The issues are fundamental but the discussion here is moderate in tone. Far from any outright opposition to the welfare state, there is general agreement that the age of the visible hand, in Michael Bliss's phrase, was something of a golden age, when the well-being of citizens was both heightened and broadened to a greater extent than in any previous generation. Equally, however, it is accepted that circumstances have changed; those who do not accept retreat as necessary are ready to recognize that continued progress has called, and will call, for shifts in both priorities and mechanisms.

Discussion within the broad centre of political opinion, rather than its extremes, nevertheless leaves scope for significantly divergent views of the economic and social policies that will best respond to the problems now confronting us. Readers will find a wide range of analysis and opinion, not only in the essays but also in the shorter contributions (by Banting, Van Loon, Osberg, and Nicholson) that are contained in the final chapter, along with some of the comments from the floor of the Antigonish conference.

In Canada it is not sufficient to define the role of government; the question then becomes, in many areas of public action, which government? The relative roles of Ottawa and the provinces, and how they can collaborate in those roles, are questions implicit in much of the discussion and explicit in, particularly, the Courchene essay and the Afterthoughts section.

The concern to which this issue leads is brought out in the Carty essay and in the related contributions (again contained in the final chapter) by Stewart, Murray, and Bickerton. Our political system is in disarray. The choice before the voters is not a consistent national choice; it is effectively between different parties in different regions. In these circumstances, there is little pressure on politicians to undertake any of the reforms – in the electoral system, in their own structures and practices – that would make political parties more reliable instruments for the democratic formulation and achievement of the public good. It may well be that this institutional atrophy, not globalisation or debt or even social polarization, is the greatest and most intransigent of the problems that we take into the twenty-first century.

Tom Kent

Allan J. MacEachen

The Honourable Allan J. MacEachen, PC, MA, LLD, LittD, was born in Inverness, Cape Breton, on 6 July 1921. He was educated at St Francis Xavier University (BA, 1944), the University of Toronto (Political Economy, MA 1946), the University of Chicago (Economics, 1948), and the Massachusetts Institute of Technology (Department of Economics and Social Science, 1951–3). Numerous honourary degrees have been conferred on him. From 1946, he taught economics at St Francis Xavier and, in 1948, was appointed head of its Department of Economics and Social Sciences.

Allan MacEachen was first elected to the House of Commons for Inverness-Richmond (later Cape Breton-Highlands-Canso) in the general election of 1953. He was reelected in 1957, but defeated in 1958. He then became special assistant and consultant on economic affairs to the leader of the opposition, L.B. Pearson. Reelected to the House of Commons in 1962, he served there continuously for the next twenty-two years. From 1963 to 1984, he was a member of cabinet except during the brief Clark government, 1979–80, when he was deputy leader of the opposition and opposition house leader.

In the cabinet, he held the following posts: Minister of Labour, 1963–5; Minister of National Health and Welfare, 1965–8 (and government house leader, 1967–8); Minister of Manpower and Immigration, 1968–70; President of the Privy Council and government house leader, 1970–4; Secretary of State for External Affairs, 1974–6; President of the Privy Council, 1976–7; Deputy Prime Minister and President of the Privy Council, 1977–9; Deputy Prime Minister and Minister of Finance, 1980–2; Deputy Prime Minister and Secretary of State for External Affairs, 1982–4.

While a Canadian minister, Allan MacEachen served as chair of the IMF Group of Ten, 1980–1; chair of the Interim Committee of the IMF;

chair of the Conference on International Economic Cooperation; and chair of the 1982 ministerial meeting of the GATT.

Allan MacEachen left the House of Commons and was appointed to the Senate in June 1984. He was leader of the government there until October 1984, and from then until 1991 leader of the opposition. His seventy-fifth birthday in 1996 brought retirement from the Senate.

He has been chair of the International Advisory Council of the Bank of Montreal, 1986–91 and a trustee of the Royal Ottawa Health Care Group, 1987–95. In 1993, he was awarded the Order of Merit of the Federal Republic of Germany and, since 1984, has been Canadian chair of the Atlantik-Brücke Annual Symposium (Canada-Germany Conference). He serves on the board of governors of St Francis Xavier University, the North-South Institute, and the board of the International Crisis Group.

Acknowledgments

Editing a book of this kind creates many reasons for gratitude. My thanks are, first, to Allan MacEachen, whose understanding and encouragement were essential and unfailing.

The task would not have been possible for me without the logistical support of the School of Policy Studies of Queen's University. For that I am particularly indebted to Keith Banting, the Director, and to Sharon Alton, whose invaluable role was played with constant efficiency and cheerful patience.

Few editors can have had such cooperative contributors. To Tom Courchene, I am especially grateful for perceptive comments that improved the Afterthoughts section, given with the helpfulness for which he somehow always makes time.

My indebtedness extends to all who made the MacEachen conference so successful. Teresa MacNeil particularly supported the concept of this book and helped to bring it to reality by subsequently spending valuable time listening to the tapes of the discussions. Martin MacKinnon, treasurer for the conference, helped in ways that considerably accelerated the book's preparation.

I warmly thank mutual friends of Allan MacEachen and myself, most particularly Tom Axworthy, for their encouragement.

McGill-Queen's University Press undertook the publication with their characteristic sympathy. I appreciate the work of all involved, including the anonymous readers who made some helpful suggestions about the typescript. Don Akenson gave welcome editorial advice. Above all, I thank Philip Cercone, Executive Director and Editor of the press.

Tom Kent

In Pursuit of the Public Good

All Those Years: Practice and Purpose in Politics

ALLAN J. MacEACHEN

The ways to get things done in government are not unique. In other organizations too, alliances have to be made, compromises worked out.
But the circumstances of political practice are considerably different
from those of other activities, not least because of the continual scrutiny that is the essence of parliamentary democracy. Often, the link between purpose and practice in government is far from agreed among
political colleagues. Theoretically, a government comes to office with a
mandate based on the party's election platform. In practice, the mandate is open to very varied interpretations by MPs and ministers,
whose purposes in politics are drawn from diverse backgrounds and
who owe their election to greatly diverse constituencies across Canada.

It is hardly surprising, therefore, that political purpose and practice
are not widely understood. My aim here is to try to offer some illumi-
nation from my own experience.

"HOW STRONG WE ARE"

The announcing of my decision not to seek reelection to the House of
Commons in the election of 1984 was surprisingly easy in view of the
lengthy process of consultation and discussion that had gone before. I
made my announcement at a press conference at the Skye Motel in
Port Hastings, NS and then went to Antigonish to unveil a plaque at
the new and relocated National Philatelic Centre. The centre is now a
money-making institution and a model of service and efficiency. But
its relocation to Antigonish from Ottawa, as part of the government
decentralization program of jobs and services, was resisted by the bureaucracy, to the point of ensuring that notices advising unsuccessful
applicants for the new jobs were delivered on the morning of the election of 4 September 1984.

s timing caused consternation and indignation among disap-
ed applicants who were entitled to believe they were mere
pawns in a power game invisible to them. The project that had been
intended to be a symbol and provider of jobs now mocked the job
seekers. "Look how strong we are," said the bureaucrats. "We are
telling you to stuff it, and we are doing it on election morning." No
doubt these bureaucrats had noted that the program had its detrac-
tors within the government itself and, in view of the way the election
was going, they knew also they might never be called upon to explain
and justify their callous and unfeeling conduct. Following the election, which the Liberals lost, I explained what had happened in Antigonish to a former postmaster general and sought his opinion as to
whether the arrival of these rejection notices on election day was an
unhappy coincidence or deliberately planned. His opinion was that
the timing was deliberate. It confirmed the view that the notices were
a parting shot by officials in the battle to prevent decentralization of
jobs and services from Ottawa.

CHALLENGING THE MANDATE

This incident is recited here to underline that change does not come
easily and that in order to achieve change the policy battle has to be
fought out at many levels. Policy conception is one phase. Final implementation is another. Within a political party, policy development
is a crucial first step. The process is easier to discern in a party in opposition as it lays out its policy objectives in the platform for the election. Elected on its policy platform, a new government may think it is
clear sailing to policy implementation.

No sooner is a new government sworn in, however, than the implementation of its policies is opposed, slowed down, attenuated by a
possible combination of new ministers and a bureaucracy skilled at
bringing forward hitherto unarticulated objections. No party is
monolithic in ideology. Hence a new minister who has never entered
the debate at an earlier stage will be inclined to join like-minded officials and like-minded colleagues to put a new and different face on a
policy that had passed the party test (it made the platform) and the
electoral test (the election was won.) It is to me still a surprising aspect of politics that policies which have been put in the window during a campaign and have been approved in the preelection process of
building the platform can be laid waste by new players who appear
on the field late in the game. These new players now rely on power
and position to advance ideas which had been excluded from previous political discussion. They had not been advanced previously,

clearly incapable of surviving any preelection political test. Power squashes principle and previous commitments. Power becomes the ally of the hidden agenda.

The scenario I have described happens. It does not always happen. It need not happen as frequently as I have seen it happen. It could be resisted by insisting more forcibly on the legitimacy of the mandate – that is, the party platform and the election result – in determining public policy. The first force which works against the supremacy of the mandate is the broad authority assumed by government, which is held to be of a higher order of legitimacy than any particular policy in the mandate. "We have been given the power to govern for the good of the country as we see it now." The second force is the gradual erosion of political resolve as the complexities of policy are explained by the bureaucracy and as ministers are systematically inducted into the sacred mysteries of government. It is within this not so clearly defined and frequently shifting environment that the two legitimacies struggle for ascendancy. The art of government manifests itself most clearly when satisfactory compromises are worked out. Getting along with the bureaucracy does not mean becoming its puppet. In its most rewarding and constructive form it impels ministers to understand clearly the specific role of the bureaucrat and to extend generously the respect and support that role demands in order to discharge its responsibilities. However, there is a line in the sand.

ROADBLOCKS

Decentralization was a settled policy of the government reelected in 1974. To declare the policy was much easier than to decide what programs from which departments were to be relocated. It was not easy to make progress in the face of opposition from the public service and Ottawa area MPs. Eventually projects were selected, including the relocation of the Philatelic Centre. This proposal was submitted to Treasury Board on 1 March 1977, approved on 5 May 1977, and announced five months later on 3 October 1977. In retrospect, the gap in time from submission to announcement was a signal of trouble ahead. The public was told that the relocation would be in place by 1979. It was modest in employment impact and well suited to the requirements and life style of the university town of Antigonish. There was also modest jubilation that this project, as well as several others, was coming to Nova Scotia. Jubilation was overtaken by frustration at delays in moving to the implementation stage. Delay also occurred from local concerns about site and land acquisition. The process was interrupted, and then put in jeopardy, by the election of the Clark government, which cancelled the relocation in July 1979.

A new phase was reached with the defeat of the Clark government and the return of the Trudeau government. We then looked to an early implementation of the program. In the meantime, however, the opponents of this policy had been given an opportunity to regroup. The scuttling of the project by the Clark government was an important gain for its opponents and one not readily relinquished. Before the 1980 election, assurances were sought directly from Mr Trudeau that the program would go ahead following the election. Despite his support and the successful outcome of the election, the program remained under siege. The endless reappraisals and delays help to explain why the unveiling of the plaque came almost four years after Mr Trudeau's positive assurances.

When I walk by the splendid home of the Philatelic Centre, as I do regularly when in Antigonish, I reframe in my mind the issues which make the project worth mentioning many years later. First, it was a commitment to the citizens of the community which I took more seriously than others. Second, decentralization was a litmus test of the government's commitment to regional development. Third, it was a measure of the commitment of the government to job creation. These considerations taken together, particularly in moments of frustration brought on by seemingly endless stalling tactics, were enough for any minister to consider calling it a day.

LEARNING FROM CONSTITUENTS

As I campaigned in the election of 1953, fresh from a two-year immersion in economics at graduate school, I was filled, or so I thought, with the latest in the subject and felt obliged to show my mastery of the material to my electors, whom I knew respected knowledge. If I showed them I had knowledge, I reasoned, they were likely to accept me as their MP. Eventually I learned that this might not be the right approach. The people, I came to understand, wanted to hear from me, not what I knew. They wanted to know what I had to offer; what I could do to meet their needs for better incomes, employment opportunities, and health and social services. My understanding of this reality deepened as my career in politics was extended. Also, I learned that an important element in the relationship between the elected person and the electors was trust, which could be gradually and surely built up, in part, by the tedious day-to-day work of representing individual and group needs. Once this trust is built up, it will not be first broken by electors.

Citizens do keep under surveillance the conduct of politicians, and more closely when they have placed confidence in their words. This aspect of political life came to the fore in a vivid encounter with a female elector. The encounter involved Mr Trudeau. In the 1968 election he talked about the Just Society. People had such confidence in his charisma that they expected it to be ushered in immediately. Naturally, they raised the matter in the 1972 election.

During that campaign, I was canvassing in the district of Little Narrows and entered a home just as the lady of the house, all dressed up, with a handbag in her hand, was leaving to attend a church meeting. However, she delayed her departure and asked us to sit down. In this district, people were attached to the church and religion. The lady of the house began the conversation by saying: "We have always been Liberals in this house. Not that we think we are any better than others. It just suits us to be Liberals."

It was a singular moment for me to hear any Liberal make such an admission. Then she went on: "Your Prime Minister is causing me great difficulty." Mr Trudeau had now become my Prime Minister. She opened her handbag and removed a press clipping reporting on a meeting in Ontario.

"It says here that when Mr Trudeau was heckled and asked about the Just Society, he replied, 'Ask Jesus Christ, he promised it before I did.'" She folded the paper and put it away, saying, "Mr MacEachen, that is close to blasphemy."

BREAD ON THE TABLE

Ottawa is never a primary source of inspiration and political nourishment. Those essential nutrients of political longevity came from other, varied and, at times, unexpected sources. Shortly after deciding not to seek reelection, I travelled in Inverness County to touch base with my constituents and listen to comments. As I stood around in the cooperative store in Margaree Forks, a constituent, who made his living on the land and in the forest, said to me, "I hear you are not running again. You certainly kept bread on the table here in the north all those years." As a compliment it was enormous. As a summation of one's political career from a citizen who made a living the hard way, it was heart-warming. His use of "bread" to identify projects and policies resulting in improved living conditions and services showed imagination and perceptiveness. Though keeping bread on the table as an aim of government has fallen into disfavour, in the mind of my chance conversationalist it was the positive face of government. His appraisal at the end of my service in the House of Commons took me

to its beginnings and why keeping bread on the table, in the
st interpretation of that expression, was the principal reason I
a university teaching post to enter politics.

Though the regular visits I made to the various communities of my
constituency – holding "clinics" – were demanding of energy and
time, they were useful as early warning signals of the issues emerging
in the country. For me they were more than exercises to maintain electoral support. They were my link with reality, a source of motivation,
and an antidote to the perspectives of the bureaucrats and politicians
in Ottawa. Even before I thought of running for elective office, I
sensed the importance of the local community. What is happening locally can be a harbinger of future national undertakings. As a professor at St Francis Xavier, and an activist in the Antigonish Movement, I
took part in one such event in April 1950, when medical care was the
subject of a discussion broadcast from the university auditorium. I
was one of a panel that included the president of the Nova Scotia
Federation of Labour and representatives of the Nova Scotia Medical
Society and the Maritime Hospital Service Association.

Lines were drawn, opinions differed sharply. The audiences in the
auditorium and the community were excited by the prospect of a
people-controlled medical care system. We hit a number of key issues
which, in retrospect, were prophetic. Universal access and comprehensive coverage of services were stressed as elements of the necessary major change in the system of medical care. Neither I nor anyone
in the over-filled auditorium on that Sunday afternoon forty-seven
years ago could have foreseen the role which the youngest member of
the panel would play in the enactment of Canada's Medical Care Act.

The formula for success and longevity in politics involves a relationship with electors based on mutual trust and on a responsiveness
which, for the local community, guarantees that their views be heard
and factored into policy formulation at the highest level.

WORKING WITH CAUCUS

In political life, getting things done involves other factors, including
relationships with cabinet and caucus colleagues. The Canadian Labour Code, for example, was a major happening for members of the
Liberal caucus elected from such industrial cities as Windsor and
Hamilton, where they always had to fend off threats from the left
flank by the NDP. Now they could argue with the evidence to back
them up, that the government which they supported had enacted the
most far-reaching, comprehensive, and progressive provisions in the
field of labour standards ever enacted in Canada by any jurisdiction.

They were entitled to make such a claim because they had a voice in the framing of its provisions through their membership in the caucus group I had established for the purpose of securing their views and later their support. It was a signal success. Those newly elected members who later became ministers, like Herb Grey and John Munro, were able to draw on that experience in outlining what could be achieved within the caucus between ministers and members working together in pursuit of common policy objectives. It was a real lesson to me in welcoming, not resisting, the voice of caucus members in policy formation.

Also important in refining the provisions of the Canada Labour Code was the contribution of ministers like Walter Gordon who, before the election, had worked on the policy proposals which were now making their way through the legislative process. At one cabinet committee meeting, Walter Gordon and I disagreed on the amount at which the mandatory minimum wage should be set. I wanted a higher rate than he, as Minister of Finance, thought was economically justified. Walter Gordon was in support of the Canada Labour Code and its provisions. But on the rate to be set he was adamant. So was I. Then Mr Gordon signalled that we ought to have a private discussion in the corridor to settle our differences. He cautioned about the danger of going too far and asking for too much.

This style of one-on-one conversation was very much Mr Gordon's way. He relied greatly on his undoubted personal charm and had a definite distaste for prolonged debate and argument in meetings. His brother-in-law, Bud Drury, remarked to me, "Walter dislikes arguing in defence of his positions. That makes it difficult."

My political tool box was enhanced by my acquisition of skills and knowledge in a critical aspect of political life: Parliament itself. Inability to operate effectively in the House is still exacting its toll on ministers. I believe that my confidence in the legislative role, when combined with my grounding in social and economic matters, was a valuable combination. Without it, I doubt whether I could have succeeded in getting through Parliament in my first two ministries, Labour and Health and Welfare, such a volume of significant legislation.

PRACTICES OF PARLIAMENT

The acquisition of my skills and knowledge of Parliament was the result of one of those sharp unexpected turns that occur in a political career. In my case, the occasion was joining Mr Pearson's staff following my personal defeat in the election of 1958. The president of

St Francis Xavier had asked me to rejoin the faculty at the university. The prospect of resuming my teaching career was appealing but was put to one side at Mr Pearson's phone call to my parents' home in Inverness, asking me to return to Ottawa to give him a hand in the daunting task that lay ahead of him. I accepted.

Joining Mr Pearson's staff had its own rewards: an inside view of the anxieties of a political leader recovering from defeat and seeking to reestablish his political status, an intimate view of the Liberal party from the leader's perspective, and an inside view of the operation of the House of Commons and the Senate from this preferred vantage point. The day-to-day challenges were more absorbing and valuable than I had expected.

The principal long-term benefit was becoming, through force of circumstances, Mr Pearson's principal adviser on Parliament and especially on the procedures of the House of Commons. These have to be fully understood in carrying out the manoeuvres required of an opposition. Mr Pearson wanted solid advice and expected his staff to anticipate all responses that might flow from any parliamentary initiative he took. He was concerned about Speakers' rulings, and what the government and other political parties might do to frustrate his moves. Hence my spending long hours pouring over the principal authorities on the subject, previous Speakers' rulings in the journals. When I became hopelessly confused in the tangle, the Clerk of the House was superb in making sense of the arcane universe of rules and precedents.

The result was that when I returned to the House in the 1962 election, I was well grounded and could take part in any technical discussion – and some quite political – involving the rules and procedures of Parliament as an institution. When I became a minister in 1963, I was equipped to put through the House unprecedented, controversial, complex, and pioneering legislation:

The Maritime Transportation Unions Trustees Act (1963), which provided for the placing of five maritime transportation unions under the supervision of trustees appointed by the government, was unprecedented. The enactment was intended to promote clean and democratic trade unionism for Canadian seamen, the stabilization of maritime shipping, and the end of the harassment of Canadian vessels in United States ports.

The Canada Labour (Standards) Code (1965) was comprehensive in its enactment of standards in employment within federal jurisdiction for hours of work, minimum wages, and holidays and annual vacations with pay.

The Health Resources Fund (1966) provided for the establishment of a fund to assist provinces in the acquisition, construction, and renovation of health training facilities and research institutions. Projects to be established with the assistance of the fund were to amount to one billion dollars.

The Canada Assistance Plan (1966) established a new and wider definition of need and for the sharing of cost between the federal and provincial governments. The concept was an important step ahead in establishing more acceptable levels of income support and shielding those in need from undue variations in provincial and municipal support.

The Medical Care Act (1966) authorized the payment of contributions by Canada towards the cost of services provided by provinces pursuant to medical care insurance plans. Through this enactment, which laid out the four governing principles of universal coverage, public administration, portability from province to province of insured status, and that insured services be provided under uniform terms and conditions to all residents of a province, Canada's medical care system was brought into being.

An amendment to the Old Age Security Act to provide for a guaranteed income supplement (1966) as a substitute for a flat rate in Old Age Security pensions, was designed to help those most in need and to deploy more effectively limited financial resources. Through this change, an estimated 600,000 Old Age Security pensioners were eligible for an increase in pension of $30 a month and a guaranteed income of $1260 a year.

One cannot overlook the role which actors outside the government can play in the political and legislative process. In the enactment of the trustee legislation, the Canadian Labour Congress played a constructive role at all stages and reflected a considerable level of trust between the labour movement and the government. Consultations were frequent and informal and labour leaders had access to the Prime Minister and ministers and vice versa.

Likewise, the support that can be provided by a career civil service is invaluable. One small but important example took place in connection with the Canada Labour Code. On ships and in the grain elevators, particular and workable regimes had to be devised to meet unique requirements. The skill of the officials in the Department of Labour in devising solutions to these problems was instrumental in inducing acceptance of the provisions and in turning aside criticism which was motivated by resistance in principle to any move of any kind to set standards for working conditions.

CABINET POSTS AND
LEADERSHIP

Another aspect of the political process is illustrated by how I became Minister of Labour and then Minister of National Health and Welfare. In the first case, personal preference prevailed. It was not the post which Mr Pearson asked me to take on in my first conversation with him following the election. His working sheet had me listed to become Minister of Mines and leader of the government in the House of Commons. In asking me to become leader in the House, Mr Pearson was passing over a number of ministers who were senior to me and who may have wanted the job. It was made clear to me by Paul Martin that I ought to back off. "Mike is giving you too much," were his words. The idea was eventually dropped. No doubt my seniors had gotten through to the future Prime Minister. That did not agitate me at all. I was, however, disturbed by the idea of becoming Minister of Mines. I told Mr Pearson that if, as I believed, I was a natural choice to become Minister of Labour, the opposite would apply if I were to become Minister of Mines. Coming as I did from a constituency in Cape Breton, on the doorstep of the Cape Breton coal area, I would be in danger of becoming a single issue minister expected to solve singlehandedly the deep problems of the industry. Mr Pearson saw my unease and told me he would think the matter over. On my next visit, he said to me quite casually, "I've decided to give you the Labour job." It was the decision I had hoped for. Now I had a harmony between past preparation and the requirements of the job.

Visiting for the first time the office of the Minister of Labour in the Confederation Building revealed that Mr King had occupied the same office when he was Minister of Labour. The office still had his desk and the wooden fixture he used to show the day, month, and year. It was still in my office thirty-three years later when I left the Senate.

The request to me to move to National Health and Welfare was for the express purpose of legislating the Medical Care Act. The House of Commons was not the strong suit of the previous minister, Judy LaMarsh.

The toolbox which I mentioned earlier was to come in handy time and time again. As my ministerial future unfolded, it became my duty to serve as leader of the government in the House of Commons in three separate circumstances, each of these in a different Parliament. Two were minority Parliaments. I also served, for a short and action-filled period, as deputy leader of the opposition. The resignation of Mr Trudeau as leader of the Liberal party, the defeat of the

Clark government, the withdrawal of Mr Trudeau's resignation all occurred in rapid succession. At critical moments, I was the de facto leader of our group in the House of Commons. Later, my years as leader of the opposition in the Senate were, at times, equally action filled.

The necessity and value of different skills were apparent in leading individuals and groups through a process of discussion to conclusions acceptable to all participants. The flip side is the endurance of prolonged frustration, at times, in the task of listening to all, coping with recalcitrant partners, taking into account, and finally reconciling, all points of view. A balance is required between authoritarianism and permissiveness. One never fully knows when one succeeds at the task. Failure is apparent when meetings drag on and, at a certain point, everybody knows they are getting nowhere. Usually it is a failure at the top.

INTERNATIONAL DEVELOPMENT

I participated in a leadership role in such processes regularly as a minister, but the three cases I single out all relate to foreign policy, especially for international development. They illustrate a much neglected and important aspect of ministerial and political practice.

Canadian development policy was reviewed in house, for the purpose of reconciling overall foreign policy objectives and the specific objectives of Canada's International Development Agency (CIDA). Michel Dupuy represented External Affairs and Paul Gerin Lajoie as president represented CIDA. They differed in style and perspective. The perspective of Mr Gerin Lajoie on the process and the weight he expected to have on the outcome were influenced by his background as Minister of Education and as a prominent political figure in his native province of Quebec. It was my task to recognize that I was not dealing with a career official accustomed to the culture of the public service, and, at the same time, ensure that policy decisions were not taken for that reason alone. Carrying out that task required time and occasional firmness. The process finally succeeded.

The resulting policy was unveiled in a speech in New York at the General Assembly of the United Nations. The reaction there was positive and enthusiastic. For the first time I encountered the UN practice of country representatives forming a long line as they waited each for his or her turn to congratulate the speaker. If the impact of the statement were to be measured by the length of the queue, as some Canadian officials believed, then the international impact of the Canadian policy statement so painstakingly put together was strong and positive.

The concept of creating a "New International Economic Order" was the subject of the Conference on International Economic Cooperation convened in Paris under the sponsorship of the then President of France, Giscard D'Estaing. Shifting the debate from the United Nations system to a representative body of limited size was more likely, he reasoned, to produce results. There were twenty-seven participants – nineteen developing countries, and eight developed members including the European Community. Seven of the developing countries were members of OPEC, whereas twelve were oil importing countries. The membership of the conference was selected to be broadly representative of the interests of the world community as a whole, with the exception of eastern Europe and China, which did not participate.

Since my focus is on political practice, on how things do or do not get done, I will set aside the substantive issues under discussion and deal with three aspects of the conference: the organization of the dialogue, the role of ideology, and the opportunity missed.

The dialogue took place at the ministerial level assisted by four commissions – energy, raw materials, development, and financial affairs. They were expected to prepare concrete proposals for ministerial consideration and decision. Usually the foreign ministers of each country were present at the ministerial sessions. Each commission had a minister as chairman. The process had two unique and important features: the dialogue was restricted and issues under review were receiving ministerial attention as required in the international capitals. The groundwork had been carefully laid; interesting proposals were prepared.

However, the ideological attitude and maximalist demands of the Group of 77 developing countries produced a disappointing result. The President of France received both cochairmen in his office at the end of the conference. He expressed his disappointment to my Venezuelan colleague, saying bluntly that the incentive for the western countries to do more could not be revived in the face of the total lack of recognition for the responses which had been made at the conference by the industrialized countries but which had been turned aside by the other participants.

The opportunity missed was the offer made by US Secretary of State, Mr Cyrus Vance, as part of a comprehensive response on the part of the industrialized countries. He proposed the continuation of the forum for an indefinite period in order to maintain work on the issues that had been raised. That, in itself, would have been a major achievement in view of the failure in subsequent periods to continue the process. But the opportunity for a continuing dialogue was rejected, and nothing of a similar magnitude has since occurred. The issues involved in the concept of a new economic order dropped out of the sights of the international community.

In becoming cochair of the joint parliamentary committee reviewing Canada's foreign policy, I confronted once again the many complicated factors involved in carrying such an undertaking to a successful conclusion. It is to be acknowledged that a committee made up of members of the House of Commons in a new Parliament, on the one hand, and members of the Senate on the other, is not necessarily in itself a recipe for success. Members of the House of Commons, fresh from their electoral victories, find themselves working as partners with fellow parliamentarians from the Senate with security of tenure. The latter, if they wish to be respected, have to bring to the table skills and assets other than the legitimacy of speaking as direct representatives of electors. It was the job of chairmanship to ensure that the two groups worked in harmony, which, on the whole, turned out to be the case.

Among the numerous challenges facing the cochairs, two were crucial to a successful outcome. First was the organization of the work to take into account the unevenness in the experience and knowledge of the committee membership in the field of foreign policy; almost all the members on the House of Commons side were newly elected. The second was to establish broad areas for consideration and, within such broad areas, to identify specific goals and problems.

The stream of knowledge was provided from numerous sources: hearings across the country and in Ottawa; specially organized exchanges between committee members and panels of experts in such areas as culture and security; the preparation of papers by acknowledged professionals in key areas of the enquiry; summaries of testimony by committee staff; and, finally, in camera discussions amongst committee members. The attendance of the House of Commons members of the committee was exemplary, as was their devotion to doing a good job.

Among the broad areas for committee enquiry was international development. It soon became apparent that CIDA, in particular, had problems. One was the financial support for structural adjustment programs, which, in general, were a major and sustained target of criticism by witnesses from nongovernmental organizations. The second was a perception that its aims ought to be more strictly defined in pursuit of specific sectors of development. The committee made an exceptional contribution to the future of Canada's international development program by offering concrete solutions to both of these problems.

FROM A MINING BACKGROUND

I delivered my maiden speech in the House of Commons on 14 February 1954. The choice of employment policy as the subject is easily understood. Unemployment was rife in Cape Breton where I grew up. Its alleviation had personal overtones for me. My experience of unemployment growing up in a coal mining town turned my interest at university to courses and professors who had a view on social and economic issues. My first election to the House of Commons followed two years in graduate school at MIT in economics. Among the gifted group of professors who guided our efforts there was Paul Samuelson, an expositor of Keynes's General Theory of Income and Employment.

The gifted essayist A.L. Rowse, in his volume *A Cornish Childhood: Autobiography of a Cornishman*, paints a vivid picture of how the beliefs and practice of his local community in Cornwall had a lasting effect. The more sensitive and imaginative the person, the more likely are the hues of his youthful existence to appear in the tapestry of his life. That is certainly the case for Rowse.

Living in a coal mining town leaves its indelible imprint. The novelist A.J. Cronin made a career writing about its special fascination. Recently, Sheldon Currie gave further impetus to the genre in *Margaret's Museum*, with its almost overly harsh treatment of the life of coal miners. Currie will not be the last author to mine this field of pain, solidarity, and heroism. In my coal mining town, virtually everybody was in the same social and economic class. We were denied the outlet of envy. In retrospect, there is a temptation to repudiate the experience and to soften its rigours. Survivors admit the hard times, but insist they were also happy times. This softening of the reality flows from loyalty to parents and community. Honesty is better than misguided loyalty. Honesty honours the best miners and especially their wives who bore their frustration in the silence made necessary by the lack of alternatives.

Mining coal economically in the seams available at Inverness was beyond the wit of management, either private or public. The unions, and there were a number competing for the support of the miners, did not succeed any better. At one point, an attempt at running the mines through a loose application of cooperative principles in a new enterprise led by the parish priest turned out to be a disaster. It produced all sorts of deep divisions in the community and fractured badly the harmony which had existed previously within and between the churches in the community. Subsequently, this episode in the community's history became the skeleton in the closet which had to be excluded from conversation. The risk of a verbal explosio unwittingly touching upon a sore point in the factional bitterne too great. Added to the economic uncertainty was the new bur social disharmony.

The mines did not operate regularly. Whether a miner would have work on any given day was made known the night before through the mine whistle: one whistle work, two whistles no work. The whistle was the impersonal voice of the unseen forces which controlled the destiny of all. It was also the harbinger of injury and death. It was an awesome sound when the whistle was used to inform the community that an accident had occurred. These accidents were, at times, fatal.

The miners usually had one suit of clothes to be worn on special occasions and always to church on Sunday. Few miners could save enough to buy a suit outright. One of three clothing merchants in town devised a system called a suit club by which miners could pay a small amount each week towards the purchase of a new suit. When enough funds were on deposit at the store, the miner could pick up his suit. The bonus for this waiting game was a tailor-made suit.

Pensions for miners were unknown. The lack of provision for future security was accepted stoically. The coal mines on the west coast of Cape Breton had been long closed when a reasonable pension system for miners was instituted in the mines of Cape Breton County, which had been taken over by the Cape Breton Development Corporation. This crown corporation was established by the Parliament of Canada, and I had the opportunity to influence key provisions of the bill as it received Cabinet consideration, in particular, giving the corporation power to open new mines. It has provided hitherto unknown stability in the coal communities of eastern Cape Breton. Devco, as the corporation is locally known, eliminated the whistle.

In July of 1995 a boyhood friend, now a retired coal miner, and I in a long conversation engaged in a social and economic account of our experiences in growing up near each other in company houses in our coal mining town in the twenties and thirties. Quietly, and without realizing what we were doing, we engaged in a sort of social and economic survey.

We lived in the north end of town in company houses built on a piece of high ground overlooking the Gulf. Between the houses and the beautiful sandy beach were the coal pits, the bank head, the coal dump, and rail lines for coal cars. All of that is now gone, replaced first by blueberry and cranberry barrens and now by nothing much at all. My father, in his retirement, following forty-six years underground, used to pick berries there instead of coal.

In our location, there were three rows of company houses. Each row had seven houses, each house had two self-contained dwellings and each of the dwelling spaces was identical to the forty-one others. There was no central heating and no inside toilets. There was running water, however, and electricity. In fact, the electricity was provided at a nominal fixed charge by the company, with the result that lights were left on day and night. People who travelled through the town late at night wondered why it was all lit up at three o'clock in the morning. Coal was supplied also at reduced rates to the miners. Even so, a preferred option was for the young boys to pick coal at the dump and, when necessary, to steal it. Stealing coal from the company was totally accepted, if not legally permitted.

The pay for a day's work was about $3 or $3.25. My boyhood friend, who still had in his possession his late father's pay envelopes, confirmed that the total weekly wage when the mines were in operation was $17 per week. In our review, we confirmed to each other that every family in that block of houses made its living in the coal mines. Every household on that high ground overlooking the Gulf, every employee, whether on the surface or underground, was governed by the whistle. The storekeepers, the clergy, the hospital, the convent were exempt in their daily lives from the direct governance of the whistle. Their households had the usual amenities, including telephones. No miner had a telephone.

The school curriculum was distant from life as it was lived in the community. The restructuring of society or the economy as ways of alleviating conditions was not a subject for discussion. The solution for many was to avoid the mines by seeking a job elsewhere or to get a higher education. The latter was my escape route.

INSPIRATION FROM THE ANTIGONISH MOVEMENT

St Francis Xavier University did more for me than provide a liberal arts education. It demonstrated, through its espousal of the Antigonish Movement, that social and economic change were possible, legitimate, and justified. It further demonstrated that there were instruments at hand, both public and private, that offered the prospect of achieving real change. It was a liberating influence. In the bleak uncertainties of growing up in a coal mining town, it was possible to sense wrongs of society and the economy. It was at St Francis Xavier where a way of change was laid out. Adult education and economic group action were Dr M.M. Coady's way of achieving significant social change. We students were stirred by his message, and his philosophy made a lasting impact upon some of us.

In the past year, because of my involvement in an examination of the current state of the Antigonish Movement, I had cause to dig deeply once again into its origins, its principles, and concrete results. In my days at St Francis Xavier, the movement and its chief expositor, Dr Coady, were each at their zenith. I never lost an opportunity to listen to Coady's eloquence, as often in private as in public. I was his disciple. I am still his disciple to the extent that his basic principles have continuing relevance.

With the perspective of time, it is clear that an essence of the Antigonish Movement was social and economic criticism accompanied by adult education leading to self-help economic action organized on the basis of cooperative principles. The results were a network of new institutions built up in the Atlantic provinces. All of this creative thought and activity was stimulating and motivational. As a member of the teaching staff at the university, I became deeply involved in these activities. Apart from participating generally in the movement, specific programs of adult education became outlets for my interest and enthusiasm.

"Life in These Maritimes" was a radio program broadcast throughout the fall and winter months, directed to the rural population and dealing with both technical and economic subjects. To serve the urban area, especially the industrial workers of Pictou and Cape Breton counties, a second series was developed entitled, "The Peoples School," a title revived from an earlier period of the university's history when Dr Tompkins brought prospective leaders from outside the university to the campus for short periods of training. The title was old. Using the medium of radio for educational programs linked through study material with discussion groups in the field was new to the area. The broadcast panel, in which I usually took part, was moved into the halls of the communities with discussion before an audience able to participate through questions and comments. Supplementing this radio phase was a series of "classes" among steelworkers and mineworkers. Nothing was more real in all my experience than these encounters.

Among Dr Coady's listeners at this time was Harry Johnson who joined the faculty at St Francis Xavier as a totally inexperienced professor for one year to fill an unexpected gap in the already small social sciences group. We who attended his first lecture (those who knew him later as a world-famous economist will disbelieve this) recall that he had to conclude well before the allotted time because he ran out of things to say. Harry Johnson was interested in the Antigonish Movement and later made a speech that distilled its principles. So thorough and accurate was Harry's distillation that Dr Coady used it in his comprehensive statement to the Royal Commission on the Taxation of Cooperatives in 1945.

rientation my activities took on in my political career was in-
l by this period. To some, it was my distinctive mark. In the
protracted debate following the 1981 budget, I was reproached because I was believed to have betrayed the principles which had been
upheld by Dr Coady. I had believed then, as I do now, that the equity
I strove to implant in the taxation system would have been ap-
plauded by Dr Coady.

BREAD AND THE STATE

If the Antigonish Movement provided the initial impetus, later influences at the Universities of Toronto and Chicago and at MIT reinforced my interest in the possibilities for change and helped to clarify
the role of the state in the pursuit of reform.

In my maiden speech in the House of Commons in 1954, I discussed the positive place of the state in reducing unemployment.
Since then, the state has demonstrated its capacity to affect decisively
the well-being of citizens. I have recounted, in this essay, a number of
measures which have made their particular contribution to citizen
well-being. The most cherished is our medical care system.

In March of 1996, I made my last parliamentary speech on economic issues, dealing with a Senate resolution establishing a special
committee to enquire into the plans of the Cape Breton Development
Corporation for the future management of the coal fields in Cape Breton. I recalled the statement made on 29 December 1966 by then
Prime Minister Pearson in setting up the corporation: "It is because of
its awareness of and concerns for the well-being of individuals and
their communities that the federal government is prepared to assist
on a massive scale." He saw the role of government in a positive
light, in much the same way as my former constituent did when he
spoke about "keeping bread on the table."

The question is: who puts bread on the table when private markets
fail to do so? The long-term role of the state will not be determined by
the necessity, in the short run, to solve fiscal problems. There are signs
now that the fashion of denying, on principle, a positive role for the
state is losing its grip. The avoidance of social disharmony makes it
imperative that those in authority will not lag behind their public in
realizing that the state has still a role in keeping bread on the table.
The people as a whole will have the final say in determining the future role of government. I am content to rely on their judgment.

Canada in the Age of the Visible Hand

MICHAEL BLISS

CANADA'S KEYNESIAN REVOLUTION

Other contributors to this volume look forward into the next millennium. My job as an historian is to set the stage with a look at where we have been, to study our country's concept of the public good, as it were, by looking through the rear-view mirror – which, as Marshall McLuhan once said, is the way that on modern expressways you see what's coming up on you. What did we think of as the public good in the half century after World War II? How did we try to realize it? And, as we study the rear-view mirror, how and how often did we go off the road?

In celebrating the forty years in public life of Allan J. MacEachen, we might begin by quoting the first sentence that he uttered in the House of Commons as the rookie MP for Inverness-Richmond. He gave his maiden speech on 15 February 1954, starting his career in Parliament with these words: "Mr Speaker, in rising to take part in this debate on unemployment, I am conscious of the concern any degree of unemployment causes honourable members in the House and the people of Canada generally."

MPs did not use the phrase "right on" in those days, but we might, for we all know how consistently Canadians have seen unemployment to be an enemy of the public good in the last half of the twentieth century. When Canada first developed national employment surveys during the early 1930s, at the height of the Great Depression, they revealed a ghastly situation, with over 25 percent of a workforce in which there was far more dependency on household breadwinners than now, looking for jobs. The Great Depression was as searing for Canada as it was for the United States and afterwards even the loosest notion of the "public good" included the idea that there must never be another period of such widespread unemployment and human suffering. Never again.

Never again such hard times. But were not hard times, like winter, like storms on the ocean, like lay-offs at the factory, simple facts of life? There was much fatalism in the Dirty Thirties, especially by those people who saw the depression as part of the business cycle – a downturn, a setback, a glutting of markets that would end once the balance of supply and demand was righted. Given time, the classical economists had taught us, markets would always clear – because of the self-adjustments brought about by the invisible hands of economic self-interest. Intervene directly in the marketplace and you might create distortions that would make things worse – in other words you might interfere with the public economic good being promoted by the activities of the free market. So, in this world-view, the best way to promote the public good was by a hands-off, a laissez faire policy. Roll with the punches and eventually Ole Man Depression would tire himself out and go away.

"I belong personally to the school of thought which affirms that with our new understanding of the causes of depression there will not occur in Canada in the future the kind of depression that afflicted us in the thirties," the member for Inverness-Richmond told the House of Commons in 1954. Allan MacEachen announced that he was a Keynesian, and, in his remarks, he celebrated the "revolution in economic thinking" wrought by John Maynard Keynes and his disciples, in showing that free markets did not necessarily find equilibrium at full employment and that there existed "certain established and recognized measures by which assistance can be given to the economy in its momentum toward full employment."

The Keynesian revolution, which had arrived in Canada by the late 1930s and was spelled out clearly in the 1945 White Paper on Employment and Income, represented a profound commitment not to roll with the punches, but instead to fight back by using the visible hands of economic managers to prod, stimulate, goad, modern economies towards full employment. There would be no more closing of the eyes, no more laissez faire, no more fatalism. The national government would now actively promote this basic public good.

(It can be argued that there had never been a period of thorough-going laissez faire in Canadian public life. Soon after Confederation, the government of Canada turned its back on free trade, the economic orthodoxy of the day, and began using protective tariffs as an instrument to mould the economy, defending them especially as a mechanism for job-creation. From 1878, macromanagement through protective tariffs was labelled Canada's National Policy, and was still the chosen instrument of the activist Bennett government during the 1930s. It was largely among Liberals of that era that Keynesianism had its greatest impact, replacing free trade, laissez faire ideas.)

CRADLE-TO-GRAVE CONSENSUS

In his maiden speech, the Cape Breton MP also instanced the work of another British social theorist, Sir William Beveridge. The Beveridge Report to the Churchill government, delivered during the height of the Second World War, became the blueprint for the postwar completion of the British welfare state, a set of programs that provided cradle-to-the-grave security for all Britons as a right of citizenship.

The idea of security from extreme hardship as a public good to be supported by the state was not new in the 1940s, and it had not been invented by the Canadian CCF in the 1930s. It had originated in the 1880s in Bismarck's Germany. Great Britain was well on the way towards a welfare state by 1914; in the mid-1930s Franklin D. Roosevelt's New Deal administration had put the United States far ahead of Canada in its commitment to this version of the public good. In those years, we talked a lot about catching up with other advanced countries in matters of social insurance. In the depths of the depression, even Conservative Prime Minister R.B. Bennett caught the vision, after a fashion, but, when we went to war in 1939, we had a lot of implementing still to do.

If there ever was an instance of using the visible hand of state power to deal with pressing national problems, it was in the operation of the war economy. No one believed that market forces could adjust quickly or equitably enough to support a total war effort. Between 1939 and 1945, the government of Canada, like that of most belligerents, implemented a thoroughgoing program of "war socialism," involving controls on wages and prices, foreign exchange, imports and exports, rationing, progressive and, at times, confiscatory taxes, the allocation of labour, and, ultimately, conscription for overseas service.

Victory in 1945 seemed to vindicate the workings of our very active, very visible hands (except perhaps in the matter of conscription). If we could use these policy tools to achieve the public good of defeating fascism, could we not also use them to achieve other public goods – including victory over unemployment, poverty, and ill health? Could we not use the power of government to build a better postwar world for Canadians?

There was little doubt, then, that the postwar era would see Canada catching up to other countries in the development of social programs (great strides were made during the war years themselves, with the introduction of national unemployment insurance and family allowances). We were ahead of some of them in our commitment to full employment. The agenda of Keynesian economic management on the one hand, and the completion and expansion of the social safety net on the other, meant that postwar Canadian governments would not be small and quiescent. In their search for economic security, jobs, and prosperity, Canadians would look to the public sector to advance the public good.

As Canada's effective governing party in this century, the Liberals were, of course, responsible for implementing much of the new public policy agenda. Mackenzie King, Louis St Laurent, Lester Pearson, and their ministers were the political architects of the age of big government at the national level. But perhaps the best symbol of the new postwar consensus came during the 1957 election campaign when the Progressive Conservative leader, John Diefenbaker, attacked the St Laurent government for only increasing the universal old age pension, born in 1951, by a measly six dollars a month. Earlier Progressive Conservative leaders, such as Arthur Meighen and George Drew, had been inclined to attack the very idea of state pensions as undermining the individual's or the family's responsibility to save for old age: that was the old left-right debate. Now, in the 1950s, a genuine bipartisan consensus had developed. Everyone was on the left where social welfare was concerned. Far from debating these issues, the major parties began trying to outbid one another as generous champions of social benefits. Diefenbaker raised the old age pension in 1958 by a further eight dollars per month.

Canadians were all Keynesians, too, by that era, with the possible exception of Diefenbaker's Minister of Finance, Donald Fleming, and the Governor of the Bank of Canada, James Coyne – both found themselves roundly and publicly condemned by the elite of the Canadian economics profession for not following "orthodox" contracyclical fiscal and monetary measures – a mistake the Conservatives would try hard not to repeat if they ever regained office.

With Keynesianism and the welfare state in place by the mid-1950s, a case could be made for suggesting that it was time to stop looking backward at the Great Depression, especially since postwar economic growth had been spectacular and sustained. In his 1954 maiden speech, Allan MacEachen cheerfully observed that "there will not occur in Canada in the future the kind of depression that afflicted us in the thirties," and went on to cite the Bank of Nova Scotia's conclusion that 1953 had set new records for employment, production, and income – so it was not a bad climate in which to be worrying about unemployment which, in 1953, averaged less than 3 percent of the Canadian workforce.

AFFLUENCE, WITH PUBLIC SQUALOR

The 1950s, in fact, were such a good decade that at the end of them another Canadian- born economist, John Kenneth Galbraith, gave the English language a new descriptive phrase when he published one of the great economics best-sellers of all time, *The Affluent Society.* To many observers, North America had broken through into historically unprecedented levels of productivity and private wealth; the state had its policies in place to fight unemployment and poverty on the macro-level. Some could argue that happy days were at hand forever.

John Kenneth Galbraith was not among them. *The Affluent Society* contained a powerful critique of the "social imbalance" economic growth was creating in North America, as the satisfaction of private wants was not being matched by equal attention to public needs – except, perhaps, in the matter of US defense policy. Galbraith wrote of "an atmosphere of private opulence and public squalor": "By failing to exploit the opportunity to expand public production, we are missing opportunities for enjoyment which otherwise we might have. Presumably a community can be as well rewarded by buying better schools or better parks as by buying bigger automobiles. By concentrating on the latter rather than the former, it is failing to maximize its satisfactions. As with schools in the community, so with public services over the country at large. It is scarcely sensible that we should satisfy our wants in private goods with reckless abundance, while in the case of public goods, on the evidence of the eye, we practice extreme self-denial."

Galbraith's notion of public goods was based on fairly well-understood notions of services that could not easily be purchased by the individual, often because they created external benefits for the whole community – access to parks, policing, scientific research, mass transportation, a clean environment. These seemed to be public goods that would have to be provided by government or not at all.

Galbraith's analysis was devoured eagerly by Canadians – even more avidly by Canadians than Americans, and especially by Canadian Liberals, who have surely provided his greatest constituency over the past forty years. (If there can be said to be one great Liberal guru of the postwar age in Canada I would suggest that Tom Kent,

Walter Gordon, even Pierre Trudeau, were outshone or at least their books outsold, by this Canadian-born citizen of the United States, who came home to speak again and again).

There was already in Canada an important tradition of the state providing public goods that the private sector was unwilling or unable to supply. These goods ranged from transcontinental rail service in the 1880s to low-cost electrical power in Ontario in the early 1900s, long-distance telephone service on the prairies, and transcontinental broadcasting and air service in the 1930s. By the 1950s, the creation of a national television network had been accepted by Canadian politicians as a public good that fell into their bailiwick. So, with the creation of the Canada Council, did the promotion through subsidy of such traditional cultural activities as theatre, ballet, opera, and writing. With the introduction of federal grants to universities, the promotion of higher education also seemed to be a responsibility of the national government.

In the Canadian federation, the provision of public goods and services was far from being the exclusive responsibility of Ottawa. The constitution assigned primary responsibility for health, education, welfare, labour, highways, the provision of municipal services, and many other powers to the provinces. A major element of the wartime and postwar reconstitution of the federal system had been aimed at creating a fiscal framework within which the provinces could better fill these traditional, but now rapidly expanding roles. By the end of the 1950s, with the baby boom generation hitting the school system and private affluence heightening Canadians' expectations for better public services, all the provincial governments were increasing their spending, expanding their activities, and beginning to press Ottawa for yet more breathing-space and tax revenues. After 1960, of course, Quebec would take the lead in demanding much more leeway to provide public goods for its people.

There always were some conservatives who believed that the private marketplace had the capacity to deliver such allegedly "public" goods as education, hospital services, and culture. But social theorists of a Galbraithian persuasion, some brought up in the thirties, some schooled in agrarian dislike of big business (Galbraith was a product of both influences), some coming out of the British or European liberal and social democratic traditions, had a deep suspicion of the private sector, indeed of capitalism itself. They thought that market failure or market oppression was the norm under capitalism, that a free market system could never generate much in the way of public goods, and that virtually all social or collective goods had to be provided by the state and funded through the tax system. Theirs was an agenda for the constant growth of government, at least as fast as the private sector, ideally much faster to right deeply rooted social imbalances. Did "social justice" involve only creating safety nets? Or did it point towards serious redistribution of wealth aimed at promoting greater equality of outcomes?

Notions of market inadequacies and inequalities of outcome took on a particular Canadian dimension when critics began to focus on structural problems of the economy of a thinly-populated federation sprawling across three thousand miles of geography. In 1954, Allan MacEachen worried to the House of Commons about the precarious state of the coal industry in his riding, for example, and meditated on whether such public works as building the Canso causeway were the answer.

THE JUST SOCIETY

Canadians had always looked to a certain amount of government spending on public works as contributing to the public good because of the employment it created, and that had been especially true in the structurally or geographically or politically disadvantaged regions of the country. Westerners and Maritimers had also traditionally argued that equalization of employment opportunities across the country was a public good to be promoted by the national government. In the 1920s, the concept of "Maritime rights" had begun to include the view that there was something wrong when people in any part of Canada did not enjoy equal employment and income *outcomes*, and that it was a public good in a country like Canada for governments to target unequal or disadvantaged regions, such as Cape Breton and other coal areas of Nova Scotia, for special help.

In the 1950s, these ideas were as appealing to a politician from the depressed province of Saskatchewan as to one from Cape Breton. Another bipartisan consensus had developed. The Diefenbaker government happened to pioneer in putting in place the first major programs aimed at stimulating regional development in the interests of equalization. The Pearson government inherited and expanded them, and, by 1968, when Pierre Trudeau talked about the hope of creating a Just Society in Canada, justice had very much to do with working to equalize opportunities and income across a very diverse nation.

A Just Society. More than a generation later it becomes increasingly striking to reflect on the amazing optimism bred in those far-off years. To think that a government of Canada in 1968 should have believed it had a chance to create what philosophers and statesmen and prophets had been contemplating from time immemorial. A just society! What optimism! What confidence! What hubris! Should we add, what folly?

If folly it was, we come to understand it by understanding the many roots of the attitudes of the postwar Golden Age of big government. The most general factor underlying Keynesianism, the welfare state, and big government generally was belief in visible hands, belief in the possibility that the visible hands of planners, civil servants, politicians, managers could do a better job of solving social problems than the invisible hands of Adam Smith's open marketplace.

It is now evident that the nineteenth-century idea of progress, largely market-oriented, was replaced in the mid-twentieth century by an even more optimistic notion of the possibility of progress through direct human action – taking charge, taking control, planning for the future, managing, even engineering, social change. Socialists believed in the possibility of planning and reshaping society. So, in fact, did the right-wing corporatists. So even – especially – did the very optimistic masters of business administration in the United States who were taking over the control of the largest private organizations the world had ever seen and who claimed that with rational planning and management they could dominate and shape their markets virtually without limits.

The visible hands were going to manage even the marketplace for toothpaste and automobiles. The most admired member of the very popular John F. Kennedy administration, next to the president himself, was the Harvard MBA and former president of the Ford Motor Company, Robert S. McNamara. McNamara was the leader of the group of "whiz kids" who had driven Ford to new heights, were going to bring the chaos of the Pentagon under proper public control, and would soon turn their efforts to calculating how to handle the job of reorganizing a relatively small backward society on the other side of the Pacific.

In staid Canada, we hardly thought of civil servants of the Clifford Clark, Mitchell Sharp, or Michael Pitfield persuasion as "whiz kids." Better to dignify them as "mandarins." But we certainly respected them. Indeed, a few jokes apart, we respected all of our civil servants, our public servants, in those years. In part thanks to the closing down of the private sector during the depression and the war, the top civil servants really were among our very best and brightest. They did seem to know what they were doing, to have the capacity to plan rationally and accurately for the future, to oversee and regulate the chaotic private marketplace, to do the job of guiding and engineering social change.

The skeptics – there were always a few – could be answered by the record of achievement by the visible hands in Canada. Look at how successful the war policies of the government of Canada had been (and notice, by the way, that they had included running enormous budget deficits, implementing wage and price controls for the whole economy, and subjecting Canadians to extremely high levels of taxation). Look at how successful postwar Canadian governments had been at keeping unemployment down, at giving out welfare benefits, at avoiding inflation, and at stimulating industries and the arts through the early subsidy policies. It all seemed to have worked, justifying the activist mentality of the government generation. For decades after 1945, Canadian politics were dominated by the "can-do" attitude that came naturally to marines storming beaches and politicians running for public office.

Even if the best-laid schemes of politicians and civil servants did not always work exactly as expected here in Canada – there were bound to be some setbacks, glitches, miscalculations – we, unlike the British or the Japanese or even the Americans, had the immense good fortune of having the ultimate social policy safety net, the immense natural wealth of our country. In a world running short of some natural resources, and destined to run short of the rest of them eventually, we had inherited (or somehow obtained from the native peoples) half a continent of minerals, wood, and virtually all forms of energy. The spectacular natural wealth of Canada, so evident during the postwar boom from 1945 to 1973, would surely support any number of government programs aimed at advancing the public good. In a pinch we could always fall back on our latent wealth, the certainty of growth. These attitudes were also furthered by the fact that until indexation in the early 1970s, the tax bracket creep generated by inflation and economic growth was pouring steady "unearned increments," or growth premiums, into government coffers.

How far could Canadians go with optimism, a glowing track record, and the confidence that no matter what happened our resource base would never let us down? In the 1940s and 1950s, we began to catch up with West European countries and, in some ways, surpassed them in the creation of our modern welfare state. In the 1960s, we expanded the welfare state all the way into the state's undertaking to finance all our health-care needs (when Allan MacEachen was Minister of Health), all the way into some of the provinces preparing to cover most of the costs of university education, some of the way into the idea of guaranteeing all Canadians a reasonable annual income, perhaps enough to abolish poverty once and for all.

As well, in our mood of national confidence, peaking perhaps in Centennial year, 1967, we could take the notion of controlling our future into new realms of protectionism, the building of new barriers restricting the less wholesome impact of, say, the mighty economy and culture to the south. We could control foreign investment. We could limit cultural penetration. We could, perhaps, create a distinctively Canadian society, becoming a different kind of North Americans – perhaps North Americans with a stronger sense of the role of the public sector in promoting the public good. We were, after all, a people who had never rejected the crown but had taken control of it and used its powers to promote the common weal. Our revolution was directed from the top down, not the bottom up; perhaps that was the essence of what George Grant was writing about in the 1960s. William Watson has recently argued that it was during the past forty years – an era when the conventional wisdom pointed to the "Americanization" of Canada – that, in fact, differences in Canadian and American levels of taxation and reliance on the state became most pronounced. The two countries were more like one another in 1954 than they are now. It seemed, in the 1960s that, in the face of American spillover and/or imperialism, Canadians could probably erect enough cultural tariffs to guarantee the country's survival.

The survival of the French language and culture in Canada had been guaranteed for more than two hundred years, perhaps mainly by the fecundity of the French Canadians, but also partly by government policies in Ottawa and, with increasing vigour from the days of Honoré Mercier, in Quebec City. In every Canadian province in the 1960s, the combination of prosperity, heavy responsibilities, high public expectations, and optimism in the capacities of the visible hands of politicians and civil servants, led to a vast expansion of government activities. In retrospect, it is surely no surprise that the government of Quebec, under various administrations, and reflecting the same optimism about the capacities of government and social engineering that was driving the government of Canada, transformed the notion of province-building into one of nation-building. The frictions of the provinces, especially Quebec, with Ottawa, are a side issue for the purposes of this essay, but all Canadians know how often and seriously in the past thirty years the alleged sideshow took over center stage.

ON TO THE CHARTER

Even as Canadians continue to argue about collectivities and their rights, including, of course, the obligations we have to the First Nations, almost all of us, including John Kenneth Galbraith and most social democrats, have believed that the collective or the public good is primarily a route towards improving the lives of individuals. Why else do we want to become employed, wealthy, healthy, and educated, if not to have more opportunities, more choices in life? However much we disagree about distinct society, Quebec's right of self-determination, *et cetera*, there is a fundamental comity in Canada to respect two official public languages, and to tolerate, even encourage, a multiplicity of private cultures.

Expanding the sphere of the individual's freedom gradually became an explicit public good in postwar Canada as policy discussion evolved from economic and cultural policies to human rights issues themselves. Dare I cite John Diefenbaker one more time, the eccentric old coot who prattled on about a Bill of Rights for Canadians, put one through Parliament in 1960, and can fairly claim to have been the godfather of the Charter of Rights and Freedoms, the most fundamental – and popular – constitutional innovation in Canada since 1867.

There was nothing per se about human rights in Allan MacEachen's maiden speech in the 1950s or in Galbraith's *The Affluent Society*. Despite the very deep roots of rights concerns, and the obsessions of mavericks like Diefenbaker, most rights issues only began to flourish in the second generation of the postwar age, beginning in the 1960s with American civil rights issues, and quickly expanding to include aboriginal matters here, the rights of women everywhere, problems of visible minorities, and, by the 1980s, gay rights. Historians will forever debate the emergence of the charter in 1981–2. Did it flow naturally from the evolution of Canadian society, or was it imposed prematurely by another maverick politician riding a very personal hobbyhorse? Whatever the answer, few Canadians outside of Quebec would dispute the view that the public good in this country has been codified in our charter of fundamental human rights. The Reform party and the gay rights issue notwithstanding, and the notwithstanding clause very much to the point, most Canadians believe it would be in the public good to strengthen the charter rather than weaken it. Surely it is in the charter, rather than in, say, subsidies for cucumber plants in Newfoundland, that we begin to implement the ideal of the just society.

In any case, the hydroponic cucumbers did not flourish in Newfoundland. As people in Atlantic Canada know all too well, many of the regional development policies of the last thirty years have had decidedly mixed results at best. Some have been utter failures. To be sure, there are wonderful success stories in postwar Canada, notably our generally high standard of living, the success of our social security net, and the feminist-driven human rights revolution of recent years. Still, in the 1990s we stand at a distance from the utopianism of the golden postwar years and are developing a healthy critical sense of the gap between aspiration and achievement. If Allan MacEachen decided to be a Canadian Strom Thurmond and begin a new career in Parliament in the next election, his maiden speech would probably be about unemployment and the problem of the coal industry, and it would contain less optimism than he expressed forty-two years ago.

What went wrong? Broadly speaking, the postwar Golden Age ended with the energy crisis of the early 1970s and the beginnings of stagflation. In macroeconomic policy we began to doubt that Keynesianism was the answer. We found that our welfare state was becoming very expensive, perhaps unaffordable in its full universal garb, and we found that certain of our safety net programs, such as liberal unemployment insurance benefits, seemed to create virtually permanent conditions of dependency.

TURN TO INDIVIDUALISM

By the 1980s, the whole range of government activities aimed at providing public goods was coming under scrutiny, not least from economists who were now scrutinizing the workings of government as carefully and critically as governments had previously examined the private sector. Could it be that many politicians and civil servants were driven by self-interest rather than ideals of selfless service? Could it be that programs to subsidize public goods, such as the arts or advocacy groups, might have much to do with politicians establishing patron-client relationships with special interest groups? Was economic nationalism a rationale for a resurgence of old-fashioned protectionism? Did planners and social engineers actually have the capacity to forecast the future, let alone change it? Were the visible hands of the bureaucrats and the politicians actually as nimble and responsive and self-correcting as the invisible forces of markets, even in the provision of public goods?

The surge of neoconservative critiques of big government in the 1980s and the resurgence of interest in market solutions to economic and socio-political problems was partly driven by the profound social changes wrought by postwar economic success. We are beginning to realize that the thrust to strengthen individual opportunities and freedoms, to create the truly autonomous individual, has been accompanied, perhaps necessarily, by the strengthening of the individual's distrust of most of the organizations that traditionally claimed a right to help organize his or her life. The affluent, self-assertive, empowerment-seeking children of the postwar age called one organization after another into question – churches, corporations, marriage and the family, then even political parties and government itself. It seems clear that Canadians of the twenty-first century wish to have control of their lives vested neither in the invisible hands of the marketplace, nor the visible hands of government, but in their own hands. The rise of what I have called "assertive individualism," or what others have labelled the end of deference, will have profound implications in defining the future directions of public life.

Canadians have suffered a particularly damaging blow in recent years in the shaking of their faith in the land itself. When natural resource prices collapsed in the 1980s, when the National Energy Program and other megaprojects were tossed into the dustbins of history, when ecologists told us that our northern lands were too fragile to support old-fashioned development, when governments began finding that there was not enough growth in the economy to generate the revenue to cover soaring deficits, it began to sink in that Canadians' ultimate social safety net, the country's natural wealth, might also be an illusion. Had Canadians actually inherited the richest country in the world, a cornucopia of natural wealth? Or had they inherited a barren, cold, wasteland, its seas even empty of fish? Particularly in Allan J. MacEachen's region of Canada, with depleted natural resources, questions like this must be asked.

At the end of what was once touted as Canada's Century, as the torch is thrown to the hands of the next generation, Canadians in public life are left with fewer illusions about the capacity of their visible hands to do a better job than the marketplace in providing public goods. The postwar Golden Age is long gone. We move into the new millennium debating the old issues of the role of government vis-à-vis the private sector all over again – and wondering whether diamonds and tar sands and Voisey Bay will do a better job of pulling us through the twenty-first century than Nova Scotia's coal and Newfoundland's cod did in the twentieth.

How best do we promote the public good? We know what we want as a people. We want to have jobs, good and steady incomes, we want to be free to choose the language we speak, the gods we worship, the ways of life we cherish. The constant aim of public policy in every generation is to find the best way of advancing these goods. If the MacEachen generation of Canadian politicians fell short in some of its goals, it can take great satisfaction in the achievement of the most fundamental ones. In the second half of the twentieth century the sacrifices of Canada's soldiers were not in vain. Those who came home, and their children and now their grandchildren, lived in a land of peace, order, plenty, and wonderfully expanding conceptualizations of the meaning of human rights.

Because I have concentrated on life and politics inside Canada, I have said very little about the outside world. At the end of his maiden speech in 1954, which was also mainly devoted to domestic issues, Allan MacEachen tried to right the balance in telling the House of Commons that "no longer" could any country exclusively control its own economy. In the last words of his speech, he called for "an increasing willingness to take part in all forms of international economic cooperation." Is this not the best of all activities to engage the visible hands and minds and hearts of statesmen?

Back to the Future: Reforming Social Policy in Canada

KEN BATTLE

INTRODUCTION

Allan J. MacEachen's enormous contribution to the progress of social security in this country makes it fitting to reflect on the present state and possible future of social policy in Canada. For this purpose, I propose to trace the intellectual roots of the welfare state and its substantive development in the postwar period. This approach is the more appropriate given the involvement, in the celebration of Mr MacEachen's seventy-fifth birthday, of several other towering figures in the history of Canadian social policy – Monique Bégin, Tom Kent, Marc Lalonde, and Pierre Elliott Trudeau.

There is another reason for framing my comments in an historical context. Provincial politicians recently have breathed new life into the ailing federal Social Security Review by embracing some promising ideas for policy reform. A couple of these suggestions are more than fifty years old and are as relevant today as when first proposed, and for the same reasons. There is a delicious irony in this fact, given the conventional wisdom in policy-making circles that we have to cast out old programs and ideas in order to "reinvent" social policy and government.

My main purposes are to explain the ongoing transformation of the welfare state and to present some reforms that could create a stronger social security system for the next century. My message is that the federal and provincial governments must build a new collaborative federalism based on national social programs – not federal, not provincial, but *national* in spirit and substance. Otherwise, the devolutionary fever that is sweeping the corridors of power will lead to national substandards in welfare and social services, the erosion of our cherished health care system, and an unravelling of the social union.

THE GROWTH OF SOCIAL
SECURITY

First, however, I shall chronicle the development of our social security system as measured by the life of Allan J. MacEachen, one of its creators. When he was born, in 1921, Canada's social security system also was in its infancy. Our first modern social program, Workmen's Compensation as it was known in those lingosexist days, had been created in Ontario just seven years earlier and soon spread throughout Canada and the United States.

Workers' Compensation was a milestone for several reasons worth remembering. It established an entitlement to benefits based on the principle of social insurance, which was to play a prominent role in the subsequent development of the theory and, to a lesser extent, practice of the Canadian welfare state. Workers' Compensation represented a state-enforced social contract between employers and their workforce, offering employees and their dependents protection against the risk of injury, illness, or death on the job by providing wage-replacement income benefits and medical and rehabilitative services. Employers, in turn, won protection from lawsuits and expensive private liability insurance premiums. The example of Workers' Compensation reminds us that social security was created as much to serve the needs of capitalists as to civilize capitalism for workers and citizens. Workers' Compensation also was significant because it was the first major provincial government initiative in social programming.

By the time Mr MacEachen was born, five provinces had instituted the first modern social assistance program in the form of Mothers' Pensions or Mothers' Allowances as they were also known. Financed and delivered by provincial governments, Mothers' Allowances recognized the problem of growing numbers of poor single-parent mothers and their children who no longer could rely upon the traditional and haphazard support of relatives, neighbours, charities, and municipal relief. When Mr MacEachen was a young boy, minimum wage laws were enacted across the country. When he was six years old, a cornerstone of our social security system was cemented in place by the Old Age Pensions Act which provided conditional federal cost-sharing of provincial means-tested old age pensions, complete with federal standards governing eligibility, benefits, and residence requirements.

Mr MacEachen was a teenager during the Great Depression, which must have had a profound formative influence on his subsequent career in public life. The federal government was dragged reluctantly, if not kicking and screaming, into a larger role in social policy as it provided financial assistance to the beleaguered provinces for unemployment relief and attempted (unsuccessfully at first) to create a national program of unemployment insurance and employment offices. The federal War Veterans Allowances program was created in 1930 and federally cost-shared Blind Pensions in 1937. The Rowell-Sirois Commission of 1937–40 recommended that Ottawa become a major player in social security by assuming responsibility for old age pensions and the unemployed and providing financial assistance to the provinces for social services and welfare.

World War II provided the means to realize the emerging demand for social security by accelerating Canada's emergence as an industrialized economy and forging a nation through collective purpose and action. Under the guidance and growing power of the federal government commanding a wartime economy, Canada developed an economic base that would require and support a modern social security system as part of postwar reconstruction. In his famous 1960 paper, *Social Policy for Canada: Towards a Philosophy of Social Security,* Tom Kent expressed it well: "People began to refuse to put up with so much misery and squalor and despair in the lives of the aged, the unemployed, the sick, the large family."[1]

Ottawa instituted Dependents' Allowances for families of the armed forces; offered grants to help the provinces provide day care for women who joined the labour force to make armaments; and built houses to ease the housing shortage for war workers. In 1940, when Mr MacEachen was nineteen, Britain amended the BNA Act to allow Ottawa to enact Unemployment Insurance, a social insurance program that grew over the years into a pillar of the modern welfare state – and, a generation later, came to be pilloried as the embodiment of the welfare state's malaise. When Mr MacEachen was twenty-three, the King government brought in Family allowances, which was the largest social expenditure to that time and Canada's first universal social program. The federal government also got involved in vocational training and other employment services.

The federal role in social policy expanded further during the 1950s, when Mr MacEachen was in his thirties. The federal government extended universality from children to seniors when it legislated the Old Age Security Act (OAS) of 1951. Ottawa also shared the cost of provincial welfare programs through the Old Age Assistance Act of 1951 for low-income Canadians aged sixty-five to sixty-nine (the age of eligibility for universal Old Age Security was seventy at that time), Allowances for the Blind (1951) and Disabled (1954), and the Unemployment Assistance Act of 1956 for unemployed employables on welfare who did not qualify for or had exhausted unemployment insurance benefits. In 1954, the federal government offered financial assistance to provincial governments and nonprofit organizations for constructing and renovating low-income housing. In 1957, Ottawa took a momentous step towards universal health insurance with the Hospital Insurance and Diagnostic Services Act, which shared the cost of provincial hospital insurance plans providing universal coverage of basic in-patient services in hospitals for acute, convalescent, and chronic care. By 1960, all provinces and the territories were in and all Canadians were covered by public hospital insurance.

Allan MacEachen entered the cabinet when the Pearson government was formed in 1963; his forties were an extraordinary period in his life and in the life of the nation. The Canada Pension Plan (CPP) and its twin, the Quebec Pension Plan (QPP), were legislated in 1965, adding to the retirement income system a new public earnings-replacement tier that covered all employees and self-employed Canadians. The CPP provided not only retirement pensions but also disability, survivor, children's, orphans, and death benefits – indexed, for another social policy first – and was jointly designed and maintained as a national social program by the federal and provincial governments. The Guaranteed Income Supplement (GIS) for low-income seniors was added the following year, creating, in conjunction with OAS, a *de facto* guaranteed income for the elderly. The year 1966 also brought the Canada Assistance Plan (CAP), merging several cost-shared categorical welfare programs into a single legislative structure which ensured a welfare safety net for all Canadians in need, regardless of cause of need, and expanded social services throughout the country.

During the 1960s, the long arm of the federal government also reached out to postsecondary education. Ottawa created the Canada Student Loans program and provided transfer payments to the provinces to support the expansion of postsecondary education. The Vocational Rehabilitation of Disabled Persons Act of 1961 provided federal cost-sharing of provincial programs of vocational rehabilitation for persons with disabilities. In 1967, the federal government enacted the Adult Occupational Training Act.

But of all these social programs, Allan MacEachen, as Health and Welfare Minister at the time, surely must be most proud of the Medical Care Act of 1966. This legislation expanded federal cost-sharing to provincial plans that insured doctors' services, conditional on provinces fulfilling the "five principles" of medicare – universality, accessibility, comprehensiveness, portability, and public administration. Saskatchewan pioneered public health insurance, but it took federal leadership and cash to develop a national health insurance system for all Canadians – and, later, the courageous tenacity of Monique Bégin and her Canada Health Act (1984) to save medicare from the infection of user fees and extra-billing.

Mr MacEachen moved on to Manpower and Immigration in 1968 and a succession of senior portfolios in the 1970s and 1980s, but the social security system he had so much advanced continued to grow. In 1971, Unemployment Insurance (UI) was enriched, expanded, and liberalized: coverage was extended to almost all the workforce; maternity, retirement, and illness benefits were added; the number of weeks required to qualify for benefits was reduced; benefits were increased; and the duration of benefits was increased for high-unemployment areas. In 1973, family allowances were tripled and fully indexed; OAS and the GIS also were increased and fully indexed on a quarterly basis. In 1975, the elderly benefits system was enlarged through the creation of the Spouse's Allowance for low-income spouses aged sixty to sixty-four and later extended to widowed persons. In 1978, the federal government created the refundable child tax credit, delivered through the income tax system to low- and middle-income families. A number of provinces and the territories established income benefits for low-income seniors, and a few provinces offered income supplements for some of their working poor.

Between 1973 and 1976, the federal and provincial governments undertook a comprehensive review of Canada's social security system. One of its key proposals was a new income support/supplementation system – a form of guaranteed income – to reform welfare and help the working poor. Another important initiative was to modernize social services and extend them beyond the poor to all who need them. But the federal-provincial Social Security Review ran afoul of multi-governmental disagreement and fiscal restraint, occasioned by the world oil shock, rising unemployment, and inflation. The review marked the beginning of the end of the expansion phase of the Canadian welfare state. Mounting deficits and accumulating debt after the mid-1970s created a chilly climate for further growth in social programming, and the recession of 1981–2 gave the federal government another reason to resist proposals to expand the retirement income system during the "Great Pension Debate" of the early 1980s.

Before turning to the transformation of Canadian social policy in the 1980s and 1990s, it is useful to reflect on just how extraordinary was the progress of social security between the time Mr MacEachen was born and his middle age. A useful measure of the growth of the welfare state is Leonard Marsh's classic, *Report on Social Security for Canada* (1943), commissioned by the Committee on Post-War Reconstruction, which was established by the federal government to explore the economic and social challenges of moving from a wartime to peacetime economy.

The Marsh report offered a comprehensive framework for the future development of the social security system. It was composed of three major elements: 1. social insurance programs to protect against employment earnings loss due to unemployment, illness, accident, disability, death, maternity, and retirement; 2. national health insurance to provide all Canadians with a broad range of health services; 3. children's allowances to help fill the gap between wages and income needs for families with children to support. Social assistance was to play a limited role since the social insurances and children's allowances would handle most Canadians' income security needs. Training, guidance, and placement programs – what we now include under the rubric "employment development services" – were to play a major and permanent role, including a federal program of income support and employment services for the long-term and chronically unemployed. Marsh also proposed a massive public investment scheme to ease the transition to a peacetime economy, though this was to be temporary and done in cooperation with the private sector.

Much of the vision of Marsh and other social reformers of the 1920s, 1930s, and 1940s was put in place, mainly after the war, as Canada's social security system grew in content, coverage, and cost. New social insurances, universal income transfers, and income-tested benefits serving large groups of the population were added; some of these programs were subsequently expanded and enriched. In 1945–6, social spending by all levels of government totalled $5.6 billion (in inflation-adjusted 1996 dollars); by 1975–6, it had multiplied fourteen times to $76.2 billion. Social spending far outpaced population growth, rising from $462 per capita in 1945–6 to $3,285 per capita in 1975–6. Social expenditures also grew faster than the buoyant economy that paid for them, increasing from 4.7 percent of Gross Domestic Product (GDP) in 1945–6 to 14.0 percent of GDP by the mid-1970s.[2]

This growth of the universal welfare state does not mean that it was universally supported or followed a smooth upward trajectory. Social programs typically were the product not of a collective commitment to widely shared values of social security (e.g., security, equality, and solidarity), but more often than not a battle between social policy doves and hawks – a conflict that often had complicating overlays of class, regional, linguistic, and jurisdictional tensions. Many Canadians have what may be characterized as a "schizophrenic" attitude towards social security; they have mixed feelings about social programs and feel a conflict between social security as a right of citizenship and social security as a cause of unhealthy dependency and a drain on the economy. Sometimes, of course, they distinguish between different social programs and view some (e.g., old age pensions) as more worthy than others (e.g., welfare). But this still means that support for social security is not as solid as supporters of the universalist welfare state would have us believe. Such conflicting views underscore the current debate about social program reform.

For all its progress in social security, Canada never achieved the dream of a comprehensive set of social and employment programs to protect all its citizens against the various risks and contingencies of modern life and to ensure a basic income. With the notable (though debatable) exception of income security programs for the aged, the objective of ensuring what was known in Marsh's day as a "social minimum" (i.e., an adequate income floor) was neither attempted nor achieved.

Welfare remains a large and widely disliked social program with all the flaws – meagre and widely varying benefits, poverty traps, provincial disparities, punitive administration, and stigma – that its critics have complained about for decades. The wartime proposal for a federal program aimed at unemployed employables who do not qualify for or who exhaust their UI benefits never came to pass, so many jobless Canadians end up on welfare. There is no comprehensive income security system for persons with disabilities, many of whom have to rely on welfare. Child benefits fail to bridge the gap between wages and needs for many families, especially the poor, and are being stealthily eroded by inflation. Despite the recommendations of a series of government reviews over the years, one of the biggest gaps in the social security system – earnings supplementation for the working poor, who make up about half the low-income population – still remains. Despite significant improvements over the years, the pension system still leaves 635,000 seniors under the poverty line. UI grew into a costly social program aimed at several purposes – none of which, the critics contend, it serves well. Even medicare, the social program most beloved by Canadians and most admired abroad, never expanded as planned by its architects to cover a comprehensive range of preventive health and dental services.

The logic of the social security model of Marsh in Canada and Beveridge in Britain hinged on the existence of a full employment economy, without which (as Marsh wrote) "the social insurances structure would have no solid foundation."[3] Social security and a healthy economy would work together in a virtuous circle: social programs would help serve as an economic stabilizer and train a skilled workforce; wages from jobs for all who want them would pay for social programs and constrain the demands for UI, welfare, and social services. The universalist/full employment model of social and economic security was a formula for sustainable social policy.

C.D. Howe did not see it that way, and he was not alone. The powerful minister in charge of postwar reconstruction would have nothing of the federal government committing itself to full employment because he believed Ottawa could not and should not guarantee such an ambitious and inappropriate objective. Instead, the government said publicly it would maintain a "high and stable level of employment."[4] Over the years, of course, that commitment proved to be very malleable.[5] After 1975, governments fought inflation at the expense of employment.

Whatever one's view of the causes of unemployment, which are surely various, there is no question that it exerted mounting pressure on the social security system both by increasing demands for programs such as UI, employment services, welfare and health care, and by eroding the tax base of the federal and provincial governments. The official jobless rate rose from 4.2 percent in the 1950s to 5 percent in the 1960s, 6.7 percent in the 1970s, 9.3 percent in the 1980s, and 10 percent in the first half of the 1990s. In 1995, the real unemployment rate – which includes people who have given up actively searching for work and part-time workers who want full-time jobs – was 15.2 percent – 60 percent higher than the 9.5 percent official rate. The average duration of unemployment went from fourteen weeks in 1976 to twenty-four weeks in 1995. The growth in the 1980s and 1990s of "nonstandard" jobs, which are typically poorly-paid, benefit-thin, careerless, unstable, and performed by women, exacerbated the mass unemployment caused by the recessions which opened each decade and led to an increase in market income inequality. There is evidence of shrinkage of employment in the middle-earnings range as the expanding services sector has divided between well-paid high-skilled and poorly-paid low-skilled jobs. Another factor in earnings polarization is growing inequality in working time since the mid-1970s. Fortunately, social programs and (to a lesser extent) income taxes to date have managed to reduce the income gap between well-off and poor and to fully offset the increase in market income inequality during recessions.[6] Nonetheless, the labour market is a major source of economic insecurity that exerts strong and seemingly unrelenting pressure on social expenditures.

Demographic and social changes have added to the burden on the social security system. The rising labour force participation of women has increased the demand for child care and squeezed many parents – mothers especially – between the conflicting responsibilities of work and home. Marriage breakdown – Canada has one of the highest divorce rates in the world – is a prime cause of poverty and heavy welfare and social service caseloads. Our aging population will exert mounting pressure on pensions, health care, and social services until the baby boomers begin to die off in the 2030s.

These external factors are not the only stresses on the welfare state. There are also internal factors involving criticisms of social programs themselves. The current mantra "the social programs designed in the 1950s and 1960s are no longer relevant to the economy and society of the 1990s" is nothing new: alter the dates, and it would be familiar to policy makers and critics in previous decades, who also thought that their changing times demanded refurbished social programs. A partial list of public inquiries over the past twenty-five years arguing that various social programs need fixing include the federal White Paper on Income Security (1970), Quebec's Castonguay-Nepveu Commission (1971), the Senate Committee on Poverty (1971), the federal-provincial Social Security Review (1973–6), the Great Pension Debate (1979–1984) and the numerous reports it spawned, the Royal Commission on the Economic Union and Development Prospects for Canada (1985), the Child and Elderly Benefits Consultation Paper (1985), the Commission of Inquiry on Unemployment Insurance (1986), the Social Security Review (1994–5), and numerous provincial inquiries on welfare and health care. Periodic calls to reform pensions, UI, child benefits, welfare, social services, health care, and federal social transfers to the provinces are an imbedded trait of Canadian social policy.

TRANSFORMATION IN THE 1980S AND 1990S

By the 1980s, Canada's social security system was a long way from the theoretical virtuous circle of sustainable social policy envisioned by its pioneers. Spending restraint in an effort to combat the debt/deficit monster became the primary policy of the federal government and the dominant driving and shaping force behind social policy reform at both the federal and provincial levels. Governments began to act on the recurrent criticisms of social programs that had been made for many years.

Over the course of two majority terms, the Mulroney Conservatives made a series of significant and, in several cases, fundamental changes to social programs that were far from incrementalist "muddling through." Under the leadership of Finance Minister Michael Wilson, the Tories laid the foundation for a leaner, tougher, more targeted welfare state and a reduced federal presence in social security – a foundation upon which the Chrétien Liberals have built.

The various twists and turns of social policy under the Conservatives and Liberals have been charted in detail.[7] For now, I will simply summarize the major changes in each policy area.

Child benefits were a crucible of change. The children's tax exemption – one of Canada's oldest social programs, dating back to 1918 – was replaced by a nonrefundable child tax credit; the refundable child tax credit was boosted; family allowances were deuniversalized and converted to an income-tested program by means of the clawback; and finally, in 1993, all three programs were replaced by an income-tested Child Tax Benefit. The Child Tax Benefit operates like the refundable child tax credit although it is delivered monthly, like family allowances, and includes a Working Income Supplement (WIS) for working poor families with children (which the 1996 budget doubled from $500 to $1,000 per family). These changes were, in my view, sensible because they replaced a distributionally irrational system with a geared-to-income child benefit that provides its greatest assistance to lower-income families and an additional payment to the working poor (who receive less than welfare families when we take into account the value of social assistance benefits for the latter's children). Unfortunately, the Conservatives partially de-indexed the child benefits system, which has shaved unreported millions of dollars worth of benefits each year and most hurts low-income families (because the threshold for maximum benefits is falling steadily and child benefits constitute a larger share of poor families' income). To date, the Liberals have left in place this part of the silently operating machinery of social policy by stealth.

UI has been tightened up periodically ever since it was liberalized in 1971. Finance Minister Wilson withdrew federal funding of regionally extended benefits, fishermen's benefits, and benefits for people in training and job creation projects, placing the full financing burden on employers and employees, who experienced premium hikes in 1990, 1991, and 1992. Two rounds of belt-cinching, in 1990 and 1993, increased the qualifying period, reduced the maximum duration of benefits and the earnings-replacement rate, and denied benefits to workers who quit their jobs without just cause. While some of the resulting savings were used to improve skills upgrading programs and maternity, sickness, and parental leave benefits and to extend coverage to workers over sixty-five, critics accused the government of financing these improvements on the backs of the unemployed.

The Liberals' first (1994) budget prescribed more of the same medicine for UI in the quest for several billions of dollars worth of savings.

Employees had to work longer in order to qualify for benefits and generally collected benefits for a shorter period. The earnings-replacement rate was lowered again, from 57 to 55 percent of insurable earnings, although low- income beneficiaries with dependents to support had their rate raised from 57 to 60 percent (where it was before the Tories lowered it in 1993).

The new Employment Insurance Act (EI), which took effect on Canada Day 1996, made more radical changes to the three key levers that affect cost – eligibility requirements, benefit levels, and duration of benefits. Its key features are:

- Eligibility is now based on number of hours worked rather than weeks worked, extending coverage to a claimed 500,000 part-time workers. The work requirement is raised by 133 percent from 180–300 hours equivalent (depending on the regional unemployment rate) to 420–700 hours.
- Benefits (now labelled EI) remain at 55 percent of insurable earnings, but average weekly earnings will be calculated over a fixed period, ranging from fourteen to twenty-two weeks, depending on the regional unemployment rate. The more that is earned during this fixed period, the higher the benefits (to encourage people to seek out as much work as they can).
- Maximum insurable earnings are reduced from $42,380 to $39,000, lowering maximum benefits from $448 to $413 a week. Maximum benefits and maximum insurable earnings are frozen until 2000.
- Maximum length of claim is reduced from fifty to forty-five weeks.
- An "intensity rule" reduces benefits for claimants who have collected more than twenty weeks of benefits in the past five years by 1 percentage point for each additional twenty weeks of insurance benefits received during the previous five years, though benefits cannot fall below 50 percent of insurable earnings.
- A Family Income Supplement (up to $413 a week) provides higher benefits for unemployed parents with family income under $25,921. Benefits, including the supplement, can constitute up to 80 percent of a low-income parent's insured earnings.
- The income threshold for clawback drops from $63,570 to $48,750; claimants with annual incomes above this level must repay up to 30 percent of their benefits. For those who have used EI more than 20 weeks in the past five years, the clawback will begin at $39,000 and increase its recovery rate in stages for increasing weeks of claims, eventually reaching 100 percent for upper-income recipients ($73,000 or more) with over 120 weeks of benefits in the past five years.

- Employee premiums are lowered from $3.00 to $2.95 for every hundred dollars of insurable earnings, employer premiums from $4.20 to $4.13. The premium rates are set to create a reserve fund that can be used during recessions so that the federal government no longer will have to bail out the EI account when in deficit or significantly raise premiums.
- These changes will cut $2 billion from the annual cost of EI by 2001-2, of which $800 million will be redirected to wage subsidies, earnings supplements, self-employment assistance, job creation partnerships, and skills loans and grants. Meantime, a three-year $300 million fund is intended to help generate economic growth and new jobs.

Because UI has been scaled back several times since 1990, there has been a drop in the proportion of unemployed Canadians receiving benefits. In 1989, 87 percent of (officially) unemployed Canadians were beneficiaries of regular UI payments. By 1995, that percentage had dropped to only 52 percent of unemployed men and women. In every province west of Quebec, fewer than half of the unemployed are collecting regular UI benefits. In Ontario, the figure plummeted from 60 percent in 1989 to just 36 percent in 1995.[8] While the new EI program will extend coverage to many part-time workers, they and everyone else will have to work much longer to qualify for benefits. The name may be new, but one effect of the EI scheme is time-honoured: it will shift a heavier share of the burden of income support for the unemployed onto the provinces.

The federal government is also devolving responsibility for employment development services to the provinces. The provinces and territories will be able to deliver a variety of employment measures funded through the EI fund, including wage subsidies, income supplements, support for self-employment, job creation partnerships, and loans and grants for skill development. The provinces will be allowed to provide labour market services currently delivered by the federal government, such as counselling and placement. Ottawa will withdraw from labour market training.

On the pensions front, the Tories took a pratfall in their first (1985) budget by trying to partially de-index OAS benefits, but Charlie Brown and his pals licked their wounds and never made a political mistake again in social policy. (I'm counting the GST as economic policy.) They converted OAS from a universal to an income-tested program by means of a partially-indexed clawback, which removed benefits from upper-income seniors but over time will cut into the pensions of more and more middle-income pensioners. Their 1986 tax reforms converted the regressive age exemption and pension income deduction to nonrefundable credits, although the age exemption is only partially indexed and the pension income credit is unindexed.

The Liberals income-tested the age credit and applied the clawback to OAS before rather than after the fact, which was a telling move because it abandoned even the pretense of universality and set the stage for the Seniors Benefit announced in the 1996 federal budget. Slated to appear in 2001, the Seniors Benefit will fold OAS, the GIS, and the age and pension income credits into a single, family income-tested benefit payable to low- and middle-income seniors. Unlike the clawback on OAS and the age and pension income credits, the Seniors Benefit and its threshold will be fully indexed, which is a major victory.

The proposed Seniors Benefit has been attacked from the left for abandoning universality (which has been absent from old age pensions and child benefits since 1989 in any event) and for denying benefits to poor wives with rich husbands. It also has rung alarm bells on Bay Street from Registered Retirement Savings Plan (RRSP) sellers who claim that their upper-middle-income clients in the fifty-five to sixty age group will do better to stop contributing to RRSPs in order to avoid the bite of the 20 percent reduction rate of the Seniors Benefit.

The only way to assuage the left would be to abandon the Seniors Benefit and go back to the profligate days of universal old age pensions for all, including the wealthy, which in my view is a dumb way to run a social security system – no matter what the state of its coffers. The impact of the Seniors Benefit on upper-middle-income seniors could be eased by lowering the reduction rate, though that would increase expenditures and so compromise the cost-curbing intent of the legislation. It is important to understand that the Seniors Benefit will not reduce future expenditures in absolute terms, which is impossible given the aging of the population, but rather will only slow the increase. By 2030, the Seniors Benefit will deliver a projected $69.1 billion or $8.2 billion less than what the old system would have cost – $77.3 billion.[9] Even with the more targeted system, elderly benefits expenditures will more than triple between 1996 and 2030.

The CPP and the QPP are, at the time of writing, under review. The federal position is that future increases in the contribution rate required under current pay-go financing will be insupportable, though it advances this argument as if it were some sort of natural law of public policy rather than through evidence. But a combination of scare-mongering and a lack of understanding of the difference between social insurance and private pension plans has caused a crisis of confidence among the public, in particular younger Canadians who believe the CPP will not be there for them when they retire. A

1994 Gallup poll found that the majority of Canadians are not confident they will receive OAS and CPP/QPP benefits, with the largest proportion of doubting Thomases among the younger age groups.[10]

Two routes to reform have been advanced.[11] The first is a relatively quick (six to eight year) acceleration in the contribution rate to achieve a so-called "steady state" rate which will be lower than the rate that eventually will be reached if the plan continues on a pay-go course. A partial fund would be accumulated that could be managed by means of a market-savvy investment strategy that would earn a higher rate of return through smart management in diverse equities and thus allow future contribution rates to be lower than they otherwise would be under the present system. Another financing option is to freeze, lower, or eliminate the year's basic exemption. Although expanding the tax base in this way would allow the contribution rate to be lower than otherwise, the change would be regressive since it would increase contributions for low-earning contributors – unless they were compensated by an increase in the tax credit for CPP contributions.

The second approach is to reduce CPP benefits in various ways, such as lowering the earnings-replacement rate, partially indexing benefits, tightening the drop-out provision, increasing the age of eligibility, abolishing the death benefit, and tightening the administration and some design features of the disability benefit. Benefit reductions could bring down the steady-state contribution rate somewhat from 12.2 percent to around the magic 10 percent of pensionable earnings level (the pay-go rate eventually might hit 14.2 percent), which appears to be the target. Unfortunately, reducing benefits is a regressive move that would most hurt Canadians working for average wages or below, which includes the large majority of female workers. The CPP is already a modest pension plan. Reducing its benefits further is not the right route to reform.

Several changes to the tax system also warrant mention. The decision to partially de-index income tax brackets, as well as personal exemptions, deductions, and the nonrefundable credits (which replaced exemptions and deductions), created a smart stealth weapon in the war on the deficit because it imposed hidden income tax increases. But it was bad social policy, resulting in regressive tax hikes on unsuspecting taxpayers and a sliding federal taxpaying threshold, which fell from earnings of $10,037 in 1980 (in constant 1996 dollars) to just $6,367 in 1996. The refundable Goods and Services Tax (GST) credit eased though did not remove the burden of the GST on low-income Canadians. Unfortunately, both the credit and its income threshold were only partially indexed, resulting in a gradual erosion of the value of the credit and hence an increase in the burden of the GST, as well as a steady decline in the income threshold for maximum credits. The lamentable result is that only poor Canadians have to pay more GST each year, and, over time, the tax will become more regressive. The well-off, on the other hand, won a lower marginal tax rate and sizable increases in the maximum RRSP deduction.

Far more significant than the politically painless abolition of universal child benefits and old age pensions was the coming of the Canada Health and Social Transfer (CHST) in 1996, a social policy change that could significantly alter the shape of our social security system. The prelude to the CHST was the Tories' decision to partially index and then freeze federal transfer payments to the provinces under Established Programs Financing (EPF) for health and postsecondary education. They also effectively ripped up Ottawa's blank cheque for provincial welfare and social service costs by imposing a 5 percent cap on annual increases in CAP cost-sharing of welfare and social service expenditures in the three "have" provinces (Ontario, Alberta, and British Columbia). These changes removed billions of dollars from provincial social security systems and ushered in a period of uncooperative federalism that soured federal-provincial relations and put one more obstacle in the way of the unluckily-named (in view of the fate of its 1970s namesake) Social Security Review led by Lloyd Axworthy.

The CHST rolls CAP and EPF into a single – and significantly smaller – block fund for provincial human services, delivered as a combined tax point/cash transfer like EPF. The CHST has sparked strong criticism from policy analysts and social groups,[12] though one prominent economist paints a cheery picture of the measure.[13]

In 1995–6, the final year of the *ancien régime* of fiscal federalism, Ottawa's total cash transfer to the provinces under CAP and EPF came to $16.3 billion. In 1996–7, the first year of the brave new world of the CHST, federal cash payments to the provinces will be $12.6 billion (in constant 1995 dollars), or 23 percent less in real terms. However, the Finance Minister heeded protests about the impending demise of the CHST if it employed the same partial indexation formula as EPF, which would have seen federal cash payments dwindle to zero by 2009–10 according to my estimate. Instead, his 1996 budget established an $11 billion cash floor under the CHST for the life of the five-year agreement for 1997–8 to 2002–3.

If we measure the trend in the federal cash transfer to the provinces in real terms, it still declines substantially from $16.3 billion in 1995–6 (the final year of the old system) to a projected $9.9 billion by 2002–3, for a $6.4 billion or 39 percent real cut. On a year-over-year basis, the cumulative reduction in cash transfer payments over the life of the CHST to 2002–3 will amount to about $8 billion. As a share of total entitlements (i.e., tax points and cash transfers), the cash portion will fall from 59.8 percent in 1994–5 to 41.2 percent in 2002–3. No matter how you measure it, the federal government will be transferring a lot less money to the provinces than it used to.

The Canada Health Act's five conditions – universality, comprehensiveness, accessibility, portability, and public administration – still apply and will be enforced by the threat of reductions in CHST payments. But welfare will be subject to only one condition that existed under CAP – the prohibition of residency requirements. One provincial government – British Columbia – already has defied the residency requirement. Gone are the other three conditions of CAP as it applied to welfare – the requirement that income assistance be provided to all people in need, regardless of the cause of that need; the imperative that provinces operate an appeals system that allows welfare recipients to question decisions made with respect to their cases; and the reporting condition that provinces supply the federal government with basic statistics on the cost-shared programs.

The loss of the needs requirement is the biggest step backward in the history of Canadian social policy and a crippling blow to the concept of social security advanced by social reformers for over half a century. One of the most important achievements of the Canadian welfare state – the guarantee of an income safety net – could disappear. If provinces are not required to provide financial assistance on the basis of need, regardless of the reason for that need, they can introduce any form of income support they like – such as work-for-welfare – or simply disqualify the "undeserving poor," most likely "unemployed employables," and return to the days of categorical welfare programs for the deserving poor. Moreover, the substantial recent and ongoing cuts to UI/EI will dump many would-be beneficiaries onto the provincial welfare rolls – a common pattern in Canadian federal-provincial social policy. The guarantee of a safety net has become all the more important, especially in the face of continuing mass unemployment, the federal government's plans to make the new EI benefits harder to obtain, and the apparent ease with which politicians can win elections and cut spending by exploiting the age-old prejudice of many voters against welfare recipients.

Equally damaging is the loss of the requirement for provinces to put in place welfare appeal procedures, which are especially important given the welfare system's maze of rules and regulations whose complex, discretionary nature invites administrative error and inconsistent treatment. All public programs in Canada provide recourse for appeals; welfare should be no different. As to the loss of CAPs data reporting requirement, we can only hope that provincial governments will agree to continue providing basic data to the federal government – or to some central data-gathering facility, be that a panprovincial agency or a nongovernmental organization.

The demise of CAP means the end of built-in countercyclical protection, which has been an important economic policy function of the federal government. The pressure on the provinces will worsen during recessions, when welfare caseloads in particular increase as rising unemployment forces many jobless Canadians onto the welfare safety net because they exhaust their UI or do not qualify for the latter, which, in any case, will be harder to get under the new EI system. The federal government no longer will come to the rescue to pay half the cost of rising welfare bills. The province of Ontario offers a sobering case study of what happens when Ottawa no longer shares half the cost of welfare; by its account, Ontario lost $7.7 billion from 1990–1 through 1994–5 as a result of the "cap on CAP." The likely response on the part of the provinces will be to cut welfare benefits or even to deny welfare to certain "undeserving categories." Ontario did not bother waiting for the CHST, slashing its welfare rates by 21.6 percent in October of 1995 in accordance with the new government's election promise to get tough on welfare.

The CHST imposes no conditions whatsoever on social services, which is not all that different than before since CAPs only requirement in this area was that funds paid under its welfare services provisions go only to nonprofit agencies. Under the CHST, provinces will be free to fund for-profit social service agencies. Critics argue that for-profit child care, for example, is typically of lower quality than the nonprofit variety. Child care advocates, who call for an increase in licensed child care spaces and are appalled by the Liberal government's failure to come through with its promised $750 million infusion of new funds, fear the loss of federal dollars which under CAP brought matching provincial money. As to postsecondary education, EPF imposed no conditions, and of course neither will the CHST.

Proponents of the block-funding concept underlying the CHST argue that it will free the provinces from the shackles of CAP's rigid cost-sharing structure. To obtain federal funds under CAP, the provinces had to spend the money on approved welfare and social services and could not experiment with innovative approaches, such as combining health and social services at the community level, or creatively mixing education and social services (e.g., Headstart-type projects), or providing income-tested (as opposed to needs-tested) benefits that would include the working poor.

I would like to think that the CHST will spark a thousand points of light and usher in a social policy renaissance, but we could just as well be headed for the dark ages – or, at least, back to the early part of this century. The provinces can now use their (much diminished) federal dollars intended for human services for whatever purposes they desire. They can spend more on health and less on welfare, or less on social programs altogether. They can "experiment" with "innovative" programs such as mandatory "participation" of welfare recipients in voluntary associations which may well not welcome such uninvited, indentured workers. They can engage in what my colleague, Sherri Torjman, has characterized as a "race to the bottom" in social policy if they so choose.[14]

I am not trying to paint a picture where provincial politicians and their officials all wear black hats and federal politicians and their officials all sport white hats, though the *federales* do seem intent in riding off into the sunset. In theory, the CHST will allow provinces to pursue innovative social policy, such as integrating children's services provided by child welfare agencies, schools, and hospitals. The rub is that such innovations often require additional upfront money to get off the ground and take years to reap the fiscal rewards of preventive social services. But the CHST is removing billions of federal dollars from provincial coffers, which will throw a bucket of cold water on the sparks of social service innovation. Far from allowing preventive social services to flower, the CHST could make that laudable goal even harder to achieve and result in further social service cutbacks and the growth of privatized for-profit services.

Remember that the total loss in federal cash transfers over the next several years will be in the $7 to $8 billion range, depending on how you measure it – about what the federal government paid out to the provinces under CAP for welfare and social services. The loss of all but one of CAPs conditions and the fact that the cut in cash transfers under the CHST will approximate what Ottawa spent under CAP has led one expert to argue that the CHST rings the death knell of the federal government's role in provincial welfare and social services.[15]

The CHST also could jeopardize the health care system, despite the cash floor that Finance Minister Martin has placed under the CHST to maintain Ottawa's capacity to enforce the conditions of the Canada Health Act. It has long been recognized that we must invest more in health prevention, health promotion, and a wider range of community supports (e.g., homemaker and attendant care) to ease the burden on expensive medical and hospital care. But homemaker and other social services will have to compete with the far more popular health and postsecondary education ministries for scarcer funds, as will welfare, which doubtless will remain at the end of the line and suffer significant budgetary cuts. The large loss in federal transfers will exert heavy pressure on provincial revenues and make even the hallowed health care system a tempting target for some provincial finance ministers. The methods are familiar and include such "zombie" notions (to borrow the wonderful phrase of health economist Robert Evans) as user fees, extra-billing, delisting insured services, and imposing an income surtax on the sick to make them pay twice for their health care.[16] By so breaching the single-payer financing system, Canada's total health costs would rise and would add to our already considerable woes.

THE SOCIAL SECURITY SYSTEM TODAY

Most of the social security system that Allan MacEachen and other social policy pioneers built over the decades is still standing, the doomsayers notwithstanding. But it has changed profoundly over the past decade. The pace and depth of change have left even policy wonks and program administrators reeling and the public largely uncomprehending. Some of the most significant changes were finessed through "social policy by stealth" – the use of arcane and poorly understood technical changes to government programs, such as partial de-indexation and clawbacks, which were imposed on the Canadian people without their knowledge, consent, or understanding.[17]

The biggest changes have occurred at the federal level, though some of them have sent shock waves throughout the provinces. Two of the pillars of the universalist welfare state – family allowances and old age pensions – were toppled, not with a bang but a clawback. But I for one do not mourn their loss, since they were replaced by fairer and more sustainable income-tested programs.

UI, oft-criticized for being part of the problem rather than the solution and taking on income supplementation and equalization functions for which it was not intended, has been simultaneously shrunk in one way and expanded in another, given more income supplementation duties, taken even further from its social insurance origins, and given a new name. Some of the savings from cuts to UI/EI have been redirected to employment development services, for which the provinces will be able to assume responsibility over the next few years.

The CPP will survive, although it probably will have to hire some seasoned pension fund managers, and workers and employers probably will see their CPP contributions double within less than ten years. Three of the most devious and regressive changes were the partial indexation of the personal income tax system, child benefits, and the GST credit – stealthy policy at its finest. Income taxes are creeping ever upwards and the taxpaying threshold is steadily falling deeper below the poverty line; child benefits are declining in value year-by-year; and the leaky umbrella of the GST credit means that only one group of Canadians face an automatic increase each year in their GST – the poor.

Federal social transfers to the provinces for health, welfare, social services, and postsecondary education have been slashed, though the Finance Minister established a crucial cash floor at least until 2002–3. However, equalization payments have escaped the knife. Ottawa's only real remaining role in provincial social policy is enforcing the Canada Health Act – which could well become more difficult in future as the provinces grapple with their lost transfers and flex their newly-fledged wings after being booted out of the nest. While the federal government has not abandoned the welfare state in general, it has abandoned welfare.

Ottawa's commitment to expenditure restraint in social policy has not been unwavering. Several tax expenditures have been enriched, including the child care expense deduction, the disability credit, the medical expense credit, the education credit, the charitable donations credit, and the credit for infirm dependents (adult children and other relatives with disabilities). The refundable child tax credit was boosted in the mid-1980s (though the decision to partially index the child benefits system is eroding these gains), and the creation and recent doubling of the Working Income Supplement improved child benefits for the working poor.

Of more dubious merit were the decisions to increase substantially the tax deduction limits for contributions to Registered Pension Plans (RPPs) and RRSPs, which are regressive and costly tax expenditures. Between 1983 and 1993, the total income of taxfilers doubled, but RRSP contributions tripled (from $6.2 billion to $19.2 billion); the boost in the maximum tax deduction from $7,500 in 1990 to $11,500 in 1991 and $12,500 in 1992 helped account for a phenomenal 70 percent increase in RRSP contributions between 1990 and 1993 (when total taxfiler income grew by only 11 percent).[18] At last estimate (1992), total net federal and provincial expenditures amounted to a staggering $12.9 billion for the RPP deduction and $8.7 billion for the RRSP deduction. Upper-income taxpayers benefit most from these tax breaks and their enrichment, since the better-off are most likely to belong to an RPP and contribute to an RRSP, contribute larger amounts, and enjoy larger federal and provincial income tax savings because the benefits are delivered in the form of a tax deduction.

But the ongoing transformation of Canadian social policy is not as simple a story as some critics would have you believe. While the imperative of expenditure restraint has driven most of the changes, not all have been bad.

Both the public and private pension systems saw some improvements during the 1980s. The creation of the GST credit, though compromised by partial indexation, at least recognized the need to ease the regressive consumption tax burden on lower-income Canadians. The conversion of tax exemptions and most deductions to nonrefundable credits was a step towards a fairer income tax system. Income tax breaks for taxpayers with disabilities or caring for persons with disabilities have been improved somewhat. The child benefits system, though infected with the partial indexation virus, is fairer now than in the past because it gears benefits to income. The same goes for the various changes to elderly benefits over the last decade, culminating in the single, fully-indexed geared-to-income Seniors Benefit to take effect in 2001. Universal child and elderly benefits never made sense to me. They make even less sense at a time of tight public money, an aging population, and persistent poverty. The federal and provincial governments have wisely resisted the siren song to privatize the CPP and QPP, and will take steps to ensure their continuing viability – without, hopefully, significantly reducing benefits.

Despite cutbacks over the past decade, social programs have continued their long-term trend of contributing to a rising share of Canadians' income and offsetting both market and regional income inequalities. The various income security programs (e.g., old age pensions, the CPP and QPP, child benefits, UI, veterans' pensions, Workers' Compensation, welfare) provided by federal, provincial, and municipal governments constituted on average 6.1 percent of family income in 1971, 7.9 percent in 1981, 11.9 percent in 1991, and 12.5 percent in 1994. Single people saw their share of income from social programs rise from 10.2 percent in 1971 to 13.5 percent in 1980, 19.7 percent in 1991, and 21.7 percent in 1994.[19] The rising population of seniors, who rely heavily on social benefits, is an important factor in this upward trend, but so too are such forces as unemployment and marriage breakdown.

Government transfers and (to a lesser extent) the income tax system greatly reduce income disparities and, so far as present statistics show, have fully offset the trend to increasing inequality in market income. For example, families in the highest one-fifth of the income spectrum had twenty-two times the share of total market income (i.e., income from wages and salaries, investments, private pensions, and other private sources) as families in the lowest one-fifth (44.1 percent versus 2.0 percent) in 1994. Once social programs and the income tax system are factored into the equation, the gap between families with high and low incomes narrowed to five times in terms of after-tax income (36.8 percent as opposed to 7.7 percent) – a ratio essentially unchanged since Statistics Canada began publishing data on market income distributions in 1981.[20]

Social programs continue to reduce regional income inequalities, especially for the poorer provinces. In 1994, the average market family income in Newfoundland was $33,233 – the lowest of all the provinces – and came to 63.4 percent of Ontario's $52,459 average market family income – the highest of all the provinces. Add income from social programs and subtract income taxes, and the average after-tax family income in Newfoundland amounted to $35,596 in 1994 – 75.0 percent of Ontario's average after-tax family income of $47,458. The figures differ, but the pattern is the same for all the other provinces except British Columbia and Alberta, which rank second and third in terms of market family income ($50,881 and $50,344) and have 96–7 percent of Ontario's family income measured both before and after taxes and transfers.

A sobering fact is that, despite the retrenchment that has been going on since the mid-1980s, social spending continues to increase. The cuts have only slowed the social security juggernaut, not reversed its direction.

Social spending has generally outpaced economic growth since the war. Average annual social spending grew in real terms by 8.6 percent in the 1950s, compared to 5.6 percent for real GDP. During the 1960s, social spending growth averaged 8.1 percent a year, compared to 5.6 percent for GDP. In the 1970s, social spending rose by 8.9 percent a year on average, versus 5.2 percent for economic growth. In the 1980s, the annual real increase in social spending fell to 4.3 percent, but GDP growth declined proportionately more to 2.2 percent. While the restraint policies of successive federal governments slowed the upward curve of social expenditures in the 1980s and 1990s, social spending kept increasing more than the economy as late as 1992–3. Only in 1993–4 and 1994–5 (the most recent year for which estimates are available) did social spending finally stop increasing, largely because of deep cuts to UI. Ontario's ongoing deep cuts to welfare doubtless will reduce social spending further.

When Marsh wrote his *Report on Social Security for Canada* in 1943, he figured that his social security dream house would cost somewhere between 10 and 12.5 percent of GDP when it was completed. Canada's actual social security structure, a much more modest edifice than Marsh sketched out, cost 14.6 percent of GDP by 1978–9, when the last major new social program – the refundable child tax credit – was added. By 1994–5, the most recent year for which comprehensive data are available, social spending by all levels of government amounted to 19.5 percent of GDP – a far cry from Marsh's 10 to 12.5 percent target. Of course, Marsh never could have predicted either the numerator or denominator of the social spending-to-GDP ratio in the 1980s and 1990s as social expenditures expanded from heavy social, economic, and demographic demands and economic growth slowed.

Nor could the social policy pioneers have foreseen the shifting pattern of federal and provincial social spending. The federal share of total social expenditures declined from 71.6 percent in 1945–6 to 57.8 percent in 1992–3. By contrast, the provinces' share of social spending rose from 25.0 percent to 40.9 percent during the same period.

Social and women's groups and labour are depressed and angry at what they consider a deadly attack on the philosophy and practice of social security on the part of Ottawa and a number of provincial governments. They lament the federal government's fiscal and legislative retreat from its traditional leadership role in national social policy. They fear that the devolutionary fever sweeping through the corridors of power in provincial capitals across the country will cripple the welfare state. They feel duped by what they view as the phony consultations of the Social Security Review and the CPP review. Social policy is being run by the Department of Finance, which, in their eyes, is a classic case of the fox micromanaging the henhouse. Canadian social security is said to be sinking down to the level of the Americans, and with it a vital part of the national identity that distinguishes us from them.

This all sounds grim, especially after remembering the extraordinary achievement of Allan MacEachen and the others who built a social security system that, for all its faults, has immeasurably improved the lives of many millions of Canadians. Are things as bad as all that?

FIVE IDEAS FOR SOCIAL POLICY REFORM

I do not take quite so apocalyptic a view of Canadian social policy, in part because I applaud some of the changes (the move to income-tested child and elderly benefits, the creation of the refundable GST credit, and the conversion of tax exemptions and deductions to nonrefundable credits) and, in fact, proposed one of them – the Seniors Benefit.[21] Moreover, there are encouraging signs of a willingness to consider more radical reforms that would strengthen Canada's social security system, and they have come from the provinces who realize the enormous implications of the new fiscal federalism. These changes involve a substantial redesign of the architecture of social security.

I can offer here only a very brief account of such ideas. They have been discussed at greater length elsewhere.[22] The proposals that follow are in no way intended as a comprehensive platform of social policy reform, but they are a major component.

1. *National Child Benefit*

The proposal that probably stands the greatest chance in the near future is for a national child benefit, sometimes called an integrated child benefit. The idea is actually an old chestnut, having appeared in various guises in reports dating as far back as the 1943 Marsh report and, more recently, in Ontario's *Transitions* and *Turning Point* reports, and the federal Discussion Paper on Social Security Reform. The Caledon Institute called for an integrated child benefit in its 1995 report, *One Way to Fight Child Poverty*, which was the first to present a concrete, costed option. Several provinces have taken a major step towards an integrated child benefit by reforming their income support programs for families with children. British Columbia and Alberta have led the way; Quebec and Saskatchewan plan similar reforms.

A national child benefit would replace the federal Child Tax Benefit and WIS and provincial welfare and other income security payments on behalf of children with a single, income-tested benefit for all lower-income families, whatever their sources of income. Such a benefit and its threshold must be fully indexed to stop the steady erosion of child benefits that is occurring under the present system.

Properly designed, a national child benefit would offer several advantages. At present, welfare families with children receive larger child benefits than the working poor; welfare families' combined provincial social assistance benefits for their children and the federal Child Tax Benefit are more than working poor families' Child Tax Benefit and WIS. Not only is this difference unfair, but it works as a disincentive for parents on welfare to move into the workforce because they lose income from welfare benefits for their children at the same time as they incur employment-related expenses and have their low incomes reduced further by income taxes, CPP contributions, and EI premiums. An integrated child benefit would remove this disincentive and help families get off welfare, stay in the labour force, and (in some fortunate cases) work their way out of poverty. It would provide working poor families with a badly needed supplement to their earnings. A new child benefit would offer a tangible commitment by both levels of government to combat child poverty. It is not a silver bullet in the war against child poverty – which is far too complex a problem to be vanquished by a single social program – but it would be a powerful weapon.

A national child benefit is more than sound social policy. It also would help renew the federation by demonstrating that the federal and provincial governments can create a new kind of creative public policy. A national child benefit could combine a larger federal base with provincially-tailored income-tested child benefits and/or earnings supplements harmonized with provincial labour market policies. Thus a national child benefit would strengthen national standards and allow for provincial asymmetry. Together, the federal and provincial governments could build an effective new antipoverty program that neither could accomplish alone.

2. Income Security for Canadians with Disabilities

Another good old idea resurrected by the provincial/territorial Ministerial Council on Social Policy Reform and Renewal is a comprehensive income security system for Canadians with disabilities. The Marsh report and a number of other studies over the years recommended social insurance for persons with disabilities. What we have instead is an unconnected collection of various public and private benefits that developed willy-nilly over the years, including Workers' Compensation, the CPP and QPP disability benefit, UI, veterans' benefits, welfare, several tax expenditures (the disability credit, the infirm dependants credit, the medical expenses credit, and the attendant care expense deduction), private long-term disability insurance, auto insurance, and criminal injuries compensation. Sherri Torjman has summarized the problems thus: "Eligibility and benefits are based to a large extent on cause of disability – how and why the disability occurred – rather than on level of need. People with virtually the same functional capacity receive very different types and levels of benefit depending upon how the disability occurred."[23] Many people with disabilities do not qualify for most of these programs, and have to turn to welfare, which, in turn, adds to their other problems in finding and keeping a job.

A new income security system for Canadians with disabilities would replace much or all of the present hodgepodge of programs and benefits. Ideally, all persons with disabilities "including both earners and non-earners, would be included in a comprehensive redesign. Right now, the only choice for non-earners with no private resources is to rely on provincial welfare. A more integrated, rationalized set of programs would reduce the complexity of the current system and would minimize costly duplication and excessive administrative costs. Partial work would be permitted, thereby (in theory) reducing disincentives to work."[24]

3. Income Security for Unemployed Canadians

A third worthy recommendation in the provinces' report is to harmonize or integrate UI (now EI) and welfare for unemployed employables. This too is a venerable but sound idea that dates back to the social reformers of the 1930s and 1940s. Caledon recommended to Minister Axworthy that the federal government create a new Employment Assistance program (providing both income benefits and access to employment development services) for people who are frequently unemployed or unemployed over a long period. This program would complement UI, which would return to its original purpose of helping those who are unemployed only occasionally or for a short time.

Such an integrated income security system for the unemployed makes a lot of sense. It would stem the wasteful and dispiriting flow of unemployed Canadians between provincial welfare and federal UI via short-term make-work jobs, and offloading from UI to welfare when UI undergoes one of its periodic bouts of belt-tightening. It would stop the unequal treatment of jobless men and women who get a better deal from UI (not just higher benefits, but also access to training and other employment development services). It would stop the warehousing of unemployed people in the welfare system.

Taken together, these three income security innovations could take Canadian social security a giant step forward. The reforms would go a long way to dismantling the welfare system, since they would provide income security benefits to the majority of the welfare caseload – children, persons with disabilities, and unemployed employables. These proposals would achieve what has never been possible in the past – national standards for virtually the entire income security system. The programs would be national rather than federal, jointly designed and maintained by the federal and provincial governments (like the CPP), though they could be delivered by either one or in combination. The measures could allow for some degree of variation from one province to another, within limits. My own preference is for a strong federal role in funding and delivery, leaving the provinces to concentrate on their own heavy responsibilities in the areas of health, social services, and employment development services.

Further asymmetry in social policy, if not political identity, is inevitable for Quebec. Whether the same degree of parallelism that exists between the CPP and QPP could be achieved for the income security programs advocated here is doubtful. However, Quebec traditionally has been an innovative and usually progressive force in social policy, and probably would be receptive to the kinds of ideas proposed here providing it designed and delivered them itself with some compensating federal funding.

I am fully aware of the prodigious labour involved in designing, financing, and negotiating the three new programs. It would take years to complete such an ambitious project of reform. If the federal government assumed full responsibility for financing, the provinces would rejoice because they would save money they now spend on welfare. Ottawa might insist that the provinces give up some tax room in return, contrary to the wishes of a province like Ontario which might like its full CHST entitlement delivered as a tax transfer. Nonetheless, income security changes of this magnitude would require some sorting out of federal and provincial revenues. Another tough issue is the appropriate blend of payroll taxes and general revenues required to finance income systems for people with disabilities and for the unemployed – both forms of taxation being highly unpopular these days.

We could begin with the national child benefit, which itself poses considerable challenges. Caledon's illustrative proposal would increase federal benefits from their current level (up to $1,233 per child under seven and $1,020 per child seven to seventeen from the Child Tax Benefit, and up to $1,000 per working poor family from the WIS) to a maximum $3,000 for the first child, $2,500 for the second, and $2,000 for the third and each additional child. The Caledon option also would convert the nonrefundable equivalent-to-married credit to a refundable single parent supplement as part of the integrated child benefit. Families on welfare would receive about the same as or somewhat more than they do now, though designing a uniform national child benefit to achieve this objective is difficult because welfare payments vary widely within and across provinces for various sizes and types of families; as a result, some provincial variability likely would be required in a final design. Working poor families would enjoy a substantial improvement in their incomes. Under our proposal, a low-wage family with two children (one under seven and one over seven) would see its child benefits increase by 69 percent – from $3,253 to $5,500.

The Caledon child benefit scheme would cost some $2 billion more than existing spending. Different designs are possible – the Caledon option was not brought down from the mount engraved in stone –

but an adequate national child benefit would require additional spending in that ball park. Less expensive options are possible, but would pack a weaker antipoverty punch and might result in income losses for welfare families. Over time, part of the additional cost of a national child benefit would be offset by savings on families which leave welfare for the workforce. Trimming some of Canada's $50 billion-plus social tax expenditure budget and/or instituting a wealth tax could make up the rest. While potentially politically controversial, such tax changes could be sold as necessary for Parliament to honour its 1989 resolution to work toward eliminating child poverty by the year 2000.

So also would a decent income security plan for people with disabilities likely cost more, since it would provide better benefits to those who are currently on welfare. Three design issues that would affect costs are the definition of disability (a thorny issue always), the level of benefits, and the method of means-testing. An income-tested program likely would expand eligibility over needs-tested welfare and so could add to the cost. Creating a new system by reassembling the disability-related elements of existing programs is a daunting task. Private insurers likely would oppose any attempt to take business away from them by expanding public provisions. There is enormous inertia in long-established programs and resistance to change. On the other hand, moving to a no-fault insurance system could produce cost savings, as would consolidating the administration of the present multi-program collection of income benefits for Canadians with disabilities.

4. Low Income Tax Credit

A proposal that I have been advocating since my days at the National Council of Welfare is a low income tax credit.[25] This measure would put a stop to the falling income tax threshold from partial indexation, which has reached a scandalously low level ($6,367) and places one more obstacle in the way of low-wage workers (including many people with disabilities). A low income tax credit would remove or at least reduce the income tax burden on the working poor. Since the refundable GST credit also suffers from the corrosive effects of inflation, it should be fully indexed. Better still, the proposed low income tax credit could integrate both income tax and GST relief for low-income Canadians in a single program. Ideally, such a low income tax credit eventually could be expanded to provide some relief for poor people in every province and territory from provincial sales taxes, which would be more feasible if we achieved some form of national consumption tax.

5. *Expanded Range of Insured Health Services*

In his 1964 report of the Royal Commission on Health Services, Justice Emmett Hall recommended that the scope of insured health services be progressively expanded over time to include home care services, prescription drugs, prosthetic devices, mental health services, and dental care for children, pregnant women, and welfare recipients. That idea was not new, even in the 1960s: the Canadian Medical Association's pioneering call for national health insurance in 1934 had recognized the need to include community-based preventive care in the ambit of insured health services.[26] Some progress has been made in broadening the scope of insured services, but nowhere near what Hall recommended.

This issue is on the table again. The provinces' report notes the growing importance of "preventative, promotive, supportive and rehabilitative services" and recommends that the provincial and territorial health ministers review and identify the range of insured services.[27] While the exclusion of the federal Minister of Health from this proposed review is not acceptable, nonetheless the Canada Health Act should be revisited with a view to expanding the range of insured health services so as to cover preventive and supportive services as well as prescription drugs – thus providing better, more efficient health care and controlling overall health expenditures.

BACK TO THE FUTURE: NATIONAL COLLABORATION

A common theme that emerges from these ideas for social security reform is the need for federal-provincial cooperation. We must revive the spirit of cooperative federalism that built the postwar welfare state which is now under reconstruction. However, the federally-driven cooperative federalism of the past must give way to a new collaborative federalism based on equal partnership and shared commitment to strong social policy and widely-held values and objectives. The answer decidedly does not lie in the current simplistic vogue for devolutionism and disentanglement. Richard Van Loon put it well when he said (I am paraphrasing) that we should not be afraid of the kind of federal and provincial "entanglement" that created vital social programs such as the CPP, QPP, and medicare.

The fact that the provincial and territorial governments have come forward with some promising ideas for new national social programs is encouraging and significant, demonstrating a willingness to move past the uncooperative federalism of recent years. The federal government should respond positively to this welcome overture, not only for the sake of strengthening social policy, but also to demonstrate through deeds rather than just words the continued viability of Canada as a federal state.

Proposals for a New National Policy

THOMAS J. COURCHENE

If capital is borrowable, raw materials are buyable and technology is copyable, what are you left with if you want to run a high-wage economy? Only skills, there isn't anything else.[1]

INTRODUCTION

As we approach the third millennium, we are embarking on a new era in social policy. With knowledge progressively at the cutting edge of competitiveness, aspects of social policy are now becoming indistinguishable from national economic policy. Of and by itself, this will transform both the conception and the role of social policy in Canadian society. There is more, however. With the information revolution empowering individual citizens relative to institutions, both corporate and government, the next century will privilege people rather than goods or services or capital. We have devoted considerable attention and research to securing our internal economic union. But in this era of internationalization, goods and services and capital will flow over, around, and under any and all borders. The new challenge is to preserve and promote the east-west internal social union, since labour is typically not mobile internationally. Of special importance is the interprovincial mobility of occupational skills and accreditation. Overlaying all of this is the process of globalization which, in turn, requires that all policy, social policy included, must effectively become international or, at the very least, be consistent with the dictates of global integration. In tandem, the result of all of this is nothing short of a paradigm shift for social policy.

One important corollary is that Canada is probably in need of a new "national policy." John A's national policy (tariffs, ribbons of steel, and immigration) built a nation from sea to sea, but has now been overwhelmed by the forces of globalization and integration. Canada's twentieth-century national policy (interregional equity and the development of the welfare state) served us exceedingly well and gave us a confident identity in the upper half of North America. But it, too, is fading away, in part because it privileged place over people and, in part, because it was conceived in an era of plenty and developed quite independently of, and often at cross purposes with, domestic and international economic challenges. Hence, Canada needs a new national policy. Lester Thurow's frontispiece provides what I believe is the answer to this quest – human capital.

Consistent with this human capital thrust, elsewhere[2] I have attempted to develop a "mission statement," as it were, for twenty-first century Canada: to be a Canadian in the twenty-first century must mean that all citizens have access to a social policy infrastructure that allows them full opportunity to develop and enhance their skills and human capital in order that they can be full participants in the Canadian and global societies and economies. Hopefully, others can improve on this attempt to outline a new national policy, but what appears certain is that the defining characteristic of Canada and Canadians in the third millennium will be the nature of our social infrastructure.

In this context, the purpose of this survey paper becomes straightforward: can we get there from here?

The paper begins by surveying the evolution of the welfare state in western democracies. The analysis draws heavily from a schema developed by Hugh Heclo,[3] in which he classifies welfare-state development into four stages – experimentation, consolidation, expansion, and reformulation. These stages are then linked to social policy developments in Canada, albeit more at the analytical than the practical or program level. Arguably, Heclo's last stage – reformulation – still applies, since it is steeped in both the neoconservative and fiscal-restraint rhetoric. However, in line with the above claim for a paradigm shift in social policy, I prefer to add a fifth stage, one that incorporates some of the features of the reformulation stage but then places key emphasis on the forces of globalization and the knowledge/information revolution.

The paper turns to focus on the process and substance of social policy reform initiatives as we approach the millennium. The analysis begins with my version of an appropriate social policy blueprint, but then focuses on the federal government initiatives and, in particular, the introduction of the Canada Health and Social Transfer (CHST) in the 1995 federal budget. This is a watershed in the evolution of social Canada. Then, in the section entitled, "A Funny Thing Happened on the Way to the Millennium," the analysis puzzles over the fact that Ottawa is embarking on a wholesale decentralization and devolution of the social envelope. Part of the answer is that social Canada has become enmeshed with priorities relating to national unity. In any event, the social policy ball is now in the provinces' court. Is it possible that they could deliver on a full-blown socio-economic union? The answer is not the emphatic "no" that might quickly come to mind. But it may not be "yes" either. In effect, we are about to witness a provincially led attempt to take more responsibility for the social envelope. No firm conclusions are drawn about this exercise, but the implication is that if the provinces cannot satisfy the social needs of Canadians, then the pendulum will again swing back to Ottawa.

Some concluding comments complete the paper.

THE EVOLUTION OF THE
CANADIAN WELFARE STATE

In his perceptive overview of the history of welfare states in industrial countries, Hugh Heclo[4] identifies four stages of development and the manner in which the prevailing paradigms in economic, political, and social philosophy interacted with each stage. These four stages – experimentation, consolidation, expansion, and reformulation – are chronicled in Table 1. While Canada does not conform exactly to this schema, the basic evolutionary chronology and analytical concepts ring surprisingly true.

For example, two important forces facilitated the transition from the stigmatizing and selective nature of most forms of Canadian social policy in the experimentation stage. The first related to the social and political aftermath of the Great Depression and the Second World War. The mass economic dislocation of the Great Depression dispelled forever the (then) widely held notion that the need for social assistance was confined to a small minority of citizens whose requirements could be met by a highly selective set of relief programs and by the "goodwill of relief offices."[5] These societal concerns for guaranteeing more socio-economic security were enhanced by the homecoming of the soldiers – a group so obviously deserving of economic security in return for their valiant efforts that the need for creative social policy initiatives on their behalf was never in doubt. Among our early successes on the social policy front were the educational programs designed to build the human capital of these returning soldiers.

Combined with political and social concerns was the second force – the advent of the Keynesian revolution. One of the central messages of Keynesianism was that the economy would not, except by accident, equilibrate at full employment. Hence, it was necessary for governments to engage in "pump-priming" policies in order to achieve full employment. More to the point, monies spent on social programs

Table 1
Stages of the Welfare State

	Experimentation (1870s-1920s)	Consolidation (1930s-40s)
Economics		
Events	• international diffusion of business cycle; dislocations of industrialization	• depression, wartime planning, destruction, reconstruction in austerity setting
Reactions	• relief of distress via *ad hoc* exceptions to "laws" of political economy	• integration of social expenditures with doctrines of demand management
Politics		
Events	• workers' movements, suffrage extensions, growth of mass parties	• discrediting opponents of national government activism
Reactions	• policy innovations seeking to accommodate liberal, conservative, and socialist principles	• all-party governments in war; emerging consensus on postwar reconstruction
Social policy		
Form	• innovation and volatility in programming "constitutional" argument on boundary problems	• unification of previous experiments
Contents	• dispensations for the deserving poor and working class; social insurance invented	• remedies for risks shared by all citizens
Value choices	• attemps to reconcile liberty, equality, and security	• demonstrations that the three values are mutually reinforcing

Table 1
(*continued*)

Expansion (1950s-60s)	Reformulation (1970s-?)
• unexpected sustained economic growth	• unexpected combinations of recession and inflation
• intensified commitment to full employment; growthmanship as solvent as economic trade-offs	• ad hoc attempts to subordinate social policy to a new sense of scarcity
• political bidding and group competition for painless policy growth	• political disaffection: electoral volatility; distrust in traditional appeals
• declining necessity for political commitment and building; "end of ideology" ideology	• competition to reduce expectations and avoid unpopularity; neoliberal attacks on tax, spending, and bureaucracy issues
• filling gaps and extending inherited approaches	• reopening "constitutional" issues; inadvertent extension in boundaries of social policy
• compensations to preserve rising living standards; group struggle for relative shares of increases	• marginal slowdowns in spending and programming; low-cost substitute means to seek same social goals
• denial that important value choices are at stake	• new recognition of "tragic" choices; search for positive-sum relationships

Source: Heclo, "Toward a New Welfare State."[2]

would not only aid the recipients but, via the Keynesian multiplier process, would provide greater employment and economic security for all. The best Canadian exemplar here is the equalization program. One could argue that Ontario's willingness to be part of a system that transferred revenues to the poorer provinces was a magnanimous gesture on Ontario's part. However, it is also true that, without equalization, the poorer provinces would never have supported the decentralization of the personal income tax system, for example. More to the point, with trade largely flowing east-west (this relates to the 1950s when equalization was instituted), and with Ontario as the principal north-south conduit, the "second-round" spending impacts of equalization transfers would likely find their way back to the golden triangle. This underscores the Heclo observation relating to the serendipitous consistency of societal values in the consolidation and expansion eras – in this case, equalization was consistent with both interregional equity and the pursuit of full employment in all of Canada. Thus, as is indicated in the row panel on value choices in Table 1, it finally became possible to reconcile the broad societal goals of liberty, equality, and security: "social policy was not only good economics, but the economic and social spheres of public policy were integrally related to each other."[6]

Working in tandem, these forces launched the beginnings of the modern Canadian welfare state. In the process, the relationship between the citizen and the state underwent a fundamental transformation. In response to the loosening of traditional ties – the family, the church, social, and friendship networks – the state was called upon to supplant the traditional source of protection and economic security. Not only was charity institutionalized but, as Scott Gordon has noted, "it was transferred from the realm of benevolence into that of justice" and, in the process, "the state conferred upon its citizens the right to receive aid from society with a minimum of reference to the sentiments of compassion and benevolence which activated the older forms of charity." Gordon links these developments to Sir William Beveridge's famous 1942 report on the UK social security system (which inspired similar blueprints on this side of the Atlantic). Referring to this report as the "Beveridge transform," Gordon asserts that "it may turn out to be the most significant change in the socio-economic relationship of western society since labour became a commodity which was bought and sold in the marketplace."[7]

Keith Banting's take on this transition from experimentation to consolidation (and, indeed, to the expansionary stage as well) is that it was at the same time both a "flight from selectivity" (i.e., a move toward universality) and a "modernization of selectivity" (e.g., a move from means testing to income testing). Banting further argues that in this time frame, the motivating force behind the social policy evolution was a "drive for mass security, for predictability, for social rights" rather than for redistribution, per se, which is why Banting suggests that the emphasis on universality dominates the modernization of selectivity: "In a sense then, the modern welfare state represented a move away from redistribution, at least in the vertical sense. Redistribution was to be from the employed to the unemployed, the healthy to the sick, the non-aged to the aged, and so on. Many of the founders of the welfare state probably thought that as a secondary consequence there would be an important narrowing of the general pattern of income inequality, but that was not their primary aim."[8]

This observation is important because, as will become clear in the ensuing analysis, one of the criticisms of the evolution of the Canadian welfare state is that its emphasis on generalized economic security did little to address the growing income inequality. Banting's response would presumably be that it was not intended to do so.

The Era Of Expansion

While the constellation of forces that forged the consolidation of the welfare state served as necessary and important catalysts, what really triggered the era of expansion was the unprecedented and sustained affluence of the 1950s and 1960s. In Canada's case, this increase came to full bloom in the Pearson era (with substantial contributions at the political and advisory levels by Allan MacEachen and Tom Kent respectively). During this period of the blossoming of our welfare state, social policy initiatives included the Canada and Quebec Pension plans (CPP/QPP), the Guaranteed Income Supplement (GIS), the Canada Assistance Plan (CAP), the conversion of equalization into a comprehensive program, the current medicare and hospital insurance programs and, somewhat later, the Department of Regional Economic Expansion and the comprehensive reformulation and expansion of the Unemployment Insurance (UI) program. Yet, despite the explosion of the social policy network, the cumulative fiscal balance at the federal level over the 1965–74 decade was a *surplus* of some $2.75 billion! To be sure, not all of this happy fiscal circumstance was due to the rapid economic growth. Two other factors were also important. First, tax rates were increased substantially during this period. The second was that this was the golden era of budgetary finance. As is clear from Figure 1, the rate of growth of Gross Domestic Product (GDP) exceeded the rate of interest by over 6 percentage points throughout 1965–74. This means that a balanced budget would lead to 6 percent decrease in the debt/GDP ratio (because the denominator was increasing 6 percentage points in excess of the numerator). Indeed, we could run rather substantial deficits and still record decreases in the debt/GDP ratio. As is evident in Figure 1, and as will be highlighted later, the recent period has been characterized by the opposite combination – a rate of interest in excess of the growth rate – with ominous implications for both the debt/GDP ratio and social Canada.

Analytically, Heclo perceptively focuses on one key aspect of this expansionist era – the declining political and economic price of social policy initiatives: "After a generation or more of expansion, the democratic welfare states had produced a policy system that was admirably attuned to – and presumed – continuous economic growth. Politically it was a low cost system whose operation generated minimum conflict and maximum, if somewhat passive, support. Economically it was in rough harmony with conventional thinking about fiscal management. Socially it avoided raising difficult questions about social values. *Commitments on the welfare state rose as commitment to it fell*"[9] (emphasis added). Coincident with these developments was a quite dramatic alteration in the demands on governments in the name of generalized "social policy." The original concerns about economic security came to encompass appeals to compensate those who lagged behind in the relative income race. Moreover, with the refinement of the principles of economic welfare and social justice, the demands on the state transcended the domain of "needs" and entered the realm of "wants." Indeed, they broadened into a very encompassing set of claims – social, political, environmental, cultural, etc. As Daniel Bell remarked, "the revolution of rising expectations, which has been one of the chief features of western society in the past 25 years, is being transformed into a *revolution of rising entitlements* in the next 25"[10] (emphasis added). It may well be the case that social policy in this era was not primarily viewed as a safety net designed to facilitate adjustment to a changing economic reality, but these developments moved it sharply further away from this framework and toward the conception that its role was to provide citizens with something akin to property rights to the status quo.[11] A large part of what is afoot today on the social policy front is a not-very-disguised attempt to unwind these property rights and sinecures.

Beyond this, there were two further characteristics of the expansionist era that merit highlighting. The first is probably unique to Canada. As Banting[12] notes, most European welfare states arose in the context of national class and political struggles at the central government level. However, much of the Canadian social policy development was

Figure 1
Dynamics of the Federal Debt/GDP Ratio

Net federal debt as a percentage of GDP

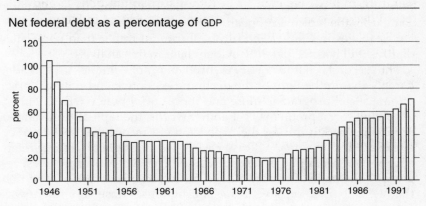

Operating balance as a percentage of GDP

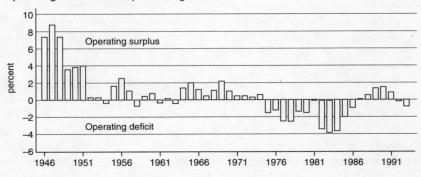

Effective rate of interest minus smoothed rate of growth of nominal GDP

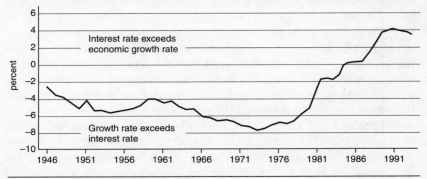

Sources: Public Accounts, Statistics Canada, and Bank of Canada. Reproduced from Government of Canada, *A Framework for Economic Policy* (Department of Finance, 1994).

inextricably tied to interprovincial equity issues. This emphasis on territorial redistribution (e.g., equalization) rather than class redistribution, per se, as the fulcrum for social policy developments sets Canada aside from the typical European welfare state. Likewise, the social policy cleavages in Canada tend to be territorial rather than pan-Canadian, as will become patently evident later in this analysis.

The second characteristic is probably not unique to Canada, namely that in the light of the declining economic and political price of new social programs "more and more social policy was ... aimed at solving social problems."[13] In other words, the rapid and sustained economic growth during the expansion era meant that social policy could be, and in Canada's case clearly was, designed without reference to key economic issues such as efficiency, work incentives, regional adjustment, etc. Indeed, we perceived ourselves to be so rich that we embarked on several social programs whose very intent was to interfere with the processes of individual and regional economic adjustment. One legacy of this period is "transfer dependency," a concept that is now widely understood, but largely incapable of being addressed because it has fallen into Daniel Bell's "entitlements" category or, as I prefer, a proprietary claim on the status quo. More generally, this is part and parcel of the earlier observation that commitments on the welfare state rose as commitment to it fell.

By way of summary, the 1960s were the good old days. During this decade, the unemployment rate hovered around 4 percent and productivity increased by 50 percent. The world economy was not only tranquil but expanding rapidly. Canada was nestled comfortably at or near the top of the international rankings of per capita GDPs. Given this environment, it is hardly surprising that Canada used its cushion of growth and its incredible resource endowment to mount a comprehensive and generous network of transfers to persons, governments, and business. This seemed wholly appropriate at the time, including the de-linking of the social and economic spheres. And it would still be appropriate if the underlying economic buoyancy remained unchanged. However, beginning with the first oil price shock in 1973–4, the economic environment altered radically, to the point where almost none of the conditions that led to the expansionary era of the evolution of our welfare state still obtained. Nonetheless, Canadians remained justifiably proud of their postwar accomplishments on the social policy front, so much so that in the great Free Trade Agreement (FTA) debate and election, our social policies came to the fore in terms of giving us a special identity in the upper half of North America. The only problem with this was that the evolutionary die was already long cast; the Pearson conception of social Canada was no longer sustainable and, equally important, no longer appropriate. Enter the "reformulation" stage of our social policy evolution.

The Reformulation Era

Virtually all aspects of the environment that underpinned the 1950s and 1960s explosion of social Canada evaporated in the decade or so following the initial oil price shock. Productivity growth stalled and unemployment rates mushroomed to, and remained in, double digits. Fiscal deficits were nothing short of staggering – the $2.75 billion cumulative federal surplus over the 1965–74 decade turned into a $125 cumulative deficit over 1975–84. And, by the end of 1994, the federal debt/GDP ratio was four-fold in 1975 value. If one adds provincial debt to federal debt, our aggregate debt/GDP ratio is now in the 105 percent range. In addition, the world economy became anything but tranquil. Economies everywhere were in full restructuring mode, and the new global economic order became much more competitive, particularly with the rise of the Asian "tigers." On the domestic economic front, the resource boom collapsed in the early 1980s, and resource rents evaporated with the result that the 1980s were especially problematic for the resource-based provinces. And the tariff walls came tumbling down, a process hastened by the FTA and the North American Free Trade Agreement (NAFTA), but inevitable in any event.

On the domestic policy front, the latter half of the 1980s were the macro equivalent to the social policy splurge of the Pearson era – personal and corporate tax reform, the FTA, the Goods and Services Tax (GST), and the Bank of Canada's shift toward price stability. While most economists would support all of free trade (the FTA), an export-import neutral value-added tax (the GST) to replace the manufacturers' sales tax and price stability, to run them together in the same time frame was, in effect, "macro overkill." As I and others have argued,[14] the bank's price stability initiative was especially problematic. By raising interest rates and dramatically appreciating the value of the Canadian dollar, the pursuit of price stability not only delayed the expected gains from the FTA, but substantially exacerbated our already perilous fiscal position – the high interest rates resulted in enormous debt-service charges, while the sharply appreciated dollar, by depressing economic activity, clobbered revenues and triggered substantial welfare and UI increases. Coincident with all of this was the global economic downturn of the 1990s. As Fortin[15] emphasizes, the worst of the price stability exercise may not be behind us, since our attempt to run a lower inflation rate than the Americans, when roughly 80 percent of our exports go south, may really be a policy of secular stagnation and permanently higher real interest rates, given the frictions associated with both the ability to achieve domestic nominal wage cuts and, internationally, to convince investors that Canadian bonds should trade at a discount relative to American bonds. These issues merit highlighting because they were important contributing factors to the watershed 1995 federal budget.

One would be remiss to neglect the positive side of all of this. After all, the mid-1980s (1984–9) represented Canada's, or at least Ontario's, longest postwar boom, although this was followed by the sharpest economic downturn since the Great Depression. And, thanks to the exchange-rate appreciation, among other factors, Canada's private sector has undergone a most impressive, although painful, restructuring. We are more competitive with the Americans than we have been for a long time. With the exchange rate somewhere around seventy-three cents, and with the purchasing power parity rate presumably somewhere in the mid-eighty cent range, it is no surprise that our exports are booming. The irony is that as long as we maintain substantially higher real interest rates than the Americans, we will be becoming, at the same time, progressively more competitive and progressively closer to a fiscal default.

The relevance of all of this for social policy evolution is that just as the unexpected and sustained growth underpinning the expansionist era allowed social policy to take on a life of its own – a residual luxury, as it were, supported by the nation's economic surplus – the equally unanticipated and sustained economic turmoil of the reformulation era (except perhaps for the mid-1980s) meant that social policy was bound to fall on hard times. As Heclo notes, the economic pessimism rekindled the traditional view that there are inherent contradictions (or "tragic choices" as indicated in Table 1) among the basic values of democratic welfare states: "It [the welfare state] was expensive, so expensive that costs of social policy were themselves posing a threat to individuals' economic security. It was ineffective, generally in providing high standards of service and particularly in making inroads into the gross inequalities of market-oriented societies. And it was dangerous, threatening to pursue welfare at the expense of individual liberty."[16]

The notion that social policy was perceived as not adequate in terms of addressing income inequalities (as indicated in the middle sentence of the above quote) reflects, in part, the shift in emphasis away from horizontal equity toward vertical equity. Intriguingly, Banting notes that this stress on vertical redistribution led to a chorus of criticism from both ends of the political spectrum: "It became commonplace for the political left to argue that the welfare state had

failed because the distribution of income had remained so frustrat-
ingly stable over the post-war period. Similarly, it became commonplace on the political right to argue that universal programs are
wasteful because they are not targeted on those most in need."[17]

As an aside, this tension between vertical and horizontal equity has
come to be reflected in our income tax system. The conversion from
family allowances to refundable tax credits with clawbacks is certainly a move toward greater vertical redistribution; but, since a family with three children earning $80,000 would pay the same tax as a
family with one child earning $80,000, horizontal equity no longer
obtains. This would have been way off side with the tax and social
policy mores of the 1960s.

In any event, the reformulation period carried with it substantial
implications for the role and design of social policy. At one level, social policy came more and more to be viewed as a vehicle to facilitate
and assist the occupational, industrial, and often geographic relocation that the new economics requires of the current generation of Canadians. Phrased differently, we no longer have the luxury of
designing social policy independently of the underlying economic environment. In particular, we no longer can afford those aspects of the
social policy network that serve to impede adjustment or entrench the
status quo. To be sure, this must be a two-way street: to the extent
possible, the general economic parameters should be conceived and
implemented in ways which recognize the needs and aspirations of
the social envelope. At another level, the environment within which
social policy is designed has undergone major changes which social
policy must address. One aspect of this relates to the "new" challenges facing the social envelope, e.g., single-parent families. Another
relates to the fact that long-standing challenges require the deploy-
ment of new instruments. For example, initially, welfare was designed
largely for the unable-to-work, while UI was geared to provide assistance for cyclical swings. Both assumed that full employment was the
natural state of the economy. Now, both programs tend, at the margin,
to be dominated by the structurally and secularly unemployed. This
requires a rethinking of the role of and incentives within these programs, let alone the appropriate interface between them.

In 1987, I noted[18] that this constellation of forces in the reformulation era was bound to be reflected in rather predictable ways in the
three social policy trade-offs – universality vs. selectivity (or targeting), centralization vs. decentralization, and public sector vs. private
sector. Specifically, the trend would be toward selectivity, toward decentralization, and toward an enhanced reliance on the private sector.
Table 2 reveals that this has, indeed, been the case for a broad range of

Table 2
Tilting Social Canada Toward
Selectivity, Decentralization, and Privatization

Program	Targeting/Selectivity	Decentralization	Private Sector
1. UI	benefits targeted (claw backs)	transfer of labour-market development to provinces	move to full premium funding (federal gov't withdraws)
2. Welfare	workfare;[1]	greater provincial responsibility (standards and financing)	workfare[2]
3. Child Benefits	shift from family allowance to refundable tax credit	N/A	N/A
4. Health	selected decreases in coverage; provincial drug plans[3]	greater provincial financial responsibility (CHST)	shorter hospital stays[4]
5. Education	–	training transferred to provinces	tuition increases and, soon, income-contingent repayment plans
6. Old Age Pensions	Negative Income Tax (NIT) proposal for 2001	[5]	–
7. CPP	Increase in retirement age (when it occurs); CPP tax credit is at lowest marginal rate	–	premium increases; real privatization if convert CPP to (Registered Retirement Savings Plan) RRSP scheme
8. CHST	Shift benefits to have-not provinces (cap on CAP part of CHST)	greater powers and financial responsibility to provinces	indirectly (see health, education, and welfare entries)
9. Federal Government	elimination of duplication and overlap	transfer of powers; curtailment of spending power	privatization, contracting out, and deregulation

Notes: 1) benefits reduced unless recipients undertake training, workfare etc. (e.g., Alberta, New Brunswick, and Ontario); 2) must "earn" welfare; 3) free drugs for elderly replaced by system based on ability to pay (Saskatchewan leads here, others following); 4) effectively privatize the recuperation period; 5) OAS was taxable, but new NIT for elderly will not be. This decreases provincial tax revenues. Part of deficit shifting.

Canada's social programs. And the evidence in the table is apart from the general grinding down of most social programs in the 1990s.

Having thus broached the 1990s evolution of social Canada, one approach would be to view this recent period as an extension of the reformulation stage of Table 1. In many ways, this might be appropriate, since the 1995 federal budget, and especially the conversion of Established Program Financing (EPF) and CAP into the CHST, was driven by many of the forces that characterized the reformulation era. However, something else is now afoot – the advent of globalization and the knowledge/information revolution – which merits its own "stage" in the evolution of social policy.

Globalization and the Knowledge/Information Revolution

In the midst of the reformulation stage and the accompanying pressures in most if not all western economies to pare down the social envelope, the emergence of the forces of globalization and the knowledge/information revolution gave social policy a new and far more pervasive and important rationale, namely that the human capital aspects of social policy were key to the competitive futures of nations and, as Thurow's prefatory quote suggests, key to running a high wage economy. To be sure, the human capital rationale for social policy was always present, but in an economy like Canada's, dominated by Fordism and resources, there were many avenues by which individuals could achieve high wages and middle class status. The last decade has altered this permanently, even though the transformation from a resource/physical-capital based society to a human-capital based society has only just begun.

Tables 3 and 4 focus on selective aspects of globalization and the knowledge/information revolution, respectively, as they relate to social policy. While delving into the detail of these tables is left to the reader, there are two aspects which merit special attention in light of developments since these tables were constructed:

- With the recent surge in trade with the United States, all provinces except Prince Edward Island now export more internationally than they do to the rest of Canada.[19] This reinforces the tension, highlighted in Table 3, between an east-west transfer system and a north-south trading system. It also lends greater credence to the regional-international interface (again Table 3) or the emergence of the "economic region state."[20] Arguably, this encompasses much of what Harris's Ontario is all about.

Table 3
Globalization and Social Policy: A Subjective "Tour d'horizon"

General Implications

- At its most basic level, globalization is the internationalization of production. Even at this level, it represents a severe challenge to social policy because welfare states in all countries were geared, incentive-wise, to their respective national production machines. What is the optimal nature of the social policy envelope when production is international?
- It is the international private sector that is globalizing, not the international public sector. Thus, economic space is transcending political space. In countervail fashion, some functions of the economic nation state are being passed upward (FTA, NAFTA, Europe 1992, Bank for International Settlements).
- Power is also flowing downward both to citizens and to international cities since it is largely via the latter that "institutions" are globalizing. The European regional science literature now focuses on the "regional/international" interface and not only the national/national interface, i.e., economic regions are cross-cutting traditional political boundaries.
- Globalization as represented by free trade pacts has other social policy implications. With freer markets, delivering social policy via cross-subsidization is more difficult. Distributional (i.e., tax-transfer) instruments, not allocative instruments, must now deliver social policy. This is a welcome development.
- Relatedly, with the spread of FTAs, whether in Europe or America, social policy issues are coming under the rubric of competition policy – hence, the increasing use of the term "social dumping."

Canadian Relevance

- As trade increasingly flows north-south, Canada will cease to be a single economy, but rather a series of north-south, cross-border economies. What will then bind us east-west is more of a social policy railway than an economic policy railway. The emerging challenge is how to mount an east-west transfer system over an increasing north-south trading system.
- In particular, the political economy of transfers will alter. When the second-round spending effects of equalization and interregional transfers tend to go south, rather than back to the "golden triangle," how will this alter Canadians' (or Ontarians') taste for transfers?
- In an increasing number of areas, a central vision emanating from the center will no longer be acceptable – the regions will be too economically diverse in that the requirements for a Great Lakes economy like Ontario will differ from those for a Pacific Rim economy like British Columbia. Part of the solution will likely be one or all of greater decentralization, greater asymmetry, and greater east-west flexibility (including wage flexibility).

Source: Courchene, *Social Canada in the Millennium.*

Table 4
The Information/Knowledge Revolution and Social Policy
A Subjective "Tour d'Horizon"

- The informatics revolution is inherently decentralizing in that individuals can now access, transform, transmit, and manipulate data and information in ways that governments at all levels are powerless to prevent. This will make old-style governance more difficult for governments of all stripes.
- With knowledge at the cutting edge of competitiveness, aspects of social policy become indistinguishable from economic policy. Regardless of what the Constitution may say, it is inconceivable that the federal government will be relegated to the sidelines in terms of social policy if national competitiveness is at stake.
- Drucker's predictions (1986) are holding up well – the manufacturing sector is becoming uncoupled from the resource sector (i.e. GNP is becoming less raw-material intensive) and, within manufacturing, production is becoming uncoupled from employment. The latest version of the latter is the prediction for a low-employment-growth recovery.
- Despite our generous resource endowment, Canada cannot avoid making the transition from a resource-based economy and society to a knowledge-based economy and society. Further success in the resource areas will progressively require the application of knowledge and high-value-added techniques.
- The middle class in this new era will include versions of technologists and information analysts. But we do not do this. We remain a professional society (as do most Anglo-American countries). Hence, the disappearing middle class. Social policy has a critical role to play in this inevitable shift from boards and mortar to mortar boards.
- In tandem with globalization, the knowledge/information revolution is altering much of the old order:
  - Interregional transfers will have to tilt from "place prosperity" to "people prosperity." To the extent that place prosperity remains important, it ought to be a provincial, not a federal matter.
  - There is emerging the notion of a global "maximum wage" for certain activities. Wages beyond this maximum wage will shift the activity offshore. As Drucker (1993) notes, this is a powerful argument for "contracting out," i.e., to enhance the productivity of these activities.
  - This is turning the original BNA Act on its head. Some of the line functions like forestry, fishing, mining, and energy can and probably should be devolved to the provinces (in any event they will continue to be driven by global imperatives) and some of the traditional provincial areas such as education and training will have to take on national, if not federal, dimensions. Since not all provinces will be able or willing to take down these areas, asymmetry will likely increase.
  - We will witness, if we are not already witnessing, an exciting and, to some, a bewildering set of provincial experiments across the full range of the social envelope. Ottawa's role is to provide the framework within which this experimentation can take place and to ensure that there is information with respect to the successes and the failures. In the same way that Saskatchewan's experimentation led to medicare a quarter of a century ago, the ongoing process is, Schumpeterian-like, creating or recreating key elements of our new social order.

Source: Courchene, *Social Canada in the Millennium.*

• Thanks to the internationalization of capital and production, the process of factor price equalization, as it relates to wages, is proceeding much more quickly than most analysts would ever have imagined. One obvious result is that high-wage Fordist-type jobs are disappearing and will continue to do so. It is not just that earnings are polarizing, but that this is ushering in other major societal changes – domestic unions are no match for international capital and production.

In tandem, then, globalization and the information revolution bring several new perspectives to the role and evolution of social policy, two of which are especially relevant. The first, and the most important, is that regaining a high-wage economy requires an upgrade in citizens' skills and human capital. In turn, this means that attention must be directed toward the means of forging an integration among the components of the human capital subsystem – schooling, postsecondary education (university and community college), training and apprenticeship, welfare, and UI/EI. (As an aside, the growing concern about child poverty in Canada, while obviously an important issue in its own right, is an essential part of the human capital challenge.) Because some of these areas are federal responsibilities and some provincial, full integration requires either substantially enhanced cooperation between levels of government or transferring responsibilities between levels of government. This issue will come up later.

The second challenge relates to the potential pressures on the social assistance and social insurance programs as citizens find that globalization has undermined their earnings potential. To the extent that Canada's social infrastructure begins to incorporate a human capital emphasis, this pressure may be alleviated, but that will take time. The problem is that UI/EI and welfare are poorly suited to addressing the needs of the working poor or the emergence of nonstandard jobs. In particular, the "binary" nature of welfare (where one is either on or off welfare) and, relatedly, the confiscatory taxation in the transition from welfare or UI/EI to work means that these programs serve more as hammocks than trampolines. This is quite apart from the existing pressures on these programs arising from the dictates of the reformulation stage of Table 1.

This completes the discussion and analysis of the evolution of Canadian social policy and the set of associated challenges. The remainder of the paper addresses the manner in which Canadian policy appears to be responding to these reform imperatives.

REFORM IN ACTION

With the election of the Chrétien Liberals in 1993, social policy reform rose to, or near, the top of the policy agenda. Part of this related to the need for social policy reform in its own right. Perhaps even more important was the role that social policy reform could contribute to the other policy priority – debt and deficit control. With the social policy commitments in the 1994 federal budget and with the release of Lloyd Axworthy's Green Paper, Canadians became engaged in what surely has been and continues to be the most in-depth and thoroughgoing policy debate on social reform in our history. Conferences number in the hundreds and scholarly papers well into the thousands. Now that the provinces are also engaged, the reform process will presumably carry on well into the third millennium.

In *Social Canada In The Millennium*,[21] I presented rather comprehensive menus of social policy reform options for several key areas – the retirement-income subsystem, UI/EI, welfare and the federal transfer system (CAP/EPF/ equalization). While the intention was to allow readers to design their own blueprint for the future of social Canada, in the concluding chapter of the book, I presented my own preferred blueprint. The thirteen-point agenda appears as Table 5.

Although the table is intended to be self-contained, several aspects are worth emphasizing. First, CAP would disappear (line 2). In its place, Ottawa would establish a new, low-income, refundable tax credit for children – low income in the sense that it would be clawed back before the claw backs on the existing child credit begin. In effect, then, Ottawa would now be largely responsible for the children as well as the elderly (and the Old Age Security (OAS)/GIS combination for the elderly would be converted into an income-tested guaranteed annual income – line 8). This would then leave the provinces responsible for adults on welfare, which would allow for the consolidation and coordination of provincial active labour market strategies since training (line 5) could be drawn down by those provinces who wished to do so, and UI/EI would revert to an insurance scheme with an emphasis on longer-term labour force attachment (line 1). A more decentralist approach to UI/EI (not shown in the Table 5 but highlighted in the accompanying text of *Social Canada in the Millennium*) would be to provincialize the program. The suggested way of doing this is to allow UI premium income to enter the equalization program, so that all provinces would have access to the five-province average of premium income per capita.

Table 5
A Blueprint For Social Canada

Program Area	Proposal	Comments
1. Unemployment Insurance	• Thirty week uniform entry. • Three weeks work for one week of benefits. • Set tax back rate equal to benefit rate to encourage labour force reentry.	• Removes UI from short-term income support. • Requires new approach to welfare because UI no longer is part of income support for temporary attachment to labour force. UI savings would be reflected in decreased premiums.
2. Welfare a) children	• Convert CAP into a new low-income refundable tax credit for children. This would be a low-income credit, unlike existing tax credit. Would be phased out before existing one begins.	• Would remove the existing inequity in CAP whereby the "have provinces" receive less than 50 percent funding, in that all children are treated identically.
b) adults	• Would remain in provincial domain. • Should be income-tested to encourage labour force reentry.	• In effect, Ottawa would look after the children and elderly. This would leave the provinces able to integrate adults into active labour force strategies, including education, training, and transition from school to work.
3. Minimum Wages	• Minimum wages are not easily reconciled with income testing, nor the changing nature of work. • Encourage greater flexibility here, especially where apprenticeship or on-the-job training is an integral part of employment.	• High minimum wages could stand in the way of increasing a person's total income (employment income plus income support) under income-tested welfare. • Provinces will presumably experiment here.
4. Postsecondary Education	• Convert cash component of PSE part of EPF into a tuition voucher. • Would be consistent with a shift to an Income-Contingent Repayment System.	• Fully mobile across provinces and across institutions (university, college, private sector training, apprenticeship), although value of voucher would differ by end use.
5. Training	• Would be subject to "Concurrency with Provincial Paramountcy." • A shift to a "training culture" requires a societal change, including curriculum revision beginning at primary school level.	• Provinces could take training down and, therefore, provide a "single window" (welfare, education, training, etc.) if they wished.

6. Workers' Compensation	• Make benefits taxable, shift to joint premiums. • Income test with respect to any new market income. • In jurisdiction of the provinces, but Ottawa controls whether wc benefits are taxable. Would "grandfather" existing benefits. Provinces will soon begin to experiment in this area.
7. Health	• Convert cash component of health part of EPF into a further tax-point transfer (equalized for personal income taxation). • Replace Canada Health Act with a new Canada Well-Being Act to reflect profound changes now underway. • Provincial schemes are undergoing immense experimentation. Ottawa needs to encourage this and at the same time set guidelines (portability, access, etc.).
8. Retirement-Income Subsystem	• Roll OAS and GIS into a single GIS for the elderly. Begin process of integrating CPP into this as well. Alternatively, begin process of converting CPP into a compulsory RRSP run through the private sector. • Begins to address the dramatic intergenerational transfer (from young to old) that now exists.
9. Canada Assistance Plan	• Would disappear and be replaced by a new refundable child tax credit (Item 2a) above).
10. Established Program Financing	• Would disappear and be replaced by a voucher for PSE and a further PTT transfer for health.
11. Equalization	• Move back to National Average Standard and remove equalization ceiling. • Convert to an NTT for provinces, so they get 70 per cent of difference between their own fiscal capacity and the equalization standard. • Equalization becomes the sole surviving federal-provincial transfer. • At present, equalization is a confiscatory tax. There is nothing that an Atlantic province can do in terms of its own legislation that would lead to an increase in its revenues. • This proposal brings dynamic efficiency into equalization. • Equalization need not fall because we could arbitrarily increase the standard.
12. Tax on Base	• Allow provinces to apply their own rate and bracket structures to the federally determined PTT base, similar to what now occurs in corporate income tax. • Would allow greater flexibility for provinces to use the PTT as an integrative vehicle for delivering social policy. • Would result only in a minor change in tax compliance.
13. Social and Economic Union	• Ottawa would be responsible for ensuring a full-blown social and economic union. • Especially important to ensure mobility of skills across provinces.

Source: Courchene, *Social Canada in the Millennium.*

Turning to federal-provincial transfers, the proposal was that the postsecondary education component of EPF cash be converted into a portable tuition voucher (line 4), which would involve Ottawa in a visible and accountable way in the creation of human capital. The health component of EPF cash would become a further tax-point transfer (line 7). Thus, equalization would remain the only federal-provincial transfer. Finally, Ottawa would be responsible for preserving and promoting the socio-economic union.

Given the not-very-disguised decentralist thrust of this blueprint, many readers will likely feel uncomfortable with its provisions (but it may well be less decentralist than the social policy path that Ottawa has launched itself upon, as will be elaborated below). Nonetheless, it has the virtue, or at least the useful feature, of integrating all the social policy components into a consistent overall system, a virtue that thus far has eluded federal reform initiatives, to which I now turn.

The Federal Reform Thrust

Ottawa's response to the social/fiscal reform challenge was as unexpected as it was dramatic. Drawing from the 1995 and 1996 federal budgets and from the commitments announced in the Throne Speech, Canada's new social policy infrastructure for the next century is beginning to take shape:

- EPF and CAP have been rolled into a single super block fund, the CHST.
- Cash transfers to the provinces under the CHST will fall from the current level of $18 billion to $11 billion at the turn of the century. The 1996 federal budget set $11 billion as the cash transfer floor.
- The cap on CAP (which limited the growth of federal transfers for welfare to the three "have" provinces) was incorporated into the CHST. The 1996 federal budget committed to remove half of this inequity over a five-year period. This refers to total entitlements (cash transfers plus tax-point transfers). Cash transfers could actually diverge further in per capita terms.[22]
- The five Canada Health Act principles will still hold, as will the prohibition of residency requirements for welfare. However, the federal government has invited the provinces to join with it to develop a new set of social policy principles to underpin the CHST.

This package, still very much in evolution, has drawn critical fire from most social policy activists and many social policy analysts.

Phrases like the "end of medicare" and a "race to the bottom" for welfare are not uncommon. In the light of the Alberta-Ottawa tussle over medicare and the British Columbia-Ottawa confrontation over residency requirements for welfare, one probably cannot rule out these possibilities. But they do seem exaggerated, especially if one takes the view that the social envelope would not, under any scenario, have been able to escape the efforts to restore Canada's fiscal integrity. I take a more sympathetic view of the CHST.[23] However, its most surprising aspect is that it is part of a much larger move toward decentralization of the social envelope, broadly defined.

A Funny Thing Happened
On The Way To The Millennium

While there are good arguments for further decentralizing aspects of social Canada (many of which were elaborated above), one could also mount a strong case that the impact of globalization and the information revolution on our social infrastructure might call for an enhanced federal presence. For example, to the extent that our national competitiveness depends on our ability to adopt a human capital and training mentality, it might make eminent sense for Ottawa to reserve a key role for itself in all of this. But quite the opposite seems to be happening. Ottawa is abandoning the field. This decentralist thrust merits elaboration.

Part of the decentralization relates to the CHST itself. The integration of health and welfare into a single block fund gives the provinces much more policy flexibility. This is appropriate since the concept of "well-being" is preferable to viewing health and welfare separately. Ultimately, however, the more decentralist aspect of the CHST will relate to the magnitude of the cuts in cash transfers to the provinces. This will have two implications. First, the decrease in cash transfers has lessened Ottawa's financial and moral authority to act as a social policy policeman. For example, the current $1.2 billion budget surplus of Alberta exceeds the cash transfers that this province now gets from Ottawa. The second implication is more long term in nature. Because of the reduced transfers, provincial health and welfare systems are undergoing comprehensive restructuring and downsizing. Eventually, this means that the provinces will be shouldering a larger share of the financing associated with their social programs. This is clearly decentralizing, even if, in the interim, the provinces prefer to view it as federal deficit shifting.

Beyond this, the 1996 Speech from the Throne signalled further decentralization:

- Ottawa agreed not to use its spending power to create new shared-cost programs in areas of exclusive provincial jurisdiction without the consent of a majority of the provinces. Any new program will be designed so that nonparticipating provinces will be compensated, provided that they establish equivalent or comparable initiatives.
- Also, as part of the Throne Speech, and probably related more to national unity than to social policy considerations, Ottawa committed to vacate the field of labour market training and, more recently, agreed to transfer the labour market development initiatives associated with UI/EI to the provinces.

At a more general level, the federal initiatives to reduce duplication and overlap, including the 45,000 reduction in the civil service, also constitute a move in the direction of jurisdictional disentanglement. And if to this one adds the Throne Speech commitments to transfer forestry, recreation, mining, etc., to the provinces, the end result will surely represent the most thoroughgoing decentralist shift in our history.

But it probably cannot stop here. As I have argued elsewhere,[24] the CHST has triggered a *path-dependent process*. The logic of allowing the provinces to consolidate health, welfare, and PSE and to acquire control of training must eventually imply provincial control or influence over UI/EI. This also makes sense from the human-capital perspective that motivates this paper: UI/EI should be integrated with training, welfare, and education. Since Ottawa has effectively abandoned any attempt to forge this integration, the challenge now falls to the provinces.

The surprising thing in all of this is that the provinces appear to be willing to take up the challenge. Part of the reason is that the three "have" provinces feel discriminated against in terms of the manner in which Ottawa incorporated the cap on CAP into the CHST. In part, too, they are increasingly frustrated with the continued regional tilting of UI/EI. For example, similarly situated unemployed persons in Ontario are only half as likely to qualify for UI/EI benefits as persons in New Brunswick.[25] And the "equalization" of the GST for the three Atlantic provinces complicated matters further. The examples thus far relate principally to the "have" provinces and the result may be to increase tension between the haves and the have-nots. But there is also common cause when Ottawa can cut cash transfers to the provinces by 40 percent, but actually *increase* the generosity of its own programs for the elderly. (To add insult to injury, the proposed guaranteed annual income for the elderly will mean that the OAS will no longer be taxable, which will substantially reduce provincial tax revenues.) The result of all of this is a degree of determination, at least on the part of some provinces, to play a much greater role in the design and delivery of social Canada.

At one level, this is a most welcome initiative. Our traditional approach to promoting the east-west social envelope has been to rely on the federal government and the exercise of its spending power. This has served Canada and Canadians well. But more is now needed. Analytically, this top-down approach is akin to what the Charlottetown Accord referred to as "negative integration," i.e., a series of "thou shalt nots" (thou shalt not extra bill; thou shalt not impose residency requirements). We now need "positive integration," namely a proactive meshing and harmonization of social programs and policies across the provinces. Obviously, only the provinces can deliver this. A good example here, and, an initiative that is long overdue, would be for the provinces to mutually recognize each other's training and accreditation so that east-west occupational mobility is ensured.

However, the system appears to be evolving well beyond this.

A Provincial Renaissance?

In December 1995, the Ministerial Council on Social Policy Reform and Renewal (representing the social policy ministers of all provinces except Quebec, although Quebec was an "observer") signed on to a quite remarkable document.[26] In large part, this was the provincial response to the federal challenge to develop mutual-consent principles to underpin the CHST. These fifteen principles, culled from the *Report To Premiers*, appear in Table 6. While some of these principles attempt to sort out jurisdictional responsibilities (e.g., principle eleven, relating to Aboriginal Canadians), in the main they exemplify an impressive statement of citizens' rights in the social policy area. As such, the *Report To Premiers* represents a potential building block for an enhanced provincial presence in Canadian social policy.

Indeed, recent documents are beginning to build on the provinces' report. For example, the report of the Group of 22[27] embraced the Table 6 principles as part of a policy directed toward renewing the federation, an important component of which is the promotion of Canada's internal social union. In turn, one suggestion by the Group of 22 is to endorse the André Burelle proposal[28] that Ottawa place the CHST cash transfers at the service of a federal-provincial oversight body rather than the existing federal oversight.

In a paper prepared for Ontario's Ministry of Intergovernmental Affairs,[29] I have taken the concept of greater provincial control over the social envelope one step further: is it possible that the provinces

Table 6
Principles to Guide Social Policy Reform and Renewal

Social Programs Must Be Accessible and Serve the Basic Needs of All Canadians

1. Social policy must assure reasonable access to health, education and training, income support, and social services that meet Canadians' basic needs.
2. Social policy must support and protect Canadians most in need.
3. Social policy must promote social and economic conditions which enhance self-sufficiency and well-being, to assist all Canadians to actively participate in economic and social life.
4. Social policy must promote active development of an individuals' skills and capabilities as the foundation for social and economic development.
5. Social policy must promote the well-being of children and families, as children are our future. It must ensure the protection and development of children and youth in a healthy, safe, and nurturing environment.

Social Programs Must Reflect Our Individual and Collective Responsibility

6. Social policy must reflect our individual and collective responsibility for health, education, and social security, and reinforce the commitment of Canadians to the dignity and independence of the individual.
7. Partnerships among governments, communities, social organizations, business, labour, families, and individuals are essential to the continued strength of our social system.
8. There is a continuing and important role, to be defined, for both orders of government in the establishment, maintenance, and interpretation of national principles for social programs.

Social Programs Must be Affordable, Effective, and Accountable

9. The ability to fund social programs must be protected. Social programs must be affordable, sustainable, and designed to achieve intended and measurable results.
10. The long-term benefits of prevention and early intervention must be reflected in the design of social programs.
11. Federal constitutional, fiduciary, treaty, and other historic responsibilities for assurance of Aboriginal health, income support, social services, housing, training, and educational opportunities must be fulfilled. The federal government must recognize its financial responsibilities for Aboriginal Canadians, both on and off the reserve.
12. Governments must coordinate and integrate social programming and funding in order to ensure efficient and effective program delivery, and to reduce waste and duplication.

Social Programs Must be Flexible, Responsive, and Reasonably Comparable Across Canada

13. Social policy must be flexible and responsive to changing social and economic conditions, regional/local priorities, and individual circumstances.
14. Governments must ensure that all Canadians have access to reasonably comparable basic social programming throughout Canada, and ensure that Canadians are treated with fairness and equity.
15. Social policy must recognize and take into account the differential impact social programming can have on men and women.

Source: Ministerial Council, *Report To Premiers.*

could mount a binding interprovincial convention with respect to the social and economic union? Were this possible, then it might also be possible for the provinces to request that the existing CHST cash transfers be converted into equalized tax-point transfers and to assume greater responsibility for UI/EI, thereby allowing them to forge a comprehensive approach to human capital and skills development. The answer is "probably not" if by binding one means constitutionally binding. But if one means effectively (politically) binding, then the answer is "probably yes." Admittedly, it is far from clear that the provinces can muster the political will to subject their provincial interests to pan-Canadian interests. Nor is it clear that Ottawa would ever contemplate a further tax-point transfer under the shared personal income tax system. Nonetheless, the political landscape underpinning social policy is shifting in fascinating and hitherto completely unexpected ways.

CONCLUSION

The purpose of this paper has been to review, in broad brush terms, the analytical evolution of postwar social policy. The policy is now in full evolutionary flight. Restructuring and downsizing are occurring at both levels of government, and it is far from clear what the eventual steady state will look like. What the analysis points toward is one firm conclusion and one tentative observation. The firm conclusion is that, with the advent of globalization and the knowledge/information revolution, the role of social policy has, conceptually, been permanently transformed: it is now about the development and enhancement of citizens' skills and human capital. Phrased differently, social policy is now an integral component of economic policy. Whether this conceptual approach to social policy can be implemented is another issue. The tentative observation is more intriguing: as social policy becomes more and more the stuff of national competitiveness, it appears that the provinces are becoming more important players in social policy design, delivery, and monitoring. Over the longer term, this trend may not have staying power. But over the near future, the recent and ongoing federal initiatives, driven largely by fiscal and national-unity imperatives, have launched social Canada in a decidedly decentralist direction. Hence, as we approach the millennium, one of the key issues on the social policy front is whether the provinces are willing and capable of accepting the degree of "pan-Canadian" responsibility commensurate with their enhanced powers.

Lessons from
the Canadian Slump
of the 1990s[1]

PIERRE FORTIN

INTRODUCTION

From the beginning of 1990 to the end of 1993, Canada experienced a long slide in economic activity and employment that was followed by a short-lived recovery in 1994 and a relapse in 1995 and 1996. The accompanying employment and output losses are still accumulating, but they already exceed everything we have known since the Great Depression of the 1930s, and they surpass the losses experienced by other industrial countries since 1990. The last decade of this century will arguably be remembered as the decade of the Great Canadian Slump.

It has thereby contradicted everything Allan J. MacEachen has stood for throughout his political career: full employment, sound public finances, and a humane social safety net. Employment has collapsed, governments are deep in debt, and unemployment insurance (UI) has been cut by 40 percent. My view of the disastrous performance of our country in the 1990s is that it has resulted from policy error: we alone, not the Americans, not globalization, not technological change, nor any of the usual scapegoats cherished by the left or the right are responsible for our current predicament. The best homage I can pay to Mr MacEachen is to tell the full story of how it all happened, so that we are not tempted to repeat, in the next century, the mistakes that have spoilt the end of this century.

Denial

A widespread attitude about the slump of the 1990s is denial. But Table 1 shows that there can be no mistake about its true magnitude. The cumulative employment loss since 1990 amounts to 30 percent of

Table 1

Size of Cumulative Employment Loss during Eight Canadian Slumps since 1929 (point-years)

Period	Size of loss	Rank	Period	Size of loss	Rank
1929–42	750	1	1967–72	28	6
1948–50	9	8	1975–7	17	7
1952–5	37	5	1982–6	107	3
1957–64	76	4	1990–6	225	2

Sources: F.H. Leacy, ed., *Historical Statistics of Canada*, 2nd ed. (Ottawa: Supply and Services Canada, 1983); and Statistics Canada's CANSIM Databank.

Note: The cumulative employment loss is the sum of the absolute differences between the actual employment ratio and its prerecession peak level, for all the years during which the actual ratio remains below the peak level. The employment ratio is the percentage of the working-age population who have jobs

the loss suffered during the Great Depression, and twice that of 1982–6. The current slump is second to none in the postwar period. A moderate estimate of 2.8 percent for the annual growth rate of potential output since 1990 would value the cumulative loss of output at some $400 billion (1996 dollars); this number would still be growing at an annual rate of about $75 billion.[2] Taking the employment ratio defined in Table 1 as a standard, the job losses relative to the level of the first quarter of 1990 added up, by the first quarter of 1996, to 5.2 million person-years. We were still currently 6 percent, or 850,000 jobs, below that prerecession level.

"We're no worse than other countries."

Another common reaction is to say that the increase in unemployment since 1990 is global and that, in the circumstances, we are not doing worse than other countries. But this perception too is wrong. Relative to the 1989 unemployment level, Canada accumulated 15.7 point-years of excess unemployment over 1990–5. According to the Organization for Economic Cooperation and Development (OECD) standardized unemployment statistics, this is significantly more than Japan (2.3 point-years), the United States (6.3), and the European Union (10.7). Our bad unemployment result has been matched only by Australia (16.3 point-years). Canada's underperformance has not been similar to other countries; it has been worse.

Figure 1
Employment/Population Ratio (jobs/1,000 adults), Canada and United
States, 1Q90–3Q96

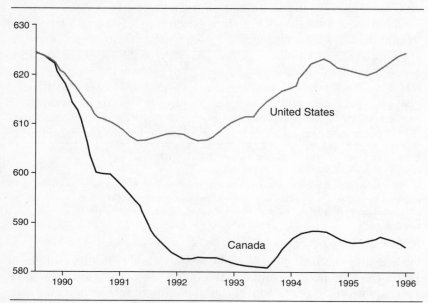

Sources: Statistics Canada; us Bureau of Labor Statistics.

The comparison with the United States is particularly instructive,
since our two countries recorded exactly the same average employment ratio in each of the two previous decades. Figure 1 underlines
the startling divergence between the paths of Canadian and us employment since 1990. The two countries entered the recession with
the same absolute employment ratio of 625 jobs per 1,000 persons
aged fifteen and over. The us ratio quickly fell by 3 percent, but has
since regained all the ground lost during the recession. In sharp contrast, the Canadian ratio took four years to decline by 7 percent, and
is still wandering 6 percent below its prerecession level.

In other words, the Canadian slump that began in the 1990s is real;
it is the worst since the Great Depression; and it is worse than in other
countries, most conspicuously the United States.

In this essay, I will pursue two objectives: to understand the causes of
the slump and draw useful policy implications. In the first part, I begin
by confronting six popular, but demonstrably false, explanations of the
slump: globalization, technological change, political uncertainty, social
policy, payroll taxes, and minimum wages. Having eliminated those

structural factors and net foreign demand as possible global causes of the slump, I argue, in the second section, that the true cause of the slump in domestic demand is old-fashioned monetary contraction and, more recently, induced fiscal contraction.

Given the central role of high interest rates in the slump, I try to understand, in the third section, why the Canadian central bank kept the real short-term interest rate differential with the United States so large for so long. The reason I offer is that, in contrast with the US Federal Reserve, the Bank of Canada has manifested a strong deflationary bias and has considerably underestimated the amount of unemployment needed to hold inflation below 2 percent. To redress the situation, I propose changes to the management structure and mandate of the Bank of Canada. The conclusion summarizes the argument.

FALSE EXPLANATIONS OF THE SLUMP

Because there is much confusion about the slump in public opinion and even among economists, I will first consider the structural explanations of the current Canadian slump, which I will show to be false or insufficient.

"Globalization and the Free Trade Agreement did it."

Globalization, the 1989 Free Trade Ageement (FTA) with the United States, and its later extension to Mexico (NAFTA) are widely held responsible for the slump. But this explanation is flatly contradicted by the fact that the nonautomotive manufacturing exports of Canada, which were the main target of the FTA and NAFTA, almost tripled in volume between the end of 1988 and the beginning of 1996. This incredible surge of nonautomotive manufacturing exports was also accompanied by a strong expansion of natural resource exports after 1991. Following the recovery in world demand for commodities, Canada's natural resource exports in the first half of 1996 were about 40 percent higher in volume than at their 1989 peak.[3]

Table 2 summarizes the overall trade picture. Real exports in the first quarter of 1996 were 60 percent higher than at the prerecession peak. In total value, the cyclically-adjusted export-to-GDP ratio stood at 35 percent, or 6 points higher than the previous postwar peak (in 1984). Real imports were held back by the slump and the post-1991 real exchange rate depreciation, but the increase from the first quarter of 1990 was nevertheless a very strong 45 percent. In short, there was

Table 2
Trends in the Composition of Real Aggregate Demand Canada, 1Q90–1Q96
(1Q90 = 100)

	Period		
Component	1Q90 Peak	1Q91 Trough	1Q96
Personal consumption:			
Durables and semidurables	100.0	87.9	99.9
Nondurables and services	100.0	98.7	108.0
Business fixed investment	100.0	90.3	97.3
Government spending	100.0	101.3	103.0
Equals: Domestic spending	**100.0**	**96.0**	**103.6**
Plus: Exports	100.0	97.5	158.7
Minus: Imports	100.0	97.1	145.4
Equals: Total spending	**100.0**	**96.1**	**106.1**

Source: Statistics Canada's CANSIM Databank.

an extraordinary jump of gross and net trade volumes over the prerecession peak. Trade-related job creation must have well exceeded trade-related job destruction.

Every effort at explaining the startling expansion of trade only by traditional factors such as the US recovery, the real depreciation, and the rebound of world demand for commodities turns out to be insufficient. It is impossible to escape the conclusion that, by whatever channel (lower tariffs, greater security, education, etc.), trade liberalization has made a major contribution to the trade boom. In fact, by propelling exports to unprecedented levels, the changing trade environment, far from contributing to the slump, has, in fact, prevented Canada from falling into outright depression. Those who attribute the slump to globalization and trade liberalization have simply got the sign wrong.

*"Technological change and restructuring
are to be blamed."*

A second popular explanation of the slump is based on the increased intensity of the reallocation of labour and capital within and across firms and industrial sectors that would have resulted from accelerating technological change, particularly the microelectronic revolution.

According to this view, "restructuring" would be the cause of the slump. But there are many reasons why this cannot be.

First, given that the United States faces the same trade and technology challenges as Canada, it is hard to believe that restructuring would have produced a large slump in Canada without having also provoked one in the United States, either simultaneously or earlier (if you believe the restructuring happened earlier there, as in manufacturing). The fact that no such depression occurred in the United States therefore makes the technological hypothesis very dubious to begin with.[4]

Second, when technological advances and restructuring allow the same level of output to be produced with fewer workers, they generate, by definition, a higher level of productivity. But, in fact, the recession began not with accelerating productivity, but with a once-over 5 percent drop in output per worker, and an even larger decline in measured total factor productivity, relative to trend.[5] This initial fall in productivity, which has not been reversed since 1991, is inconsistent with a causal interpretation of the slump based on accelerating technological change.[6]

Third, the negative link between technology and employment is straightforward from the microeconomic and partial equilibrium perspective most people adopt, that technological progress destroys jobs in the sector where it occurs. But we know that this story is incomplete from a macroeconomic and more complete perspective. Technological progress also generates lower costs and prices in the sector affected. This benefits consumers, who are left with residual purchasing power to spend elsewhere in the economy. There is decreased labour demand in the sector affected by the technological development, but also increased labour demand in other sectors. There will be at least partially offsetting job creation.

The full macroeconomic prediction is, therefore, that accelerating technological change will increase *both* unemployment and the job offer rate. However, this is not at all how the slump developed in Canada. Unemployment did increase markedly, from 7.5 percent in 1989 to 11.3 percent in 1992. But, instead of increasing, as the full technological story would have had it, the job offer rate dropped by 60 percent.[7] Hence, accelerating technological change and restructuring cannot have caused the slump.[8]

Let me be very precise about what to conclude from these observations. There is no question that the reallocation of labour and capital has intensified markedly during the slump. Partly, this intensification followed technological innovations, and partly it was a *sauve qui peut* response to the slump. But all the evidence reported indicates that the restructuring itself cannot have caused the fall in aggregate employment and output, and that the slump cannot be interpreted as a response to accelerating technological change.

"It's political uncertainty."

A third explanation of the slump is the political uncertainty sur- rounding Canada's three- decade old constitutional quandary. A key implication of this conjecture is that the deterioration in economic performance from that source would have been most pronounced in the region that has been the main cause of the difficulty, namely Que- bec. But this prediction receives no empirical confirmation for the pe- riod 1990–6. Since 1989, Quebec's employment performance relative to Ontario's has not worsened, but has considerably improved. The gap between the employment ratios of the two provinces shrank steadily, from eighty-two jobs per 1,000 adults in 1989 to forty-seven in the second quarter of 1996. Such a small gap has not been seen since the mid-1960s.

Ontario, of course, has had political and economic problems of its own, which could have dominated the effect of constitutional uncer- tainty on the Quebec-Ontario employment ratio differential. But if so, that would simply prove the point that Quebec-related political un- certainty has had, at most, a secondary influence on the economic sit- uation. Moreover, if we look instead at the comparison with Atlantic Canada, it turns out that the employment ratio differential with Que- bec has remained stable since 1990. It has not deteriorated to Quebec's disadvantage as implied by the political uncertainty explanation. The economic consequences of political uncertainty, if any, seem to belong to the future, not the past.

"Our generous social programs have destroyed the work ethic."

A fourth explanation of the large drop in employment since 1990 is simply that less people work because less people want to supply la- bour. Two important developments underlie this view. First, aggre- gate labour force participation declined by 4 percent (from 67.5 to 64.8 percent) between 1989 and 1996, contrasting with the relatively constant participation rate (66.5 percent) in the United States over that period. Second, the proportion of the total population on welfare has increased substantially. Between March 1989 and March 1994, the rate of social assistance increased from 6.8 to 10.6 percent nationally and, most surprisingly, from 5.8 to 12.7 percent in Ontario, leaving even Quebec and Atlantic Canada behind at 10.8 percent.

Three major events of the late 1980s and the 1990s are key to understanding the decline in the participation rate and the increase in welfare recipiency: the recession itself; the federal restrictions on UI benefits and eligibility rules; and, for a time, the increases in real social assistance (SA) benefits, most notably in Ontario and British Columbia.[9] The labour force participation rate has naturally reflected the usual discouraged-worker reaction to declining employment opportunities in the recession, but UI cuts and larger SA benefits probably also depressed participation and encouraged welfare recipiency.

On welfare recipiency, I have recently, with the help of data for the ten provinces, produced evidence showing that business cycle fluctuations and changes in UI generosity and real SA benefits together have no trouble explaining the pattern of increases in provincial social assistance over the years 1975 to 1993.[10]

On labour force participation, two pieces of evidence are very suggestive. First, there is definite indication of a decline in structural unemployment between 1992 and 1996. In those years, the unemployment rate declined by 1.5 points, while the job offer rate did not improve at all. This is exactly what should be expected from changes in the economic environment, such as social policy initiatives, that reduce unemployment for reasons other than increases in aggregate demand.[11] Second, about half of the 4 percent drop in participation from 1990 to1995 can be attributed to the employment decline, but there was also a cumulative "unexplained" downward shift of 1.5 percent in participation over the 1992–5 period.

Let us assume for the moment that this 1.5 percent shift, which involves about 230,000 dropouts, is permanent and due entirely to the changes in UI and SA (and not, for example, a product of the extraordinary magnitude and duration of the current slump). The strategic intent here is to exaggerate the role attributed to UI and SA changes in causing the downward shift in labour force participation to see what upper bound this imposes on the fraction of the employment drop that can be explained by social policy.

How much negative impact would that have on aggregate employment? The answer is: much less than 1.5 percent, and more likely around 0.5 percent. The reason is that, since the dropouts were previously much more often unemployed than employed, their withdrawing from the labour force must have reduced unemployment to a much larger extent than employment. To fix ideas, make the additional reasonable assumption that the dropouts were previously employed only 30 percent of the time. Then, on first approximation, the 1.5 percent drop in participation will translate into a 1 percentage point decline in the aggregate unemployment rate, and a reduction of just 0.5 percent in employment (3 jobs per 1,000 adults).[12]

There are two implications. First, the calculated upper bound of 0.5 percent for the drop in employment induced by social policy initiatives can account for only 8 percent of the total decline in aggregate employment from 1990 to 1996 pictured in Figure 1. We should not look at social policy for a global explanation of the employment slump. The second implication, which is strongly suggested by the decline in unemployment not accompanied by an increase in the job offer rate, is that in 1996 any given unemployment rate reflects a larger amount of labour market slack, perhaps up to 1 percentage point, than in 1989. The "nonaccelerating-inflation rate of unemployment" (the NAIRU, or the level of unemployment beyond which inflation starts to increase) must have declined to that extent.[13] If previous estimates putting the Canadian NAIRU at 7.5 percent[14] are to be believed, the current NAIRU could be 6.5 percent.

"Higher payroll taxes have killed jobs."

The last two popular explanations of the slump are that increased employer payroll taxes and higher minimum wages have depressed employer demand for labour, particularly for the low-skilled and the young. Between 1989 and 1995, employer payroll taxes were increased by 4 percent of total wages and salaries, and provincial minimum wages by 8 percent more than the average hourly wage.[15] There is clearly an element of truth in the argument that these policy measures have harmed employment, but the quantitative extent of the damage can easily be exaggerated.

The thrust of the econometric literature on the incidence of payroll taxes is that, while they affect employment negatively in the short run, they are largely shifted to workers in reduced real wages after a while, with little permanent effect on employment.[16] It is, in fact, remarkable that countries with roughly comparable levels of productivity have comparable labour costs despite huge variations in the level of payroll taxation.[17] There is, however, reason to believe that the zero-inflation environment of recent years may have delayed the absorption of higher payroll taxes into lower real wages: if productivity and prices increase very slowly and nominal wages cuts are resisted, then by definition the absorption process must also be slow.

To capture the order of magnitude of the transitory disemployment effects, make the simple assumption that employer payroll tax increases take three years to be shifted to employees, with the employer burden declining linearly from 100 to 0 percent, and make the further standard assumption that the aggregate labour demand elasticity is -0.5. Then, the simulated disemployment effect of the payroll tax hikes relative to control rises from 0.3 percent in 1990 to a peak of 1.2 percent in 1992,[18] and then falls to 0.3 percent again in 1995. The example is specific, but underlines the general point that, if the negative incidence of the payroll tax increases on employment was important in 1991–3, it has by now receded to modest proportions and does not seem to account for more than a small fraction of Canada's total employment shortfall. It is an effect that is dying out as time goes by.

"It's provincial minimum wages."

Recent Canadian research has found significant negative employment effects of minimum wage increases, with particular concentration among young workers. The average elasticity of aggregate employment with respect to minimum wage changes that can be derived from two recent studies,[19] on the basis of three decades of provincial data, does not exceed 0.04. The fact that the average of provincial minimum wages increased 8 percent more than the average hourly wage would hence have reduced employment by no more than 0.3 percent (two jobs per 1,000 adults).

A prudent assessment of the existing literature, given, in particular, recent American results that find employment insensitive to minimum wage changes,[20] is to view the disemployment effects as nonlinear, being small at low levels of the minimum wage and large at high levels. Since the recent increase in Canada started from a two-decade low in the ratio of the minimum to average hourly wage (36 percent in 1989), the 0.3 percent figure for the cumulative disemployment effect over the period 1989–1995 must be seen as a strict upper estimate of the true effect.

To summarize this section, I have first shown that explanations of the 1990–6 collapse in output and employment based on globalization, technological change, and political uncertainty are not consistent with existing evidence. I have then tried to estimate generous upper bounds for the disemployment effects of the federal restrictions to UI benefits and eligibility rules and the provincial increases in relative minimum wages. The upper-bound estimate for the drop in employment from these two sources in combination is 0.8 percent (five jobs per 1,000 adults). This represents a little more than 10 percent of the total employment decline since 1990 (forty jobs per 1,000 adults). The social policy changes may have reduced the Canadian NAIRU by as much as 1 percentage point, to around 6.5 percent.

THE DEMAND-SIDE
EXPLANATION OF THE SLUMP

Since explanations of the slump based on supply-side disturbances are unsound, by elimination, the true story can only be found on the demand side. Table 2 characterizes trends in the composition of real aggregate demand from the absolute peak of the first quarter of 1990 to the trough of the first quarter of 1991, and then on to 1996. The major conclusion that emerges from this picture is that Canadian aggregate demand has recently suffered from some sort of schizophrenia. The contrast is indeed extraordinary between the persistent stagnation of domestic demand and the very strong turnaround of net foreign demand after the trough of 1991. The behaviour of net foreign demand was examined in the previous section. It therefore remains to investigate the causes of depression in domestic demand.

Table 2 also indicates exactly why our domestic demand has remained depressed since 1991: the most interest-sensitive demand categories, consumer durables and business fixed investment, have remained below absolute prerecession levels; and real public sector spending has been flat.[21] This gives us a clue to the true cause of the great slump of the 1990s: old-fashioned monetary and fiscal contraction. I argue that monetary policy has been the leader, and that the fiscal contraction was *induced* by the monetary contraction. Let me present the evidence in some detail.

Ten Years of Tight Fiscal Policy

Figure 2 demonstrates that discretionary fiscal policy has been tight each and every year since 1985. In other words, as a result of both tax increases and program spending cuts, the "cyclically-adjusted operating balance" of the public sector has never stopped increasing from one year to next as a percentage of trend Gross Domestic Product (GDP).[22]

The inescapable implication of this fact is that, contrary to widespread belief, the large increase in government deficits from 1990 to 1993 was not caused at all by spendthrift fiscal policy, but by the economic feedback, from high interest rates and the accompanying recession, on debt service costs, tax revenues, and social expenditures. The public finance crisis of the 1990s is, therefore, essentially a product of the monetary contraction and the economic crisis.[23] Large public sector deficits have, in turn, led governments to slash program spending in 1994 to 1996. This has clearly further increased the structural operating balance in those years, as Figure 2 shows, while contributing to renewed stagnation in 1995 and 1996, through standard multiplier effects.

Figure 2
Cyclically–Adjusted Operating Budget Balance, All Levels of Government, Canada, 1981–95 (% of GDP)

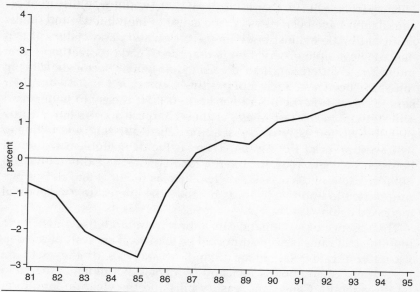

Source: Based on data from Statistics Canada.

I am not at all arguing here that we should not have had fiscal austerity, or even more fiscal austerity at times (particularly in the late 1980s). The slower long-term growth environment of the last two decades clearly required the public sector to downsize permanently. I am simply making the four following points: one, the assertion that fiscal policy has been lax at any time in the last decade is false; two, the large government deficits of the 1990s essentially resulted from the high interest rates and the accompanying recession; three, the fiscal retrenchment in reaction to those deficits has been instrumental in prolonging the slump; four, as a result, the downsizing operations in the public sector have been carried much farther than would have been otherwise necessary.

The assertion that the large fiscal deficits of the 1990s were caused by high interest rates seems to squarely contradict the opposite view, which is held with great conviction by financial analysts, that it is the deficits that have caused the high interest rates (through larger risk premia). There need be no contradiction here. Interest rates may increase first and generate a recession and larger deficits that in turn raise the premia on government borrowing. Vicious circles are possible.

What must be rejected, however, is incompetent causal analysis limiting the story to the partial impact of large deficits on interest rates and omitting the previous impact of high interest rates on deficits.

The particular view that large fiscal deficits and resulting debt accumulation have been a systematic cause of high interest rates faces an uphill battle against both simple observation and statistical evidence. The simple observation is that the Canada-US real long-term interest rate differential and the Canadian public sector deficit-GDP ratio have been negatively, not positively, correlated in 1989–95. Their simple correlation coefficient has been -0.44. It is easy to understand why. Canadian interest rates got their sharpest boost relative to US rates in 1989 and early 1990, just as the deficit-GDP ratio was falling to its lowest point of the decade. Then, as the debt problem worsened between 1990 and 1993, the international interest rate differential did not increase, but decreased slowly. Then, as the debt and deficit picture started to improve in 1994 and 1995, the interest rate differential increased again.

The absence of systematic causal link from large fiscal deficits to high interest rates is also supported by statistical analysis of the deficit-interest rate relationship. Standard analyses of the yield on long-term Canada bonds focus on two key determinants: the yield on three-month Canadian treasury bills and the yield on long-term US treasury bonds. It is usually found that the long-term US interest rate exerts a predominant influence on the long-term Canadian interest rate, and that the impact of the short-term Canadian interest rate is smaller, but significant.[24] To capture short- and longer-term debt accumulation effects, it is natural to add to the list of determinants the current and lagged values of the public sector deficit-GDP ratio. When this is done, however, the systematic impact of the deficit variables on the domestic long-term bond rate is found to be statistically negligible. The fact that deficits seem to have no systematic positive influence on interest rates does not, of course, exclude the possibility of temporary effects in specific months or quarters. The same observation applies to the ups and downs of the political situation.[25]

The Canada-US Real Interest Rate Differential

Beside the flat profile of real public spending, domestic demand growth has been mostly held up by the disastrous performance of interest-sensitive categories. This strongly suggests that high interest rates must be at the core of any serious explanation of the slump. In fact, the only factor that has been sufficiently important, persistent,

Figure 3
Real Short-Term Interest Rate Differential, Canada Minus the United States,
1Q81—1Q96

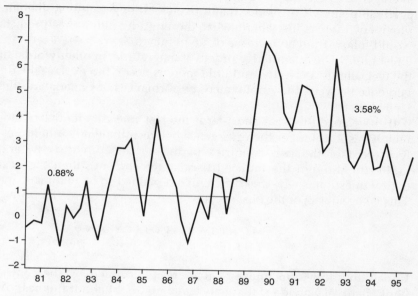

Sources: Bank of Canada; Statistics Canada; us Federal Reserve; us Department of Commerce.

and powerful to explain the coincident sharp and prolonged divergence between the output and employment performances of Canada
and the United States in this decade, as well as the previous absence
of such divergence, is the very large average real interest rate differential between the two countries since 1989. Figure 3 shows that the
Canada-us real short-term interest rate differential averaged 0.9 percentage point in 1980–8, but jumped to 3.6 points in 1989–95.

A strong reduced-form connection between short-term interest
rates (acting as a summary variable for the stance of monetary policy)
and aggregate output has been established by the voluminous Canadian and international literature on the determinants of real economic
activity.[26] Raising short-term rates brings higher long-term rates, an
exchange rate appreciation, stricter credit rationing, and lower
wealth, which reduces consumption, investment, net exports, and
government program spending, and depresses output and employment. Although there are different views on the exact nature of the
monetary transmission mechanism, there is no controversy over the
fact that monetary policy has an extremely powerful impact on real
activity, at least for the short and medium terms.[27]

When Figures 1 and 3 are compared, it is found that, in 1990–6, the gap between the employment ratios of Canada and the United States averaged 2.6 percentage points, while the real interest rate gap averaged 3.6 points. It turns out that a decrease of 2.6 points in the employment ratio is just about what the empirical literature predicts would follow from an increase of 3.6 points in the real short-term interest rate.[28] The quantitative orders of magnitude, in other words, fit the facts almost perfectly, and little more is needed to explain the divergence between the employment performances of Canada and the United States.

If the Canada-US real short-term interest rate differential is ultimately responsible for the divergence between the employment performances of the two countries in the 1990s (both directly, and indirectly, through the induced fiscal retrenchment), then the next logical question is why that differential remained so large for so long. This is the subject of the next section.

MONETARY POLICY AND THE SLUMP

Canadian short-term interest rates are determined by the central bank. Bank of Canada statements leave no doubt about this fact. At his 1995 HERMES-Glendon Lecture, after making the *caveat* that "the widespread existence of uncertainty makes it evident that monetary policy cannot be conducted in some sort of mechanistic way,"[29] Governor Thiessen reminded the audience that "neither should one go to the other extreme and conclude that … the market controls interest rates and the Bank has no capacity to pursue a monetary policy geared to Canadian requirements." Deputy Governor Noël later repeated that the Bank of Canada has all the power it needs "to target fairly precisely the level of the 3-month treasury bill rate."[30]

Since interest rates matter enormously for short- and medium-term economic performance, and the central bank believes it has all the needed power to guide interest rates, the only serious question is why the Bank of Canada kept the short-term real interest rate differential with the United States so large for so long in the 1990s. The answer to this question has two parts: first, from 1989 the central bank focused exclusively on the goal of zero inflation; second, contrary to expectations, achieving this objective has forced it to impose permanently higher unemployment through higher interest rates. I will examine these two statements in turn, and then proceed to make specific proposals to redress the situation.

The Exclusive Focus on the Goal of Zero Inflation

The first part of the answer is that the only objective the Bank of Canada has pursued since 1989 has been to establish and maintain the inflation rate at "zero level," which it sees as a Consumer Price Index (CPI) inflation rate that is "clearly below 2 percent."[31] The Bank, in other words, has played the game of pure inflation targeting. With official support from the Conservative government from February 1991 on, CPI inflation-control targets of 3 percent by the end of 1992, 2.5 percent by the middle of 1994, and 2 percent by the end of 1995 were initially set; a target range of plus or minus 1 percent was allowed around midpoint. Upon nomination of the new governor by the Liberal government in December 1993, the inflation target specified for the end of 1998 was maintained at 2 percent.[32]

The Bank of Canada settled to its task with extraordinary zeal. It achieved the December 1995 target of 2 percent four years in advance, and has spent 85 percent of the time since 1991 in the lower half of the specified target range, thus keeping CPI inflation at 1.4 percent on average in the last five years. The Bank has acted as if it has been following an "epsilon policy," according to which, instead of targeting the midpoint itself, it would aim for an inflation rate *below* the midpoint so that the probability of trespassing the midpoint would not exceed some small epsilon.

By contrast, no official inflation target has ever been set in the United States. In practice, since 1989 the Federal Reserve has been satisfied with achieving an inflation rate of around 3 percent. In setting the interest rate, it has continued to pay explicit attention to real economic growth and employment, with the result that the US unemployment rate has been in the 5 to 6 percent range. How then are we to explain the Bank of Canada's exclusive focus on the inflation objective and its apparent deflationary bias, as opposed to the more balanced approach followed so far by the US Federal Reserve?

The Bank of Canada has stated its strong view that the economic benefits of reducing inflation, say from 4 percent to below 2 percent, are "many and large," and that the unemployment costs are "transitory and small" by comparison.[33] The basis for the first statement is the standard textbook list of efficiency costs of inflation.[34] The second assertion rests on two ideas: the classical idea that, in the long run, the aggregate unemployment rate is unaffected by whatever level of inflation is achieved by the central bank;[35] and, second, the idea that, if the central bank's commitment to zero inflation is made *credible* and has a direct downward effect on expected and actual inflation, then the unemployment costs of disinflation are small even in the short run.[36] The policy implication of this view of the world is that monetary policy should focus exclusively on demonstrating its ironclad commitment to the zero inflation objective. The real economy will take care of itself, suffer minimal short-run costs, and reap large permanent benefits.

Both statements, on benefits and costs, are highly speculative and questionable. The assertion that zero, as opposed to low, inflation has a permanent favorable effect on the standard of living has no reliable quantitative evidence going for it (see the review by Fischer[37]). It is also clear by now that the hoped-for "credibility bonus" from the commitment to zero inflation in labour and product markets has materialized neither in Canada[38] nor elsewhere, even in Germany.[39] I argue below that even Friedman's proposition that aggregate unemployment is independent of the level of inflation in the long run is contradicted by recent Canadian experience.

So, why has the Bank of Canada focused exclusively on the zero inflation objective (as a number of other central banks also have done) despite the lack of hard quantitative evidence either that there exist any significant benefits from zero inflation, or that policy credibility reduces the unemployment costs of disinflation to any extent? I see at least four reasons. First, the notion that any positive rate of inflation is a terminal evil is probably held with much more conviction by the new generation of central bankers, who got their basic training in the high-inflation decade of the 1970s, than by the old generation, who had lived through the Great Depression.

Second, the religious fervour and mutual support which bond together the world fraternity of central bankers seems to have played an important role. In the latter part of the 1980s, there was a genuine strong convergence of opinion, mainly among European and Australasian central bankers, that zero inflation was the way to go, that central banks lacking a credible commitment to zero inflation *must* have an inflationary bias. Such opinion was bolstered by the impressive performance of the German and Swiss central banks, and the radical reform of the sister central bank of New Zealand in 1989. Fervour and dedication to the cause were reinforced by the very tight internal power structure and intellectual atmosphere of the Bank of Canada, which ensures that the zero inflation ideology percolates through every aspect of the life of the institution.

Third, the Bank of Canada enjoys all the independence it needs to translate its strong preference for zero inflation into concrete action. Any major divergence of opinion between the central bank and the government would put the government into an impossible situation. It would, by statute, have to explain its position in public and issue a directive to the Bank of Canada, giving it precise orders. There is a 100 percent chance that such an occurrence would immediately trigger a financial and currency market crisis. No sane Minister of Finance would ever dare to start such a process, with the consequence that, in practice, the Bank of Canada enjoys near-complete independence from the government, except once every seven years on the day a new governor is appointed.

Fourth, the fact that the Bank of Canada has acted since 1991 as if it were following an "epsilon policy," leading to an average CPI inflation rate (1.4 percent) situated well below the midpoint of the target range, is probably not a chance occurrence and likely reflects the Bank's deflationary bias; it may initially have been positioning itself for a lowering of the target range to 0–2 percent by 1998. But the foremost reason for the deflationary bias is that the Bank of Canada has been striving to establish its reputation as a tough central bank in capital markets. The Bank has tended to react to every weakness in the exchange rate with a degree of tightness that even faithful supporters of its monetary strategy have found inappropriate.[40] In addition to the excessive concern for "orderly markets," the less hawkish reputation of Governor Thiessen compared with his predecessor may have convinced the Bank that it had to demonstrate its toughness again in 1994–5, at a time when the employment ratio was still 6 percent below its prerecession level and even the Bank's own measure of the output gap was still in the 4 percent range.[41] This important policy error, which coincided with the US slowdown and domestic fiscal retrenchment, contributed to bringing the recovery to an abrupt stop in 1995. Only with the threat of deflation (the GDP deflator falling at the annual rate of 0.8 percent in the first quarter of 1996) did the Bank rush to reduce interest rates.

The US central bank is also independent from Congress and the administration. However, the broad institutional and political context in which it operates is set to enhance intellectual vitality, diversity, and competition in a systematic way. First, the Federal Reserve System is divided into twelve districts which enjoy a fair amount of intellectual independence and display a wide array of tendencies. Second, the Federal Reserve Board is run by seven full-time governors, including the chairman, who are drawn from a regular turnover of direct nominations by the President, come from all quarters of economic life, and make it impossible for insiders, such as the district presidents, to monopolize the field. Third, in addition to congressional oversight, there are many important private institutions devoted to public policy analysis, covering the political spectrum from the extreme right to the centre, that add to the internal-external intellectual competence and balance. In Canada, we have only two major think tanks, which are both conservative and predictably supportive of the current central bank strategy.

Two consequences follow. First, the radical assertion that the benefits of zero inflation, as opposed to moderately low inflation, are large would immediately be met in the United States by a flurry of papers and statements that would demonstrate the lack of reliable domestic and international evidence in support of that proposition. Second, given the different institutional and political context, it would be very hard for the Federal Reserve to formulate and implement a monetary policy that would be so narrowly focused on achieving zero inflation and oblivious of unemployment, and would be so completely and clearly at odds with the preferences of the general public, as is the case in Canada. Contrary to Canadian monetary policy, US monetary policy under Chairman Greenspan has been perfectly consistent with the spirit and letter of central bank legislation, which asks the institution to find a compromise between inflation and unemployment. This mandate is more complex than pure inflation targeting, but, as I shall argue below, it is perhaps wiser to have a complex mandate that is the right one than a simple mandate that is the wrong one.

Zero Inflation Requires Permanently Higher Unemployment

The second reason why Canadian real short-term interest rates exceeded US rates so much for so long is that, rather unexpectedly, pursuing the extreme goal of zero inflation has *forced* the Bank of Canada to impose permanently higher unemployment through higher interest rates. Maintaining CPI inflation around 1.5 percent since 1991 has required a national unemployment rate above 10 percent on average. By contrast again, the United States has been able to achieve a 5.5 percent unemployment rate by conceding an inflation rate slightly in excess of 3 percent. The difference between the inflation rates of the two countries has been small, but it is a difference that seems to have been very significant for their diverging employment performances.

Previous accounts of the tradeoff between inflation and unemployment in Canada held it that in a calm supply environment the annual inflation rate would continue to fall by 1 percentage point per 2 point-years of excess unemployment above the critical (NAIRU) level.[42] The experience of 1990 to 1992 initially confirmed this rule of thumb: inflation fell by 3.5 points (from 5.0 to 1.5 percent), while cumulative excess unemployment above 7.5 percent amounted to 7.3 point-years. Over the period 1993 to 1996, with unemployment averaging 10.2 percent, the same Phillips curve assumptions would have predicted a further decline of 5.5 points in inflation, to a *de*flation rate of 4 percent. The puzzle is: why has this not happened?

It is unlikely that this inflation stickiness has resulted from a structural increase in the traditional NAIRU since 1992. On the contrary, as argued in the first section, the NAIRU must have declined, by perhaps up to 1 percentage point, in the wake of social policy changes. Arguments based on the "hysteresis" idea, that the experience of persistent high actual unemployment has by itself pulled up the NAIRU, are not very convincing either. The comprehensive review of Canadian and international evidence on the hysteresis hypothesis by Jones[43] indicates that some mild increase in structural unemployment is as much as can be expected. This upward pressure would at any rate be smaller than the downward pressure on the NAIRU arising from the UI cuts.

The most sensible explanation of the inflation stickiness of the last five years is that, except in extreme conditions, nominal wage cuts are strongly resisted by employers who are worried about the negative impact on employee morale and turnover, and by employees who think absolute wage cuts are unfair. In short, the micro response to excess supply has a floor at zero wage change. That floor may not be of great macroeconomic importance when the median wage change is about 4 percent, as was for example recorded among the 1,230 large Canadian non-COLA wage settlements over 1986–8. At that time, only 12 percent of settlements hit the floor of zero wage change. But the zero constraint can take a large macroeconomic bite when the median wage change is itself around zero, as was observed over 1992–4. Figure 4 clarifies this point by showing the distribution of the 1,149 large non-COLA wage settlements in that period. There were 47 percent cases of wage increases, 47 percent of wage freezes, and only 6 percent of wage cuts.

The macroeconomic significance of the nominal wage floor was explained by James Tobin[44] in his 1971 Presidential Address to the American Economic Association. For inflation rates as low as 3 or 4 percent, such as occurred in Canada in the second half of the 1980s, the scope for relative wage adjustment across micro markets seems quite satisfactory, given our productivity growth rate a bit in excess of 1 percent per year. No extra dose of permanent unemployment above the NAIRU which characterizes the traditional vertical long-run Phillips curve is needed to maintain inflation there. But if inflation is to fall to a very low level, such as the 1.4 percent of 1992–6 in Canada, and stay there, the proportion of wage earners that are pushed against the wall of resistance to wage cuts must increase sharply. The long-run marginal unemployment cost of lower inflation in this range

Figure 4
Percentage Distribution of Negotiated Wage Changes (non-COLA), Canadian
Wage Settlements (500 Employees +) 1992–4 (N=1,149)

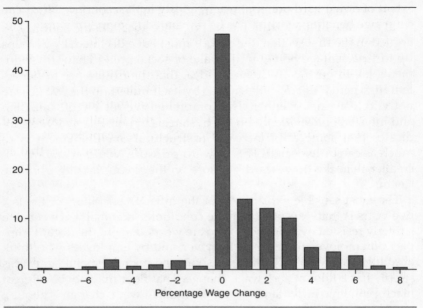

Source: Labour Canada.

is not zero, but positive and increasing. Geometrically, the long-run
Phillips tradeoff is vertical at the old low NAIRU level until inflation
falls below, say, 3 percent. But for inflation rates below 3 percent, the
tradeoff is negatively sloped, convex, and eventually flat.[45]

The contrast between the 1986–8 and 1992–4 situations for Canadian wage settlements supports the conjecture that the curvature of
the long-run Phillips tradeoff begins very suddenly around an inflation rate of 3 percent, and is very pronounced. Approaching zero inflation in a country like ours, where labour productivity grows very
slowly, has exactly the same effect on the laws of economics as approaching the speed of light has on the laws of physics. Nothing
seems to happen (i.e., the Phillips curve remains vertical) until you
reach a certain threshold. But if you cross the Rubicon, everything
breaks down. This stark nonlinearity can explain why the United
States can entertain a 5.5 percent unemployment rate with an inflation rate of 3 percent, while Canada seems incapable of lowering its
unemployment rate below 9 percent with an inflation rate less than
two percentage points lower.

There are three counter-arguments against the above theory. The first is that the above Canadian evidence on resistance to wage cuts, based on negotiated wage settlements, greatly exaggerates the true extent of downward nominal wage rigidity in the economy. Firms can cut fringe benefits; workers can be prevented from moving up within fixed pay scales; layoffs and new hirings give some flexibility; wage cuts are more prevalent in the nonunion sector, etc. But such phenomena are unlikely to turn the evidence from contract data around. Working with many US data sets, Akerlof, Dickens, and Perry[46] have recently provided detailed statistical evidence that the no-wage-cut norm is generalized in labour markets, and that the other ways to cut wage costs provide no practical macroeconomic escape from it.

The second counter argument is the apparent contradiction that, in the decade 1955–64, Canada was able to achieve an average inflation rate of 1.5 percent. It must be pointed out, however, that labour productivity in that decade was growing so fast that wages were able to increase at an average annual rate in excess of 5 percent, a situation in which very few cases of forced wage freezes must have occurred. Likewise, it is currently possible for a country such as Japan to target zero inflation without having to accept permanently higher unemployment, simply because labour productivity there grows much faster than in Canada.

The third counter argument is that the resistance to wage cuts will go away if only we persist with zero inflation a few more years. This assertion is contradicted by the experience of the last five years, and also by the history of the Great Depression, where the extremely high rates of unemployment led to stronger, not weaker, institutions to prevent absolute wage declines. To bet on the contrary in the rest of the 1990s is to take an incredible chance with a very uncertain proposition and continue to take risks that are costing Canada many tens of billions of dollars annually in depressed output and employment.

*Public Preferences and the Inflation-
Unemployment Tradeoff*

The large and persistent differential in real short-term interest rates between Canada and the United States that caused the Canadian slump of the 1990s is the result of two errors of monetary policy. First, the central bank displayed a strong deflationary bias that has not reflected adequately the true state of knowledge on the effects of zero inflation, the true preferences of the Canadian population, and the spirit and letter of the Bank of Canada Act, which reflects those preferences by stipulating a reasonable balance between inflation and unemployment objectives. Second, the central bank misjudged the nature of the tradeoff between inflation and unemployment in the range of very low inflation rates to which it has led the Canadian economy. The unemployment costs of zero inflation have turned out to be not transitory and small but permanent and large.

Two implications follow naturally from this verdict. First, the Bank of Canada must be brought to reflect the preferences of the general public more adequately. Second, the objectives pursued by the Bank must take explicit account of the costly tradeoff between inflation and unemployment at low inflation rates.

Central banks are very powerful political institutions that must reflect social preferences. They must be accountable to the public through its elected representatives. But they must also protect the public against the "eternal temptation of the Prince," to debase the currency. They should, therefore, be allowed some degree of independence from government. A practical compromise between accountability and independence must be found and reflected in the nature of the mandate and the way it is executed and monitored.

The problem that has emerged in the 1990s is not lack of central bank independence but lack of accountability to the public. The public must be protected against the inflationary bias of the government, but also against the deflationary bias of central bankers who are, in Stanley Fischer's apt metaphor, "cocooned within an anti-inflationary temple,"[47] and tend to minimize the consequences of the zero inflation strategy for output and employment. It is true that the Bank of Canada has made every effort to explain this strategy though public speeches, appearances in Parliament, research papers, *Annual Reports* and, more recently, *Monetary Policy Reports*. But it is also true that these have often been exercises in advocacy of a controversial and extreme policy orientation rather than genuine dialogue with the public.

It is critical that the balance be redressed and that the Bank of Canada be brought to better reflect the preferences of the public. One suggestion[48] that has been floating around for some time and that I strongly support is that policy responsibility be conferred not on one inside governor with a seven-year term, but to a board of five full-time governors, led by a chairman, for overlapping ten-year terms. There would be a majority of outside appointees. One nomination every two years instead of one every seven years and a larger board would bring a better balance of power between the central bank and elected representatives while preserving the stability and independence of the institution. The nomination of an outside majority would better protect the institution against the cocooning problem. Intellectual vitality, diversity, and internal-external competition would be enhanced.

Concerning the inflation-unemployment tradeoff, the preceding analysis has two crucial implications for monetary policy, one negative and the other positive. The negative implication is that targeting an inflation rate "clearly below 2 percent" instead of a rate, say, around 3 percent is a disastrous strategy to follow on elementary grounds of cost-benefit calculus. On the one hand, there exists no reliable quantitative evidence that "going zero" can raise the general standard of living significantly. On the other, if forcing inflation down to 1.5 percent instead of 3 percent requires keeping unemployment permanently above, say, 9 percent instead of 6.5 percent in Canada, then the true cost of the policy is not small and temporary. It is large and permanent, amounting to some $50 billion of national income lost every year. This cost is not "behind us" as is sometimes argued: it is past, current, and future.

The positive implication for monetary policy is that it should try to aim for the lowest achievable inflation rate on the vertical arm of the long-run Phillips curve, where the unemployment rate is also the lowest sustainable. This target inflation rate could be 3 percent, and the corresponding NAIRU 6.5 percent. These numbers make no claim to precision, but they look reasonable in view of recent US experience (3 percent inflation and 5.5 percent unemployment), the recent trend growth rate of our labour productivity (1.3 percent), the actual distribution of wage changes in the 3-to-4 percent inflation environment of 1986–8 (only 12 percent of wage freezes), previous estimates of the Canadian NAIRU (around 7.5 percent), the UI amendments of 1990–6 (worth perhaps up to a 1 percentage point reduction in the NAIRU), and the recent shortfall of employment relative to the pre-recession peak (6 percent).

This change of strategy could be implemented smoothly. The first step would have the central bank continue to hold down short-term interest rates in Canada, as it has done very appropriately in recent quarters, even if they rise in the United States, and even if the exchange rate shows temporary weakness. Then, as the economy begins to respond to the monetary stimulus, the Bank of Canada should let the recovery process run its course. Because we are so far below potential, our current growth capacity is enormous, and the full recovery will take many years. The Bank must avoid the kind of premature and inappropriate tightening that killed the recovery in 1995–6. Most crucially, it must recognize the basic implication of the nonlinear Phillips curve that some increase in inflation, likely to the 3 percent level, will have to be allowed for output to recover fully and unemployment to decline to below 7 percent. In other words, between now and the end of 1998, the increase of inflation into the upper half of the current inflation-control target range (between 2 and 3 percent) must not be a cause for panic, but must instead become a reasoned objective of policy.

Such a new monetary strategy would have to be widely explained, but it should be easy for financial markets and the general public to understand and approve. Concern about the slump currently outweighs preoccupation with inflation; the theory makes sense and has empirical support; and the practical implications are extremely attractive. The real economic outlook will be substantially improved, inflation will remain under control, Canadian monetary policy will resemble the US strategy, and Canadian fiscal performance will quickly become better than that of the US. The natural last step will be to make the change of strategy official for the post-1998 period by returning the specified inflation-control target to 3 percent and the related target range to 2–4 percent (as in 1992).

The proposed evolution is both moderate and radical. It is moderate in that it would basically require "only" an increase of 1 percentage point in the official inflation-control target. But it is also radical because macroeconomic performance seems very different according to whether you operate the economy in the lower half of the 1–3 percent inflation target range or in the upper half of the 2–4 percent range. This small difference that matters arises from the sharp nonlinearity of the long-run Phillips curve at low inflation rates.

The main difficulty with the proposal is that it is politically delicate, because it requires the Bank of Canada to end eight years of commitment to the zero inflation strategy, to embrace instead a balanced strategy and implement it with conviction. But it must absolutely be done because the stakes for Canada are so enormous.[49]

CONCLUSION

I began by pointing out that the Canadian slump of the 1990s exceeds everything we have known since the Great Depression. The cumulative employment losses since 1990 already amount to 30 percent of the corresponding losses of the 1930s, and are still accumulating. The cumulative output losses since 1990 now exceed $400 billion, and keep growing at an annual rate of $75 billion. After being almost identical to the US in the 1970s and the 1980s, Canada's relative employment performance has been a disaster in the 1990s. My purpose has been to analyze the causes of this surprising and sad development, and to draw useful implications for policy.

I have eliminated a number of popular, but false, explanations of the slump: globalization, technology, political uncertainty, social policy, payroll taxes, and minimum wages. Those rationalizations are either contradicted by evidence, or much too limited in scope to explain more than a small fraction of the slump. Given the failure of supply-side factors to provide a satisfactory explanation, and given also the extraordinary expansion of net export demand after 1992, the slump must have reflected sinking domestic aggregate demand.

The flat profile of real public spending and the depression of interest-sensitive components of demand leave only one satisfactory explanation of the slump: old-fashioned monetary contraction and induced fiscal contraction. The large differential in short-term real interest rates between Canada and the United States is the only factor that has been sufficiently important, persistent, and powerful to explain the coincident sharp and prolonged divergence between the output and employment performances of Canada and the United States. High interest rates and the recession, not lax spending, have been the unique source of large fiscal deficits. The deficits brought fiscal policy to increase taxes and slash spending, and hence to prolong the slump in 1995 and 1996.

There are two reasons why the Bank of Canada kept Canadian short-term interest rates so high for so long. First, it focused narrowly on achieving zero inflation (in practice, an average CPI inflation rate of 1.4 percent since 1991), while the Federal Reserve has been satisfied with an average inflation rate of 3 percent that has allowed the US unemployment rate to fall below 6 percent. Second, the Bank of Canada has misjudged the nature of the inflation-unemployment tradeoff in the previously uncharted territory of very low inflation rates that it has explored since 1991. Driving down CPI inflation and keeping it down has, rather unexpectedly, forced the Bank to impose permanently higher unemployment. Strong resistance to nominal wage cuts in labour markets is the likely explanation for the marked flattening of the long-run Phillips curve at inflation rates below 3 percent. The United States has simply avoided falling into that trap. The inflation rate differential between the two countries has been less than 2 percentage points, but it is a small difference that has had big consequences.

The policy implications from this analysis are that the Bank of Canada must be brought to reflect the preferences of the general public more adequately. Its objectives must take explicit account of the costly tradeoff between inflation and unemployment at very low inflation rates. My suggestion is that the pure zero inflation experiment be terminated, and that the Bank of Canada aim instead for the lowest inflation rate on the vertical arm of the long-run Phillips curve (about 3 percent), where the unemployment rate is also the lowest sustainable (perhaps 6.5 percent). In order to support recovery from the slump, the Bank should first let inflation increase into the upper half of the current 1–3 percent target range. Beyond 1998, the target range should be reset at 2–4 percent, thus allowing much greater hope for Canada to emulate the recent good macroeconomic performance of the US economy.

Given the current realization by public opinion in many countries that the promised "large benefits" from zero inflation are actually a mirage and that the "small" unemployment costs are actually huge, and given the rapid evolution of knowledge in this area, I would not be surprised if a number of central banks, even in Europe, soon begin to support the more moderate strategy that I am proposing. The question may not be whether the Bank of Canada will change its strategy, but whether it will be the first or the last to do so. I hope for Canada that it will be a leader rather than a follower.

Canadian Economic Growth: Perspective and Prospects

RICHARD G. HARRIS

INTRODUCTION

The recent Canadian economic experience is often discussed in negative terms, both in the policy literature and in the media. Falling real wages and high unemployment are the two topics which have received the most attention. This focus on the recent past, however, ignores the remarkable economic achievements of the period 1950–90. There is little doubt that the federal government played a major role in fostering and promoting an environment in which the living standards for most of its citizens increased on a scale unprecedented in history. One objective of this paper is to review that experience and discuss what economists have learned about the causes of economic growth. It then goes on to discuss the "other half" of the history of Canadian economic growth, which is the large-scale structural transformation of the economy particularly in the last decade. The paper closes with some comments as to what lessons can be drawn from the growth history of the postwar period with regard to economic policy in the future.

THE RECORD

The record of Canadian economic growth since World War II is shown in Figure 1. Over the period 1960–90, the Gross Domestic Product (GDP) grew at an annualized rate of roughly 4.3 percent. Reporting of growth rates does not adequately convey the remarkable impact over the long-term that economic growth has on living standards. In Figure 1, output per capita is given for the entire four decades, 1950–90. Depending upon exactly how one does the calculation, real living standards per person have approximately tripled over this period.

Figure 1
Economic Growth in Canada, 1950–92 (output per capita)

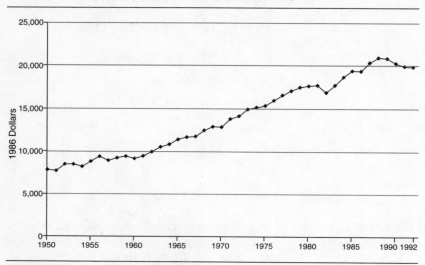

Source : Statistics Canada.

The economic measure of well-being used here is the standard constant dollar measure of produced goods and services – the GDP per person. There are two major caveats to this statistic. First, it overstates social and economic welfare as it includes expenditures that, while necessary, are a response to a deteriorating social and economic system – for example increased protection against violent crimes or health expenditure due to a poor environment. On the other side of the ledger, changes in GDP do not measure the dramatic reductions in working time that have occurred over this century. Despite much research, it is not evident that a more comprehensive measure of net welfare would give a dramatically different view of the longer-term record of economic growth.

We think of the 1980s as a difficult decade, but this perception is less than self-evident in the data. One major problem with the GDP statistic is that it fails to include corrections for the improved quality of new goods. The car you are driving today is a lot better than the one you drove twenty years ago. Some estimates for Canada by Diewert suggest that the bias in the cost of living index for the 1980s, a period of strong technical change, could amount to an overestimate of as much as 1 percent as compared to the officially reported Consumer Price Index (CPI). If this is correct, then the growth slowdown of the 1980s could be a statistical illusion, and much of the recent concern about fall-

Figure 2
Relative Income 1970 (US Dollars)

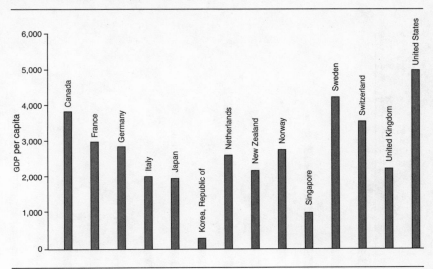

Source: World Bank.

ing productivity growth could be misplaced. With this caveat in mind, what can be said of Canada's performance relative to other countries?

The international comparisons are indicated in Figures 2 and 3 for 1970 and 1993. The benchmark here is per capita income expressed in current US dollars. These comparisons do not use the controversial Purchasing Power Parity (PPP) adjustment. What is clear from these figures is that the world has changed a lot since 1970. Canada has moved from third place to seventh or eighth depending on the details of the calculation. Many view this shift in relative position as alarming. There are two points to make about this. First, exchange rates have a powerful effect on these rankings. Generally we now think that the Canadian dollar in 1993 was well below its long-run PPP value. The high ranking of a number of European countries is due, in part, to this difference. On the other hand, much of the relative change is real enough. Understanding why some countries did better than others is a major challenge to scholars of economic growth and of obvious concern to policy makers. The rapid growth rates of a number of former developing countries, particularly in Asia, has meant that the size of the industrial country "club" is much larger and Canada is much less unique on the income scale than it was even two decades ago. Much of our economic angst probably has as much to do with the change in the relative international standing of Canada as it does with lower growth rates.

Figure 3
Relative Income 1993 (US Dollars)

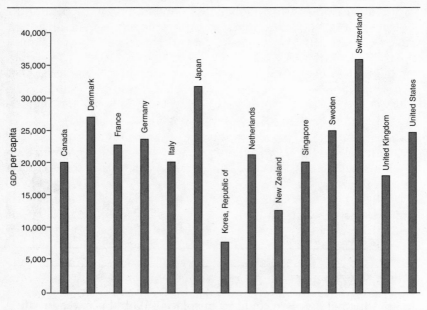

Source: World Bank.

ECONOMIC GROWTH 1950–73[1]

High incomes are the consequence of high productivity, as measured by output per hour worked. Why was productivity so high and rising in Canada until 1974? Why might productivity growth have slowed thereafter?

In the broadest terms, economists traditionally categorize economic growth as being driven by four alternative sets of factors. First, Solovian growth or growth driven by the accumulation of larger amounts of physical capital (or, more bluntly, machines) per worker. The second type, referred to as Smithian growth, is that due to productivity gains driven by increases in market size, an increased division of labour, and larger-scale production which accompanies such specialization. In open economies, Smithian growth is usually associated with international trade.

The third type of growth is knowledge-based growth emphasized in some of the "new growth theory" pioneered by Paul Romer and Robert Lucas. In this view, a combination of new technology and the accumulation of skills by the labour force lets economies escape the law of diminishing returns. Growth becomes linked to the levels of investment in research and development and expenditures on human capital development. In a global environment, one must account for the fact that technology, wherever it is developed, is generally available. Consequently, poor countries can grow faster as they catch up to the technological leaders.

Finally there is the staples-led growth associated with the name of Harold Innis. This is economic growth that comes from resource extraction and harvesting. It has played an important role in Canadian experience, but is usually viewed as being nonpermanent, as resources are depleted or inevitably come at much higher cost.

In addition to the broader determinants of economic growth, there are the particular historical and geographic circumstances unique to each country. But to understand the remarkable Canadian economic growth in the 1950s and 1960s, one must appreciate that the same thing was happening in the United States, both in magnitude and timing. The best explanation of US postwar growth is given in the work of Richard Nelson and Gavin Wright[2] who propose three important explanatory factors.

First, Solovian growth: the maturation of the technology associated with mass production of industrial and consumer products. Often termed Fordism, after the plants of the Ford Motor Company which typified the switch to assembly line production methods, this method of production achieved its preeminence during the immediate postwar period across almost all manufacturing industries, promoting large-scale economies in production and associated productivity gains.

Second, Smithian growth: Reductions in transport and communication costs facilitated the emergence of a large integrated market in the United States, with corporations that were genuinely national in scale. The large market and the competition within that market were unprecedented in scope and allowed the United States an enormous opportunity to make productivity gains through a more efficient allocation of resources both within companies and across regions.

Third, staples-led growth: The United States was richly endowed with raw materials and a national infrastructure which facilitated the efficient extraction and exploitation of these resources. This last feature of the US growth experience tends often to be forgotten, but detailed studies of US exports have consistently shown their very high natural resource content.

How then does Canada fit into this picture? Starting with the obvious, Canada got rich by being a major resource supplier to the US market and the newly emerging global industrial market. Wheat, forest products, aluminum, minerals were all exported in large quantities to the United States using a well-developed and highly efficient transport system. Prices for these products were kept high by demand which was growing ahead of available supply. Productivity in exploiting resources was both high and rising; Canada's labour force was highly trained and much of the nation's engineering and science was devoted to resource extraction of one sort or another. Resource exploitation was also highly capital intensive, with the result that large amounts of capital had to be imported. This requirement for capital imports, together with the vertically integrated nature of basic industry, led to a rising degree of US ownership of Canadian industries.

A second factor was the emergence of the integrated US market. Canada indirectly benefited from this as the manufacturing sector became more open to US competition through the successive reductions in tariffs that occurred under the early General Agreement on Tariffs and Trade (GATT) rounds. Careful studies by Baldwin and Gorecki[3] have shown how slow and gradual this process was, though a dramatic example of continental rationalization of product lines was that of the big three auto firms under the 1965 Canada-US Auto Pact. The point often made both by the Wonnacotts and myself was that opening up our domestic market to US competition meant the necessary adoption of Fordism within Canada if the industry were to locate here and be competitive.[4] This, in turn, meant that Canada benefited slowly but surely by integration into the large US market, with the attendant low prices and high wages that market was generating.

The last factor has already been alluded to: the maturation of large-scale mass production methods. This was obviously less important in Canada than in the US, but it became significant as markets opened up sufficiently for economies of scale to be achieved through export. I do not want to downplay, however, the importance of mass production methods for Canada. Studies show that, for example, in the industries processing natural resources, economies of scale and productivity levels in Canadian plants were similar to those achieved in the United States. Even within branch plants, similar methods of production were adopted, albeit over shorter production runs than in comparable US plants. Therefore, many of the technological improvements in US plants were also relevant for Canadian branch plants.

GLOBALIZATION AND THE GROWTH DECLINE

Productivity growth declined in virtually all industrial countries at about 1974, the same year as the first oil shock. This is also the date that most economists use to mark the beginning of the transition to the global economy and the decline in the rate of economic growth in the then-prominent industrial countries. For Canada, the oil shock, while bad for global productivity in the short term, had a number of beneficial side effects – notably the creation of a commodity boom in western Canada.

The oil shock diverted attention from a major structural change that was occurring in the background: the growth in the world economy outside Europe and North America. The Japanese success in the early 1970s was the first visible sign of this trend, but the rapid emergence of manufactured exports from the Asian tigers in the later part of that decade provided a clearer indication of what was to come. The basic technology that had succeeded so well, first in North America and then in Western Europe, quickly found its way to other parts of the globe. This meant, from the industrial countries' perspective, a large increase in the number of industrial competitors. The pressures of the new competition became evident in the trade policies of the industrialized countries. While trade between the rich industrial countries was liberalized up to and including the completion of the Tokyo Round in 1977, imports from the nonindustrial countries were increasingly restricted by a variety of nontariff barriers to trade.

Global development had profound implications for the structure of wages in the industrial countries, although this did not become evident until the middle 1980s. By and large, the products of the new industrializing countries involve relatively standardized production methods with a substantial input of unskilled labour. The generally low level of wages in these countries, therefore, meant that the same goods could be produced more cheaply than in the older industrialized countries. The simultaneous results were to raise the level of world income but also to increase substantially the effective supply of unskilled labour to world industrial markets. Wage levels in the industrialized countries came under increasing pressure, most notably in manufacturing. Not only did real wages to unskilled manufacturing labour fall in those countries; the relative returns to higher skill levels increased significantly.[5]

From the world perspective, the wages of workers in the newly industrializing countries were growing at a much faster pace than were wages being reduced or jobs eliminated in the industrialized countries. This, in turn, was reflected in the much higher growth rates of the tigers. The process is far from over. The initial export successes of countries such as Taiwan, Hong Kong, Singapore, and Korea, based on low wage cost advantages, are now being lost as labour intensive industries move to countries with still lower wages, such as China, Indonesia, and India. The low-skilled labour market has become a

Figure 4
Natural Resource Trade (Share of Canadian Exports)

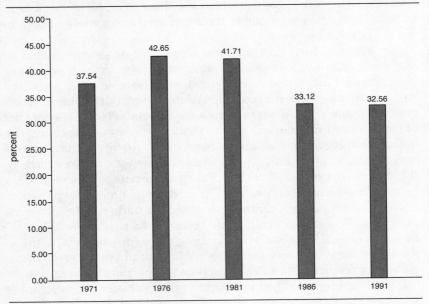

Source: Statistics Canada.

global market. In the absence of policy intervention, wages for such jobs will continue to be pressured by the large available supply of workers in Asia, Latin America, and now eastern Europe and the former Soviet Union.

Of particular importance to Canada during this period were developments in natural resource markets. Historically the trend in resource prices has been one of decline. Technological progress has, on balance, been geared to reducing the material input to goods production, and growth in supply has been more than sufficient to meet demand. The rise in oil, mineral, and agricultural prices during the 1970s was one of the periodic aberrations against what has thus far been the longer-term downward trend. The implications are indicated in Figure 4, which shows the shift in natural resource trade in Canada. From 1974 through 1982, there was a distinct increase in the natural resource share of the value of total trade. The commodity boom contributed to a false sense of economic security in Canada for a period lasting a little less than a decade. The belief that Canadians could continue to earn high wages by selling oil and other commodities came to a symbolic end with the fall in oil prices in 1985. Not only oil prices but all other commodity prices fell in real terms for the rest of the 1980s.

It is conceivable that the long-term trend in commodity prices may be reversed by a high rate of growth in world demand, particularly as Asia accelerates. But, for the present at least, our natural resource trade has gone back to about 30 percent of total exports.

FACTOR INPUT GROWTH
IN CANADA

While their relative importance changes over time, natural resources, physical capital,[6] human resources, technology, and organization are the principal "factor endowments" that determine economic growth and income generation. An assessment of the recent record of factor input growth in Canada provides some context against which to judge alternative policy prescriptions for increasing the rate of economic growth.

Savings and Investment in Physical Capital

There is a considerable debate amongst economists as to whether a high savings rate and thus a large share of GDP devoted to investment is a significant source of economic growth. My reading of the evidence is that that high rates of equipment investment (thus excluding investment in real estate) are clearly associated with high rates of economic growth.[7] If so, countries that can maintain environments favourable to investment will grow faster on average than those that do not.

However, the national supply of investment funds has received less attention, in policy discussions of the global economy, than the attraction of investment. In a world with highly mobile financial capital, it is sometimes argued that investment levels in small countries should be unrelated to their rates of national savings, and thus savings rates are not important determinants of economic growth. The evidence on this is far from conclusive, and, indeed, the whole proposition that capital is perfectly mobile, after allowance for risk, is far from self-evident. Most of the evidence on financial capital mobility pertains only to the government bonds and treasury bills of industrial countries. Evidence on the international mobility of equity capital is far less conclusive. The contrary view, that countries with high rates of national saving will have high rates of investment, deserves a lot more weight than it has recently been given. For a variety of political, cultural, and institutional reasons, domestic savings by and large seem to stay at home in most countries. Quantitatively, the most obvious way to raise the rate of capital formation in Canada would be to raise the rate of national saving. Countries that save a lot are likely to grow faster than those that do not.

Figure 5
Growth in Real Business Capital Stock per Person Employed

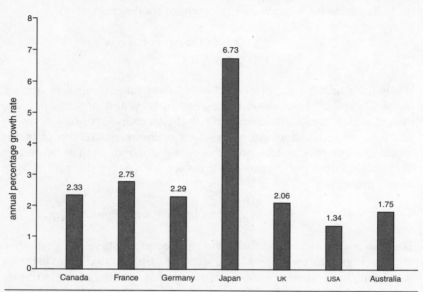

Source: D. Slater, "The Contribution of Investment and Savings to Productivity and Economic Growth in Canada" (Ottawa: Investment Canada, 1992).

The case for capital accumulation as the cause of growth is certainly debatable. Evidence for industrial countries is indicated in Figure 5. With the exception of Japan, most countries have had annual increases in real capital per worker of about 2.5 percent over the last two decades; they did not have vastly different growth experiences. Japan and many of the successful "tigers" (Singapore, Korea, and Taiwan, for example) had both high rates of labour productivity growth and high rates of capital accumulation. This evidence contradicts the view that technological change is the growth driver, and that capital accumulation merely accompanies growth, if one assumes that all countries were subject to roughly the same set of technological opportunities. The fast growers were the ones in which investment rates were high.

The issue becomes even more interesting when you look at the composition of investment. In Figure 6, the shares of investment in machinery and equipment and of public sector investment are graphed over the 1950–90 period. Machinery and equipment investment has taken off since 1974, steadily increasing with the exception of the dips in the last two recessions and almost doubling relative to its 1970 level. If machinery and equipment investment is an engine of economic growth,

Figure 6
Investment in Canada, 1950–92

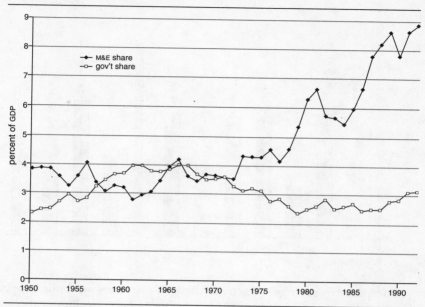

Source: Statistics Canada.

why has this increase not shown up in growth rates? There are two answers. First, the 1974–81 increase can be largely explained by the energy/commodity boom in Canada. Growth in that sector was offset, in part, by lower productivity growth in nonresource manufacturing. Since 1984, the structural shift to manufactured and service exports has been accompanied by large-scale investments in computers and electrical equipment. It has been suggested that the productivity improvements in those sectors have been offset by a host of other negative factors – high real interest rates, an overvalued currency, and political uncertainty. Much of the trade evidence is consistent with this view.

The other feature of the investment data is the small but significant decline in public sector investment. Part of the fallout of our national fiscal crisis has been a shift in public expenditure away from investment towards transfers and debt service. There has been an active, but inconclusive, debate as to how much of the weak 1980s productivity growth experience can be attributed to the decline in infrastructure investment. My own guess is that it has been significant but may not yet be showing up as a decline in private sector productivity due to the long lags involved.

Figure 7
Comparative National Savings Rates

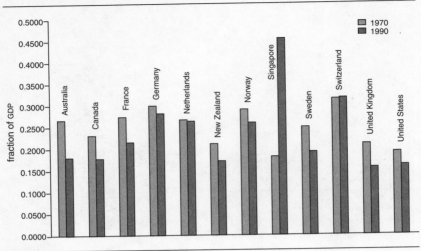

Source : World Bank.

Comparative savings rates for industrial countries are indicated in Figure 7 for 1970 and 1990. Canada has had a large decline in its national savings rate, from 23 to 17 percent over this period, and, as of 1990, stood in the middle of a large number of low savings/poor growth countries including Australia, New Zealand, the United Kingdom, and the United States. In comparison with many of the high-growth, newly industrializing countries, these savings rates are much lower – often 10 to 15 percentage points lower. The usual excuse offered is that high income countries do not need to save as much as middle income or industrializing countries; it is not clear that the evidence of the past two decades is consistent with this rather complacent view.

Education and Human Capital

Perhaps the most fundamental determinant of wealth generation in modern economies is the level of human capital. It is certainly the case that, in studies of economic growth over the period 1950 to 1985, human capital consistently shows up as an important growth determinant. Indeed, some studies show it as the only significant variable.[8]

The Canadian record is fairly good on investment in human capital. One way to measure this s to look at the cost of inputs to the education "industry." In Figure 8, it is indicated that after reaching a peak in 1971 of about 8.1 percent of GDP, total inputs (public and private)

Figure 8
Canada's Investment in Human Capital
Expenditure on Education (Public and Private)

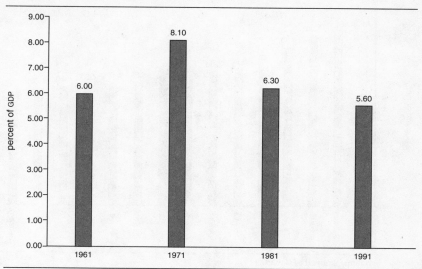

Source: Economic Council of Canada, *Education and Training in Canada* (Ottawa: Supply and Services Canada, 1992).

to the education sector have declined to about 5.6 percent of GDP. Looking only at the public sector spending (Figure 9), Canada stood fourth in the OECD in the late 1980s.

The debate about the contribution of human capital to economic growth is unresolved and highly contentious. Estimates of the contribution of education to the growth rate range from less than 10 percent to over 50 percent. Recently, Jorgenson and Fraumeni have argued that there is massive underestimation of the stock of human capital for the United States. They suggest that properly measured, the value of human capital exceeds the physical capital stock by a factor of eight! If they are correct, the earlier studies, for which the magnitude is about 1.5 to 2, vastly understate how important human capital growth has been for total economic growth.

The human capital debate has taken a new twist with the rise in the wages of skilled (i.e., educated) workers relative to unskilled workers in most industrial countries. The most popular explanation has been labour-saving technological change – the substitution of "chips for neurons" in the second industrial revolution. The issue is whether growth is caused by the computer or by giving people skills to work

Figure 9
Public Sector Spending on Education

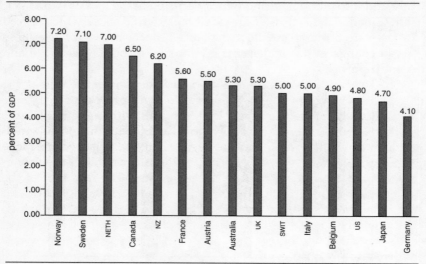

Source: Economic Council of Canada.

with the computer. It is possibly both, and the increased importance of human capital (as reflected in the skilled wage premium) may show up in future growth accounting studies with an increased weight on the factor of educational input.

RESTRUCTURING

The structure of all advanced industrial countries has been changing over the last decade, and it has long been recognized that change and growth are closely related. Schumpeter's gale of creative destruction, as new industries emerge and old ones die, is a standard metaphor. In more pedestrian terms, there is a widespread consensus that the end of the 1984 recession marked the beginning of a period of large-scale structural change, and that this is having a noticeable effect on the growth performance of the advanced countries.

Both the role of the industrialized countries in the world economic system and the structure of their own economies are changing. Much of this occurs without the visible hand of government. It is most acute during recessions, when it becomes evident that certain forms of economic activity are inefficient or unprofitable; uncomfortable and hard decisions are forced upon workers and firms.

Occasionally structural change can occur without the help of the business cycle. One prominent example was the move out of agriculture and into manufacturing which occurred at the end of World War II in Canada. The war itself provided the external shock which served to facilitate a massive shift in resources. But a necessary condition was a change in the underlying technology of both agriculture and manufacturing.

The 1984 and 1990 recessions facilitated the emergence of massive structural change in the world economy. The process of economic growth unfortunately appears to be linked with periods of large change in which there are many visible losers. With the globalization of manufacturing, small countries such as Canada must become niche exporters who are relatively specialized and can achieve the economies of scale necessary for competitive export. The first part of the adjustment toward this new economic structure involves plant closures and layoffs as it becomes apparent at the company level which activities are not competitive. Often the process is unpredictable and gut-wrenching to the people involved. Unemployment rises and skills that were once thought to be useful are rendered obsolete.

The second part of the rationalization process involves investment in new plants, new technologies, building new skills among employees, and investing in the distribution and marketing network to service the larger external market. Many would have us believe that technological change is the main or only source of structural change in the economy. While this is no doubt an overstatement, the overwhelming significance of technology must be recognized. New developments in microelectronics – the Smart Machine – are replacing labour across a wide range of both service and industrial jobs.[9] The problem about such change is, of course, that the net social productivity gains that it brings come only with a long lag, and the jobs created are often more demanding in terms of the skill levels required.

Other aspects of technological change are also causing major reorganizations. Consumers have become more price conscious, thereby inducing a substantial change in the way retailing is done; the move to just-in-time inventory systems has forced suppliers to keep a much tighter control on quality and cost; the hierarchical structure of firms is changing as new information technology reduces the need for a lot of middle management. And so on. Adjusting to new technologies is a complex and unpredictable process.

A further source of restructuring is the ongoing shift in the composition of final demand as countries grow wealthier and the real price of manufactured goods continues to fall. The demand for services is growing faster than income, while the demand for many basic consumer durables is becoming less responsive to income. Once the average family is fed, housed, clothed, and has a car in the garage, most discretionary income falls on services – travel, entertainment, recreation, education, dining out, child care services, hobbies, and so forth. In Canada, close to 70 percent of the workforce is now employed in the so-called service industries. Some of these services are not driven by final demand but are intermediate inputs to the production of other goods and services. It is important to note that in this way service production is intimately linked to the trade side of the economy. David Cox and I calculate that every dollar of manufactured exports in Canada contains about 38 cents worth of service sector output.[10]

Reliable evidence on restructuring in the last few years is just beginning to emerge. Work by Baldwin and Rafiquzzaman at Statistics Canada probably provides the best available data. Their conclusions are what one would more or less expect. Resources and low-wage manufacturing have been in decline. Scale-based industries continue to expand, reflecting our catch-up to US Fordism. Product differentiated and science based industries are expanding. The other major finding is that exit and entry of firms, and job turnover associated with this process, are far greater on an *intrasectoral* than on an *intersectoral* basis. The implications of this are far from clear. One possibility is that traditional industrial classification schemes are simply breaking down; "sectors" are being redefined. The other hypothesis, more plausible in my view, is that Canadian manufacturing industry is being globalized across the board. New firms are entering into new niches, often with export markets in mind. Some existing firms are failing; many are restructuring themselves through a combination of cost reduction, shedding old product lines and adding new ones, targeting new markets, and giving up old ones. All this shows up in the statistics as intrasectoral turnover.

Globalization ultimately shows up as an increase in the volume of trade, much of it occurring in previously nontraded services. In this regard, the Internet may well turn out to be one of the most spectacular trade promoting innovations in history, rivaling the introduction of the railroad and the steamship.

Openness, as measured by the sum of exports plus imports divided by GDP, is reported in Figure 10. The trend, beginning in 1972, has been steadily upward, starting from a fairly stable 40 percent to a number now well in excess of 60 percent. More recently, there were large increases in the volume of both export and import trade with the United States. Increased openness can lead to Smithian-type growth due to improved productivity achieved by increased

Figure 10
Openness of Canadian Economy

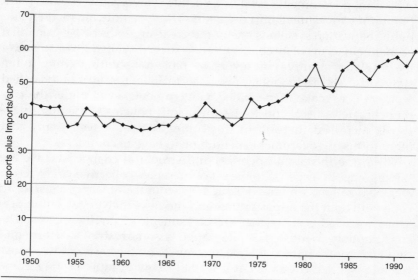

Source: Statistics Canada.

specialization, but as yet we have no established methodology to put a reliable number on how much of recent growth can be accounted for by this factor.

BACK TO GROWTH

What can be learned from all this? I think there are two basic messages. First, there is hope. There is no reason to believe that economic growth has ceased, or that Canadian institutions are incapable of adapting to the necessary changes. While there have been some difficult times, there is much to be proud of in what has been achieved. Second, government has a role to play in facilitating economic growth through the environment it creates. Policies for creating growth demand a long view that we all too often neglect and politics often undercut. I would emphasize three types of policies to which governments need to pay closer attention.

First, Canadian governments need to be concerned about the national savings rate. An increase in the rate of national savings is, in my opinion, the most certain way to secure an increase in long-term living standards. Balanced budgets and taxation of consumption, as opposed to savings, are two basic principles of economic policy that contribute towards this goal.

Second, governments need to be actively involved in securing and promoting investment in education. There is little doubt that our public education system is one of the great strengths of the Canadian economy in terms of its contribution to social equality. It is also one of the single most important levers we have for securing rising living standards. The right policy response to falling wages of unskilled workers is to make them skilled. Governments, even under the current climate of fiscal constraint, must shift policies at the margin towards increased investment in people. That may well imply that other forms of government spending will have to contract.

Third, the increased openness and structural change that we are undergoing, in response to the set of pressures collectively referred to as globalization, are unavoidable for a country of Canada's size. To cope with both the opportunities and the risks that globalization presents, we need policies that are investment-oriented as opposed to consumption-oriented. The alternative is an industrial structure and human resource base that have to compete on the basis of low wages. Canada is a rich country; but if we fail to invest more of the income that wealth is generating, it is a status that will not endure.

Realism and Moderation for the Public Good

JAMES SCHLESINGER

In this volume honouring Allan MacEachen for his long years of service – as statesman, colleague, negotiating partner, and friend, to Nova Scotia, to Canada, and to the Free World – my special responsibility is to provide international flavour. That goes beyond the rather pointed reference in your national anthem: "O Canada, We Stand on Guard for Thee." It has been clear to us Americans, at least since the War of 1812, just who it is that you are on guard against. It is *therefore* not my intention to justify either the extraterritorial reach of American law or the Helms-Burton Act. I prefer first to refer back to an earlier, and more harmonious, period in US-Canadian relations, when I got to know Allan MacEachen well. It was early in 1978, and the topic was gas transportation from Alaska and the Mackenzie Delta. I soon found out how tough a negotiator my genial counterpart could be, fulfilling his obligation to stand on guard for thee, O Canada.

So dedicated a public servant is appropriately honoured by examining the lessons for the future public good that may be drawn from the experience of his times. In these last forty years, we have learned much about our capacity – and our limitations – in discerning and promoting the public good. Until the last decade or so, it was naïvely believed that the task of discovering and promoting the public good was relatively straightforward. Increasingly since the 1970s, we have discovered the complexities of that task and our own limitations in furthering it. I shall focus primarily on those limits.

Yet, while that is the current fashion, today's *Zeitgeist*, we should not ungratefully forget the marvels of these last forty years. By and large we have enjoyed a degree of economic growth and levels of employment unimaginable during the 1930s and believed difficult to attain during the years of the Second World War, when the general assessment was that the industrial world would likely sink back into the depressed economic conditions of the 1930s. Thus our principal economic challenge was to achieve some degree of growth and to sustain something approaching full employment. The ingenuity of our policies and the soundness of the institutions that were created in those years have meant that the world has generally enjoyed a period of unprecedented prosperity since 1945, a period of international expansion and of relative peace and security difficult to conceive in the troubled thirties. And that has been accompanied by extraordinary accomplishments in social policy.

Let me cite an incident from the Reagan years which illustrates both the achievement of institutions in terms of the public good and our latter-day inability to appreciated that immense accomplishment. My mother-in-law came from a small town in northern Missouri. Its citizens regularly express contempt for those politicians in Washington. They denounce not only welfare queens and welfare expenditures, but the very concept of welfare. One day, during the recession of 1983, it was announced that the local bank had failed and was shutting its doors. The town's reaction was what you might expect. "This is a disaster! Our resources are tied up in that bank! What will become of us?"

The next morning a notice appeared in the bank's window indicating that it had been taken over by the Federal Deposit Insurance Corporation (FDIC). "Unfortunately we will be unable to reopen this morning, but we shall reopen at noon for normal transactions. The FDIC apologizes for this delay and inconvenience."

This was a conservative town, skeptical about Washington and its ways. But suddenly that skepticism about Washington and its hopeless ineptitude evaporated. "The Blessed Feds have come. Our deposits are saved! Thank God for the Federal Government!" To be sure, with the passage of time, the old refrain regarding Washington's folly resumed. The episode illustrates both how far we have come since the 1930s in providing institutions to serve the public good, and how time erodes our appreciation of those benefits.

Having paid tribute, however brief, to our capacity to discern and promote the public good, I turn to analyzing the limits: our belated discovery of the barriers to using public policy to promote the public good. Our awareness of those limits has grown since the early seventies – the end of fixed exchange rates, the collapse of the Bretton Woods system, the oil embargo, inflation, and slow economic growth. We moved from exaggerated faith in government to exaggerated skepticism about government. The modern industrial state, Karl Marx might have suggested, is beset by a number of internal contradictions. They are not necessarily crippling, yet they do provide warning flags that we would be unwise to ignore.

The first of these contradictions is the well-known "revolution of rising expectations." In this context, it might more precisely be described as "the revolution of declining gratitude" or the "revolution of rising forgetfulness." Over time, government services tend to "morph," to use a term from television, into entitlements. Regrettably, the public is not very good at arithmetic. Take, for example, the case of Social Security. The American people generally believe that through their contributions to the Social Security system they have fully paid for their benefits. In reality, the liabilities of the system dwarf the payments that individuals have made. While the public is prepared, in the abstract, to consider adjustments of entitlements, it is far from receptive to concrete proposals. When pollsters ask Americans whether they are willing, in pursuit of a balanced budget, to accept curtailment of entitlements, some 65 percent say Yes. But you ask people whether they are prepared to cut Social Security or Medicare, the 65 percent shrinks to 35 percent.

Such attitudes are accompanied by a sense of being put upon. For example, a large majority in the United States believes that 20 percent of the federal budget goes to foreign aid, whereas, in reality, less than 1 percent does. Such misconceptions underlay a widespread unwillingness to pay the taxes necessary to sustain the benefits that the public demands. In the American case, those benefits include the level of defense expenditures that the public is willing to support. That resistance to taxation was most dramatically reflected in Proposition 13 in California, which placed constitutional limits on taxation – and which also set off two decades of experience in resisting tax increases and demanding tax reductions.

The demand for tax reduction has been associated with one of the zanier beliefs of supply-side economics that by cutting taxes one can engender a gusher of revenues that will more than offset the reduction in revenues coming from reduced tax rates. The upshot of these problems in arithmetic, the feeling that one is being put upon, the zanier faith in the benefit of tax reduction, plus sheer political irresponsibility have resulted in the immense deficits that have occurred here in Canada, as well as in the United States. Such deficits divert the very capital that has sustained economic growth and rising living standards in the industrial nations – and thereby helped to sustain social peace. The "fiscal train wreck," as it is sometimes referred to, goes a long way to explaining why confidence in government's ability to promote the public good has diminished so sharply.

The second contradiction with which our society has to cope flows from the globalization of the world economy and the severe limits this has placed on the capacity of governments individually to pursue the public good. Free trade conflicts with national determination of economic policy. The globalization of the world economy means the government must be increasingly sensitive to the balance of payments. Concern over the balance of payments prevents governments from adopting domestic policies that they might well adopt in the absence of such concern. Today capital flows dwarf the money flows that come from trade, enormously increasing the volatility of the balance of payments.

In addition, the pattern of world trade has been altered dramatically. In the past either political insecurity or the perception of financial irresponsibility precluded the flow of capital and of technology to Third World countries. Today that has changed substantially. In some areas, there is significantly more political security, and many Third World nations pursue policies of financial responsibility that are the envy of the industrial nations. As a consequence both technology and capital flow to much of the Third World, in pursuit of lower costs in a reasonably secure environment. The effect has been to undermine manufacturing employment in the industrial nations. Whatever the benefits of free trade, relatively few of those benefits have flowed to semi-skilled workers, who resent the competitive pressure on wages. Free trade not only imposes limits on what governments can do, it has led hard-pressed semiskilled workers in the West to view suspiciously the actions of government. It has done little to improve the public mood, at the same time that it imposes limits on the freedom of action of governments.

In the extreme, the quest for freer trade conflicts with national sovereignty itself. Perhaps the most dramatic example can be found in the European Union. The pursuit of closer integration now encroaches on the preservation of national sovereignty as well as on national economic self-determination. As Canadians well know, the North American Free Trade Agreement (NAFTA) has created some similar problems. All in all, the globalization of the world economy has severely constrained what individual governments can do in pursuit of the public good.

The third contradiction is the widespread loss of political cohesion. A spirit of national unity and civil-mindedness emerged in World War II and its aftermath. It marked the "civic generation," now largely gone. Today we are marked by a vigorous, not to say rampant, individualism. That might be praised by a latter-day sophist viewing the individual as the measure of all things. But government action to be effective depends upon a sense of community. The diminished sense of community and the undue stress on the solitary family unit thus have weakened the capacity of government to act in the public

good. And, of course, these trends have been reinforced by the loss of
a common enemy. While it existed, the Soviet Union served to bind
together not only the West but also the publics within each of the
western countries. In the United States, the disappearance of the Soviet threat has resulted in a diminution of bipartisanship, of mutual
goodwill, and of the long-time belief that politics should stop at the
water's edge.

That lost sense of common purpose has resulted in the fragmentation of the electorate and is increasingly reflected in the rise of voting
blocs. That has severely and adversely affected the sustaining of a coherent foreign policy. In fact, in the United States, foreign policy has
increasingly become the serial propitiation of domestic groups, as
Canadians recognize from the motivation that lies behind the Helms-
Burton legislation. I refer to this development as the Balkanization of
foreign policy. To some extent, it is the unavoidable concomitant of
the loss of homogeneity in the society, resulting in lessened political
cohesion. In the United States, the melting pot is no longer honoured.
A new "ethnicity" is all the rage. In Canada, the expanding mosaic
has had a similar effect.

The rise of economic voting blocs also batters the sense of common
purpose. The most prominent example today is that of the elderly,
who have become dependent upon government benefits and are determined to protect those benefits. This is a principal source of the
problem of budget deficits discussed above. In the United States, the
Republican party is learning for a *second* time not to tamper with entitlement programs. Republicans had their first taste of the political consequences in 1986, when it was believed that they would tamper with
Social Security. That year they lost control of the Senate. In 1996, they
were burdened by their attempt to restrain the growth of Medicare,
providing President Clinton and the Democrats with an opportunity
they were quick to exploit. While control of the entitlements programs
is probably indispensable for the fiscal health of the country, it will be
some time before anyone has the temerity to raise the subject again.

The fourth of my contradictions is the steady growth of disenchantment, disillusionment, even cynicism on the part of the bodies politic
throughout the western world. In Canada, the problems of Meech
Lake, the continuing disputes over the status of Quebec, as well as
fiscal problems have had a massive impact on the public's attitude. In
the United States, it may have started with Vietnam and with Water-
gate, but disenchantment continues to blossom. Clearly Whitewater
has had an effect on the attitude towards the Clintons, although we
cannot as yet assess the ultimate impact. The attitude in Quebec
towards former Prime Minister Trudeau and present Prime Minister

Chretien is both puzzling and suggestive. In an earlier era, they both would have been embraced with pride as native sons of Quebec.

The contrast with older attitudes towards government is stark. Seventy-six percent of the American people in 1964 could say that the government did the right thing most of the time. Ask that same question today and only 24 percent of the public will say that government does the right thing most of the time. In brief, the public has become cynical. I do not know how much cynicism the American society can tolerate. The United States is not France, but the American people have now become somewhat like the French in their cynicism. Almost 70 percent of the American public says that Hillary Rodham Clinton did something either illegal or unethical in the Whitewater affair. Almost as many say that President Clinton did something illegal or unethical in the Whitewater affair, and more than half declare that Bill Clinton is not a trustworthy man. My point is not to deal with the validity of these views but to recognize their significance. They undermine the degree of public support essential for governments to pursue the public good. They represent a remarkable change in the underlying attitudes of the public toward the presidency, for, despite this skepticism, Bill Clinton easily won reelection.

To what can we attribute the growth of public disenchantment? One of the powerful sources is television. Its impact is substantially to dilute and even to destroy authority. In the past, authority was represented by clergy, university officials, business leaders, professionals like lawyers and doctors – people who were presumed to be knowledgeable and to whom one could turn for informed judgments. Television's impact is so powerful that the individual citizen feels much more able to make up his own mind about issues, without seeking any kind of external authority or informed opinion. This may contribute to the public psychology that, without any obligation, we are entitled to the benefits that flow from government programs. That, in turn, tends to undermine any feeling of gratitude about the existence of these programs – until such moment that there is an attempt to reduce them.

By its nature, television is a powerful attack medium. That has resulted in a continued assault both on political figures and on agencies. Indeed, in the United States, the civil service itself is under assault. The general attitude of the public is one of contempt for government servants.

The final point in this connection is that such disenchantments are world-wide phenomena, affecting all the industrialized nations. In none of the major western nations is the present leadership in a strong position. Even the deferential Japanese suffer from disenchantment with government.

The problems, the "contradictions" in advanced democratic states that I have suggested point to certain conclusions regarding the pursuit of the public good in the third millennium. What conclusions should we draw regarding the capacity and the limitations of the government? While the capacity is substantial, we have come increasingly to appreciate the real limitations. Government, no doubt, provides a powerful tool, but one that is not omnipotent. We would not wish it to be. Despite the substantial potential in governments to pursue the public good, it is wisest not to attempt to push it too far. In the years ahead, the appropriate guideline for public policy would seem to be modesty and moderation. Canada appears to have reached that judgment.

In a free society, one is obliged to keep the voters with one. The voters are most inclined to be generous, or to think about the public good, when their own living standards are rising. In recent years that has not been the case. Certainly the American public's present view about government is that there has been far too much meddling, far too much nurse-maiding, far too much hectoring. There has also been far more tolerance of antisocial behavior than the public is ready to accept. Despite past accomplishments of government in pursuing the public good, it is time for a respite. Consequently my own conclusion is both simple and conservative: do not try to do more good for the public than the people can tolerate.

There is a belief – I would say an illusion – drawn from high-school civics that somehow or other governments can regularly generate comprehensive solutions to problems. But that can take place only when the public is in a benign mood. The premise, drawn from civics, suggests that if one simultaneously gores many oxen, one can engender broad public support; the public will put its shoulder to the wheel. That may well happen during times of emergency. It can also happen during times of rising prosperity. But it is unlikely to occur in a period in which there is widespread public skepticism and in which the cohesion of the society has been weakened.

These thoughts may appear to be somewhat gloomy regarding the near-term prospects of governments seeking the public good. For a variety of reasons these have been troubled times. Democracies tend to go through periods of discontent. But then – for reasons no one can understand – they spontaneously revive. A classic case occurred in France in the early years of this century before World War I. It was called *la belle époque*, and it came after a period of divisive controversy. Perhaps in the next millennium we can look forward to such a recovery. In any event, we can always draw some comfort that in a democracy, inevitably the people get the government they deserve.

For the Third Asking: Is there a Future for National Political Parties in Canada?

R. KENNETH CARTY

THE SIGNIFICANCE OF 1993

What are we to make of the 1993 general election? Was a stake driven through the heart of the Conservatives, the nation's founding political party? Was social democracy removed from the national political agenda? Are we going to be condemned to a system of regional parties unable to speak for a broader Canadian interest? To put it simply, we might just ask: has the national party system really crashed? Three possible answers to this question suggest themselves – No, Maybe, and Yes.

First, the No answer. There was no party system crash in 1993. The three old parties commanded about two-thirds of the vote, and the parliamentary result was just another case of the single-member plurality electoral system playing havoc with the popular vote. Those who would argue for this answer recall 1979 when the Conservatives won with almost half-a-million fewer votes than the Liberals, or 1984 when the Liberals got only forty seats, the smallest number in their long history. By this reckoning, 1993 is just an exaggerated case of this old story, and the pendulum will swing back. Though this analysis has rarely been advanced in popular accounts of the 1993 electoral earthquake, it seems implicit in the belief of many, especially in the older parties, that time will inevitably restore the traditional party alignment.

Second, the equivocal Maybe answer. On the one hand, it seems obvious that at least two of the established parties crashed, and that, for only the second time in our history, we have a majority government with limited support from Quebec. But, on the other hand, it is also true that one of the country's great national parties was returned to office with a healthy majority. Given that the Liberals have been in power for three-quarters of the last sixty years, most Canadians may well think, plus ça change ... .

Third, the real answer is surely Yes. There was a major crash of the national party system in October of 1993. Both the Progressive Conservatives and New Democrats were handed unprecedented set-backs, and two new parties disrupted long-standing electoral balances. And both those new parties managed to challenge and disrupt national party competition by defining the existing pattern of party politics as the problem. For its part, the Bloc Quebecois argued against the very idea of a modern Quebec staying in the Canadian system. That claim resonated amongst those least tied to national party politics: half the Bloc's support came from individuals who had not voted for a national party in 1988.[1] At the other end of the country, Reform successfully appealed for a new politics in which relations between politicians and voters, and among MPs, would be transformed. For them, the very character of representation, and our practices of responsible government, were the source of most public ills.

Now there is something hauntingly familiar about this. In many ways, the country's current politics echoes the electoral crises of both the early 1920s and then the 1960s. While 1993 did not produce the minority governments of those previous periods, the election does seem to mark another significant turn in the cycles of Canadian party politics. It is salutary to recall that after those two earlier disruptions the national parties were forced to set about reinventing themselves. In the process, they redefined leader-follower relationships, rebuilt their organizations on new principles, reforged communication channels, and refinanced electoral practices. By doing so, the parties survived those electoral debacles and went on to become powerful vehicles for revitalizing our public life.

A PARTY COUNTRY

This is a peculiarly Canadian practice, this relegitimating of the national community by rebuilding its political parties. Other societies use old monarchies or new constitutions, religions or revolutions, civil wars, or centuries of civil peace, but Canadians depend on party politicians rebuilding national parties to restore community. In part this is because we have been, from the beginning, a democratic people, our first common act being to hold a general election. For that, and the Parliament it produced, we knew we needed working political parties. And we still believe that: three-quarters of the electorate recently told the Lortie Commission on electoral reform that, however much they dislike them, parties are necessary for democracy.[2]

But although political parties are critical organizations in all democracies, they are especially important to Canada. Unlike almost any other place, Canada is uniquely a party country. It was the deliberate creation of party politicians, acting in good part from party-driven motives, and it has been the task of party politicians to nourish and defend a national interest. When Nova Scotians sent a phalanx of separatist MPs to Ottawa in the election of 1867, it was Macdonald's Conservative party that had to set about accommodating them in the national interest. And party politicians have been doing the same thing ever since. It may be possible to think about countries like England or France without thinking about their politicians and parties, but not so of Canada. We define ourselves by their works.

It is this truth that leads to an explanation of our cycles of electoral crashes and party renewal. When Canadians get angry about politics, dissatisfied with public policy, or disillusioned with their governments, and decide something has to be done about it, their instinctive response is to start by changing their political parties. So, in the 1920s, westerners decided that the direct route to more acceptable social and economic policy was to reform the parties and the system of representation. Then, in the 1960s, those left behind in the wake of the Quiet Revolution protested by mobilizing to build a new party. Progressives, socialists, Créditistes all took it as an article of faith that you could not change Canadian public policy until after you had first broken and replaced the party system.

If those third parties had simply been offering new programs, our earlier electoral earthquakes of 1921 and 1962 would not have provided a fundamental challenge to the system.[3] But they represented groups that wanted to build new kinds of parties, practising new forms of politics, and organizing new patterns of governance. At the heart of their diagnoses of the country's political failures were the issues of the proper role of political leadership, and the appropriate relationships between voters and parliamentarians. They believed that if MPs would put their constituents' interests above those of party then the public good would be served. Party was to be reformed by abolishing party discipline and replacing it with constituency discipline, and populist devices like recall or referenda.

Of course, the parties that burst into our political world determined to change it radically have had limited success. The realities of operating in Parliament prove more difficult in practice than theory as Reform's internal caucus struggles in the thirty-fifth Parliament have again demonstrated.[4] But the problems third parties have had with the politics of legislative give and take have not been the whole story. After previous electoral collapses, the major parties recognized their world was changing and moved successfully to adapt to those changes. And just as there has been a common pattern to previous party system crashes, so too has there been one to the patterns of party renewal.

Before considering how national parties responded to earlier electoral upheavals, it is necessary to ask why Canada has had to endure these cycles of popular challenge and party collapse. Leaving aside the political issues of the campaigns of 1921, 1962, or 1993, admittedly a big aside, this question takes us to the very heart of the dilemma facing Canadian political parties.

PARTY DISCIPLINE,
FICKLE ELECTORATE

Parties are, first and foremost, organizations which hinge a society to its institutions of government. In democracies they are the channels which structure and deliver the ideas and leaders thrown up by the social order, and the vehicles which organize the political face of its government. National party systems inevitably reflect the society that has spawned them and the institutions within which they live and work.

If we were to describe Canadian society in a word, surely that word would be American, in the sense of North American. It is one of the world's newest nations. It is a plural, ethnically diverse, mobile, growing, geographically open society. One in six Canadians comes from somewhere else, anywhere else: none of Vancouver's five Liberal MPs was born in Canada; one in two of us move during the five-year life span of a Parliament;[5] our electorate doubled in the first three decades after the Second World War, a growth rate eleven times that of Britain's; and, as Mackenzie King was known to complain, geography continues to overwhelm history. It is this tumultuous sprawl that parties must organize, mobilize, and connect to their government.

The central institutions of Canadian government might, in a word, be described as European. We inherited a system that is, in the words of the old British North America Act, "similar in principle to that of the United Kingdom." Though our versions of federalism and the Charter modify it, Canada's governing institutions are old, monarchical, parliamentary, disciplined, and bureaucratic. Parliament works to allow the executive to predominate over the elected legislature; party discipline forces elected representatives to toe a common line; and the closed world of bureaucracies centralizes and secretes decision making.

The central problem for Canadian parties is to connect an American society to European institutions. It is no easy task for we have no models as to how it can be done. American and European parties were designed to meet the distinctive political challenges of their very different political systems.[6] While we have tried to use European-style parties to conduct national campaigns which will capture and sustain unified majority governments, the very fluidity and diversity of Canadian society rebels against being captured and long held by such un-American-style parties. It is in this demand for an unnatural balancing act that we find an explanation for the distinctive characteristics of Canadian parties and the occasional collapse of our party system.

The solution Canadian parties devised to reconcile this tension between a loose society and tight institutions was a simple organizational trade-off: local autonomy for Ottawa discipline. Constituency associations have traditionally had almost complete freedom to run their own affairs. That has included both organizational and financial matters and, perhaps most importantly, it has also meant the right to name their own candidates. Choosing candidates has included the right to remove them, and there has rarely been an election in our history in which some MP was not dumped by his or her riding party. While the national parties have sometimes tried to interfere with or constrain riding freedom, it has survived since 1867 as a basic, defining feature of our party life because it reflects the reality of our diverse society.

But no matter how free local parties are to manage their own constituency politics, when MPs get to Ottawa our party bargain has insisted that they be disciplined soldiers in the parliamentary battle. In part, this is because the parliamentary system we use rewards parties that stick together. But surely it is also because the country's political leaders fear that, without a fair amount of discipline, a system populated by locally oriented politicians might easily come apart. Over time, parliamentary discipline has come to be regarded as a good in itself, and Canadian parties are amongst the most tightly disciplined of any free parliamentary system. Margaret Thatcher or John Major might often have looked longingly at Brian Mulroney and wished for the comparatively easy ride his caucus provided him.

Canadian parties evolved to combine maximum local organizational autonomy with minimal parliamentary autonomy for their members. It is a peculiarly unique combination which no other democratic parties have to live with. These two dominant elements are forever in precarious balance, and the result has been a set of national parties that are inherently unstable. Holding them together has been one of the principal tasks of our party leaders. It is for this reason that party leadership has been so much more important to the survival and health of Canadian parties than those elsewhere.

But for all the Herculean efforts of party leaders, Canadian parties have had a difficult, sometimes precarious existence over the past three generations. Though Liberals and Conservatives have dominated, they have continually been challenged by minor parties, and the Tories even resorted to taking the Progressives' name in a attempt to appeal to that party's protest voters. As the country grew, the distance between the institutional centre and the societal grassroots has continued to stretch and, by the 1960s, parties began to divorce some of their provincial affiliates in an attempt to manage the growing tensions.[7]

Though the country's two old national parties have been remarkably resilient, the fact is most individual Canadians understand that local autonomy for national discipline is a poor exchange. Such parties cannot be relied on if what is needed is an effective mechanism for pressing the demands of changing communities on remote governments. In that circumstance, it seems almost inevitable that commitments to any particular party will be fluid. The result is that Canadian parties have, by comparative standards, the shallowest roots imaginable and only the most limited capacity to withstand the winds of popular electoral fortune.

Think about the make up of our national parties. Out in the constituencies, they ultimately depend on their voters. But most of those people are an exceptionally unfaithful lot. Only about two-fifths of Canadians have enduring partisan allegiances. That translates into very irregular voting patterns. Just 22 percent of the electorate was faithful to one of the three national parties over the last two general elections; in fact, the largest single group of consistent Canadians from 1988 to 1993 were those who abstained in both elections, hardly the basis for a healthy party system.[8] Nor for a stable one. With voters like these, Canadian election outcomes are notoriously volatile. Seat turnover rates are regularly much greater than those in Britain or the US:[9] about 80 percent of all Canadian constituencies have been represented by MPs from more than one party in the past decade.

There is no solid base of loyal party members to make up for this fickle electorate. Compared with other democracies, Canada's national parties have very low and unstable memberships which fluctuate a good deal.[10] After all, members realize that they are free to work hard to choose a candidate and run a campaign, but, once the election is over, party discipline is again the order of the day. They know that their membership fee has become little more than a poll tax which purchases a vote at a nomination meeting. Political parties which induce individuals to leave and rejoin in time with the electoral cycles, and which devalue their memberships by turning them into commercial transactions, end up with unstable and vulnerable local organizations.

If party members are unreliable, the core of party activists seems hardly more committed. Somewhere between one-fifth and one-third of all delegates to the two old national parties' leadership conventions of recent decades admit to once having been members of other parties.[11] Such individuals bring to the critical task of choosing a new leader limited party experience, tenuous connections, and uncertain loyalties. For instance, one-third of the British Columbia Liberals who participated in their provincial leadership contest in 1993 voted for some other party in the national election a month later.[12] And enduring partisanship seems no stronger at the very peak of the parties. Twenty-seven percent of the three established parties' candidates in the 1993 general election reported that they had once been active in some other party.[13]

So, from bottom to top, Canadian party organizations are populated by ambivalent partisans. They are ambivalent because the party system is a very imperfect instrument for connecting them, and their continually changing society, to government. Parliamentary practice demands a discipline that stifles the expression of local views and so voters, members, activists, and even would-be candidates respond by moving parties as it suits them. The genius of our traditional parties has been in their ability to manage all this movement by constantly rebrokering popular demands and mediating conflicting interests. But there have also been moments in our history when this fundamental tension between our American society and its European institutions became too great for the existing parties to cope with, and the system snapped. The current party crisis is but the third such episode.

REFORMING NATIONAL PARTIES

Like 1993, previous party system breakdowns saw the rise of new parties determined to change the political order, starting with a new party system.[14] The demand was for new political organizations which would alter the party equation by reducing party discipline and expanding the rights of ordinary members so that the impulses of a changing society might blow through Parliament to the government. On each of those earlier occasion, the Liberals and Conservatives, determined to preserve their place, developed a two-pronged strategy that combined institutional reforms with a remake of their own organizations.

The years after the First World War marked the first collapse of our party system. It did so in the wake of enormous population shifts in the early years of this century, and a popular clamour for democracy.[15] The Conservatives were displaced as the second party by a band of political reformers from the West. For the first time in our history there was not a majority government, and several provinces fell into the hands of third parties. The system responded with a series of major institutional reforms: the adoption of a universal franchise, the abolition of constituency-based party patronage as the organizing principle of government, and an end to the excesses of gerrymandering. But the parties also moved to incorporate the demand for more popular input and control over their internal affairs.

They started by building formal national party organizations so that, for the first time, individuals could actually join them. Conventions were held that allowed local delegates to discuss policy, and more importantly, to choose the party leader. Given the special pre-eminence held by leaders in Canadian parties, the decision to take the choice of the leader from the caucus, and give it to a convention of local delegates, was a major shift in the balance between society and institutions towards recognizing the demands and interests of the grassroots.

The 1960s saw another party system collapse and three five-party minority parliaments in quick succession. That attack on the traditional pattern of party competition reflected the politics of a new, rapidly growing, urbanizing society, the quick disintegration of an old Quebec, and the confusion following the realignment of the prairies from a Liberal bastion to a Conservative stronghold. Major institutional changes designed to cope with the new demands quickly followed. They included the emergence of executive federalism, the reform of election financing and broadcasting laws, and the formal recognition of parties in Parliament.[16]

Again the parties changed to adapt themselves to the new demands for a more participatory politics in order to maintain their primary place as the working hinges between a volatile society and its long-standing parliamentary institutions. Regular conventions increased the policy-making role of individual members and facilitated enhanced accountability. The federal and provincial wings of several parties split, freeing the national organizations to focus on developing their own public agendas. And party leadership politics changed dramatically. Members seized the right to remove as well as select their leaders, and leadership competition mobilized large numbers of individuals as the conflicts reached down into highly contested battles for local delegate selection.

In neither of these episodes, during which the patterns of our politics were rethought and reorganized, were either proportional representation (PR) or relaxed party discipline seriously considered by Canadians. That is worth noting because those have been two principal responses in other democracies to the problem of accommodating changing social organization with parliamentary government. Most European countries have adopted some form of proportional electoral system, and New Zealand had its first PR election in October 1996. The United Kingdom remains one of the few parliamentary systems to have resisted PR, but the British have dealt with the tensions of modern politics by allowing MPs at Westminster much greater parliamentary freedom than exists in Ottawa.

Only in Canada have the parties been forced to absorb all the tension between society and government within themselves. Given that Canadian society is more volatile and dynamic than that in most other democracies, this is a near impossible task. As we have seen, the consequence is system breakdown every few decades, leaving us to then engage in a major rebuilding of our national parties. And this brings us back to 1993.

LOOSER REINS

The outcome of the 1993 general election confirmed what had been obvious for several years: the party system had once again been stretched beyond its capacity to reflect the underlying society. The Charlottetown referendum had exposed the yawning gap between politicians and voters and the record number of parties (14) and candidates (2155 – up 27 percent from 1988) in the election indicated that growing numbers of Canadians were no longer satisfied with old choices and old practices. The new parties that muscled their way into Parliament did so by promising to change the system. Their problem, like that of both western and Quebec-based protest parties before them, is to find a way to do so. Our past experience suggests that playing the parliamentary game will drain them of much of their reformist impulse.[17] It also reminds us that parties rooted in communities of protest have never been able to develop genuinely national constituencies for their grievances. Canadian society is too diverse for that.

Parties like Reform and the Bloc failed in the past, but not just because they succumbed to the embrace of Ottawa. Established parties responded to the threat to their position by adapting their organizations and practices to incorporate the demands of disaffected citizens. That process has already started again.

One response to the current party crisis can be seen in the report of the Royal Commission on Electoral Reform and Party Financing.[18] The commission took as one of its six principal objectives the strengthening of the national parties as primary political organizations. It concluded that our national parties must: regularize members' ability to participate in their decision making, develop enhanced policy-making capacities, improve the transparency of their financial (electoral and nonelectoral) practices, and accept more public regulation and accountability in all these activities. The report then made dozens of specific recommendations about how those objectives might be achieved by both local and national party bodies. The commissioners' analysis, arguments, and proposals provide the starting point for serious reform efforts, and any party with national aspirations will ignore them at its peril.

The other clue that the parties are responding can be seen in their leadership politics, always a critical early warning indicator of party change in Canada. The highly manipulated, expensive, winner-take-all leadership campaigning of recent years – practices that were then too often emulated in nomination contests – are being rejected by individual party members who are demanding a direct vote in leadership contests. While the national parties seem to be moving towards some such inclusive processes, several provincial parties have already pioneered in the development of a new leadership politics.

Direct leadership votes will transform the relationship between leaders and party members. By altering our notions of party membership, they will force us to reconsider the very status of parties in the political system. The selection of Ralph Klein by the Alberta Conservatives provides a case in point. In theory, Klein was chosen in an open vote of all Alberta Conservatives; in practice any Albertan who showed up at one of the party's polling places, and was prepared to pay a modest five dollar (party membership) fee, could vote. Over 52,000 did for the first ballot, and then, seeing how close the contest was, 78,000 turned up for the final deciding vote.[19] The party's leadership process had been transformed into an open US-style primary to choose the province's premier. This precedent, establishing primary-style party politics, may be hard for any Canadian party with hundreds of thousands of members to resist in the future.

However Klein was not elected in a publicly regulated primary. It was a party vote, and Canadian parties remain, for all intents and most purposes, private associations free to conduct their affairs as they happen to choose. The big issue facing our parties, raised by both the Royal Commission and this new leadership politics, is to what extent can or should our parties remain private organizations. It now appears to be time to accept the fact that political parties are public institutions, what we might call public political property. That being so, there will have to be a much greater public structuring and regulation of their electoral activities, including candidate nomina- tions and leadership selections. Such changes will take us in the di- rection of American party organization, recognizing that national parties operate as the public utilities of electoral democracy in societ- ies as diverse as ours.

We are also going to have to rethink how we want Parliament to work. Proportional representation is seen by many as a solution to the problems of parties with a national vocation who are threatened by regional movements. We are told that, in 1993, PR would have given the government more seats in Quebec and the Conservatives more seats everywhere. Perhaps. I suspect, however, that the geo- graphic diversity of Canadian society would conspire to defeat any nationalizing impulse of PR, and the more probable consequence would be a fragmentation of party competition with more narrow in- terest or regional parties and weakened national ones.

The British alternative of relaxed caucus discipline may well prove to be a part of the solution to the problem of national party survival. Commons votes in the spring of 1996 on same sex benefits and New- foundland schools saw the Liberal caucus divided as its members struggled to represent their communities and the range of views that exist in the country. The party survived, and having done so should find it easier to repeat the experience in the future. By loosening the reins, they will make it easier for individuals from a wide variety of backgrounds to come into and to support the party. And it is just that capacity to attract support from all corners of Canadian society that is the mark of a genuinely national party.

CONCLUSIONS

It seems that the answers to our starting questions really are Yes, Maybe, and No.

Yes, there really has been a major breakdown of the national party system. But we must remind ourselves that we have survived similar disruptions in the past. Maybe this one will be different. Reform is con- scious of and determined not to repeat the experience of the Progres- sives. However its very character conspires against it. As a regionally- rooted protest party struggling to articulate particular grievances, it still shows little capacity to become a genuinely national party. Maybe national parties are passé, but the whole character of Canadian political life denies that proposition. Canada is about national party politics.

No, we need not have a system of regional parties; no, the national party system is not yet dead. But, as before, the national parties must reinvent national politics by reinventing themselves. There is nothing automatic or inevitable about this process. It will require that the parties recognize that they are themselves public institutions. And, like other public utilities, our modern society will demand that their norms and operating practices be transparent and subject to public regulation and accountability. It also means that national parties must find a way to allow their parliamentarians to vote as public representatives as well as party politicians. If they cannot, they should not be surprised when voters continue to desert them for parties of protest or system destruction. If they can, they should be able to reestablish themselves as the dominant players in our politics.

These will not be cosmetic changes. They have the capacity to transform Canadian government, but then that is what voters always expect their parties to do. They are also not likely to prove permanent. If we have learned anything, it is that we ought to expect another party system crash in the national general election of 2025.

Debating the Public Good, with Afterthoughts

TOM KENT

SETTING THE STAGE

In their first form, as papers for the MacEachen conference at Antigonish, the preceding essays were followed by varying periods of discussion. The purpose of this chapter is to preserve main features of the discussions and to try to draw from them some further observations about the ways to advance the public good as we move to the twenty-first century.

Briefly to set the stage, the conference was attended by some 170 people. They included the Prime Minister to whom Allan MacEachen was deputy, Pierre Elliott Trudeau, as well as a number of former cabinet colleagues, present MPs and ministers, senators, Nova Scotia politicians, distinguished members of the Roman Catholic hierarchy, former and present public servants, and many other friends and admirers. Marc Lalonde, the conference chair, melded grace with appropriate firmness and dispatch. Senator Joyce Fairbairn chaired the seventy-fifth birthday lunch at which warm and eloquent tributes to Allan MacEachen were paid by political opponents as well as colleagues. Chairs for the various sessions included Sylvia Ostry, William Mulholland, and Francis LeBlanc (who, as the MP for the riding where so many were so proud of "our Allan J.," was appropriately the lead organizer of the conference). The formal respondents to the main papers on social and economic policy were Keith Banting (Queen's), Richard Van Loon (Carleton), Peter Nicholson (BCE Inc.), and Lars Osberg (Dalhousie). The paper on political parties was accompanied by a panel chaired by Linden MacIntyre and consisting of Senators John Stewart and Lowell Murray, Pierre Pettigrew (then newly a cabinet minister), Ian McClelland MP (the Reform party), and James Bickerton (St Francis Xavier).

Surprisingly, there was not much discussion of exactly what we mean by the objective of the public good. Ian Stewart made a forceful plea for the importance of public goods in the economist's sense: the benefits from their consumption cannot be appropriated by one person; they remain available for others. He cited the classic example of lighthouses but suggested that many products and services have some degree of the character of public goods. The challenge is to ensure that they are provided "efficiently and effectively," and by their nature that is not a matter for the market alone.

It was an economist, Lars Osberg, who offered a broadened definition of the public good. The well-being of a society is not measured just by the average well-being of its members, if some have a great deal and others have very little. The public good is also about relationships within the community. It also requires policies to enable all citizens to participate meaningfully in a democracy, which means that there are "primary goods" all should have. In these, Osberg included the standard political and civil rights; but he argued that a realistic conception of personal freedoms, in the sense of capabilities for functioning in society, also requires the possession of social and economic rights as expressed in the "Universal Declaration" of the United Nations. In other words, the public good relates to minimum incomes, social security, health, and education; and it is about the degree of equality in a society as well as its total wealth.

The conference began with Michael Bliss's analysis of our postwar history. Its perceptions did not save it from dissent. Was it inevitable that, after the successes of the 1940s to 1960s, the visible hand should falter so badly in face of post-1970 market forces driven by technology and globalization? Pierre Fortin, for one, thought otherwise. Anticipating the theme of his own paper, he said that our problems are not related to technology, and they do not lie in the rest of the world; they lie in Canada, among us.

From a rather different viewpoint, Sylvia Ostry complained that we are too preoccupied with a phenomenon of the Western world. If we look outward, to East Asia, we see a confidence and optimism compared with which ours of a generation ago seem mild. One of our illusions then was that the West would dominate the world for ever. Eastern nations are now climbing the ladder very fast and their miracle, as she called it, is education-led. Another of Ms Ostry's points was that the proliferation of information without context contributes powerfully to alienation. It creates the scope for ideology to provide the context, the rise of cults to provide the context, the Oklahoma militia to provide the context.

Richard Cashin took up the topic of education from the viewpoint of areas such as Newfoundland and Cape Breton. People without a tradition of education worked hard at jobs that no longer exist. We must find a way of ensuring access to education from childhood on. If that is not a priority, we are allowing a "cancer" to develop in our society. Cashin anticipated a theme to which other sessions returned.

So did Thérèse Arsenault, who suggested that today's pessimism is deeper than that of the Great Depression. Then, faith in government did survive. People continued to look to government as the institution to define and provide for the public good. What is terrifying about present attitudes is that government has lost this credibility. If we do not look to government for it, will we, in future, have any notion of the public good?

KEITH BANTING

There were two scheduled respondents to the social policy papers of Ken Battle and Tom Courchene. Rather than debate specific points, Keith Banting chose to build on their analyses to provide his own reflections on the objectives of social policy.

The postwar welfare state, he suggested, can be thought of as representing a balance among three basic objectives: security, redistribution, and social integration. The first was the most fundamental. It was to provide protection from the major risks of contemporary life: protection in the case of unemployment, illness, or disability, and protection against poverty in old age. Against the backdrop of the depression, the emphasis was on security for the population as a whole. The risks were not confined to a specific group labelled "the poor" but were seen as confronting all Canadians, and as a result, security came to be associated with the idea of universality, with social insurance and with social rights to benefits. This emphasis was so strong that the postwar welfare state was essentially a "security welfare state."

Vertical redistribution, from rich to poor, was clearly a secondary goal. Indeed, compared with the welfare provisions of the 1930s, the postwar welfare state was a move away from redistribution as the primary goal of social policy. The transfers were now to be primarily horizontal: from the employed to the unemployed, from young to old, from the healthy to the sick and disabled, from those without children to those with children. There was implicit redistribution to the poor in these programs, but that was not the basic purpose.

There was, to be sure, a secondary trend in the later 1960s; the modernization of selective or targeted programs through the Canada Assistance Plan (CAP) and the Guaranteed Income Supplement (GIS).

But these were not seen as central instruments of social policy, and the basic purpose of the security welfare state continued to be to lift people off selective programs such as welfare.

The third objective was the integration of the Canadian society. Social policy is often seen as an instrument for building social cohesion, for moderating social conflicts by creating spheres of shared experience that transcend divisions that otherwise separate us in our daily lives. Since Bismarck in the 1880s, social policy has had a role in easing or mediating class divisions, but in Canada the postwar welfare state also came to be seen as an instrument for integrating Canadians on a regional basis. National social programs are one of the limited number of things we share as citizens, irrespective of our language or region. This may not have been a conscious objective of the builders of our social programs, but the welfare state has come to be seen as part of the social glue that holds Canadians together, a symbol that there is – at some level – a social meaning to our common citizenship.

Banting went on to discuss social policy in the "new" world that he saw defined by global economic integration, changing social divisions, new fiscal realities. A major shift in the balance of objectives has occurred. Most importantly, the conviction that social policy can be an instrument of protection from the risks of an uncertain world is fading. It has not disappeared completely; health care remains an instrument for the population as a whole; and retirement income is a mixed case. But certainly in the case of the unemployed population, the postwar conception has eroded. The modern emphasis is on flexibility, adjustment, and an "active society" in which social policy does not attempt to shield people from disruptions in their lives. Increasingly, social policy is seen as an instrument of change, a hand maiden of economic transformation.

This emphasis can be seen as a direct challenge to the concept of security that was at the heart of the postwar welfare state. Increasingly, security does not mean protection *from* change; such security as is available in this world is the security that comes from the capacity *to* change. Hence the new instruments of social policy: training, education, human capital. How profoundly the changed approach challenges traditional conceptions of the welfare state is seen most clearly in the case of unemployment insurance. It embodies all the contradictions between the conceptions of security as protection from change and security as the capacity to change. Our inability to integrate the two has left the new Employment Insurance legislation without conceptual clarity.

The receding of the security welfare state has generated a new redistributive welfare state. In other words, the welfare state is less and less about protecting Canadians as a whole from the inevitable risks inherent in modern life. The operating assumption is increasingly that the primary purpose of social policy is the provision of support for the poor. The trend has, indeed, been underway for decades, initially reflecting criticisms of universality on both the left and right, and then responding to the fiscal constraints of the 1980s and 1990s. The shift can be seen most clearly in income security expenditure. Whereas in 1960, some 80 percent of all income security dollars flowed through universal programs or social insurance, in the 1990s, the proportion is only about 50 percent. Even this is an underestimate because income-testing is sneaking into unemployment insurance.

In addition, the greater social diversity of contemporary life has generated new views of equality, maintaining that it does not necessarily mean the same treatment for all people. This has also contributed to more complex redistributive politics and more differentiated social programs.

The shift of emphasis to redistribution has been most important in helping to stabilize the distribution of income in Canada, notably in comparison with the United States. We can be less sure, however, about the extent social policy continues to serve as an instrument of social cohesion. There are two fundamental trends at work. The redistributive welfare state is inevitably less adapted to social cohesion, because it does not treat all citizens the same, as universal programs did. The effect is intensified by the decentralist trend arising from the politics of our federal system and the fiscal weakness of the federal government. In consequence, the nature of Canada is coming more openly into question. Are we a community of communities, or a common political community that shares a social citizenship? In response, there is a search for new mechanisms to reflect a common citizenship, with some people looking to new forms of federal action, some to a social charter, some to an interprovincial agreement.

By this route, Banting came to pose his questions about the future of social policy. At its core, he argued, it will resemble the past in the sense of having the same three purposes. But we will need to find a new balance among security, redistribution, and social integration, a balance that is consistent with the underlying economic, social, and political realities of changing times. We have only begun to come to grips with the policy implications of security as dependent on the capacity to change. How far will we sustain our commitment to a redistributive welfare state that can offset the economic dynamics generating higher inequality? And will that state retain a capacity to act as an instrument of social cohesion? Can we find ways of sustaining social policy as an expression of shared Canadian values? Will

Canadian citizenship retain a social dimension? Will we retain a sense that, at some level, we are a people that does important things together? Or will we have to find other areas altogether to define our shared life? These, in Banting's view, are critical issues that we are bequeathing to the third millennium.

RICHARD VAN LOON

Richard Van Loon's contribution complemented Banting's in the sense that it took up these questions while also responding more directly to the papers of Ken Battle and Tom Courchene. First, however, he commented on the history of the past forty years. We should ask how we managed to do so many things right. We devised and implemented a set of social policies that were quite appropriate to their age; and we produced, as a collateral benefit, a federal system that – warts and blemishes and all – worked well too. What went wrong mostly happened after 1974–5, when we started to borrow heavily.

The indisputable brilliance of Tom Courchene's paper did not inhibit disagreement with it. His mission statement for social policy was paraphrased by Van Loon as meaning that all Canadians must have access to a social policy infrastructure that allows them to develop and enhance their skills and human capital in order that they can be full participants in the Canadian and global society and economy. This, in Van Loon's view, is necessary but, for two reasons, insufficient. First, it does not deal with child poverty; at least 25 percent of our children have a start that practically precludes them from succeeding in Courchene's terms. Second, the "high skill" jobs that are so much emphasized are not for everyone. If "high" means anything it means "above average." All the 50 percent below average may not be condemned to poorly paid jobs or none, but many will be. We will, therefore, still need a social policy that provides income supplementation, to the working poor as well as the unemployed and unemployable.

Income transfers are essentially a national function. The provinces in 1996 recognized this through the now famous "Report to Premiers," and the federal government has moved towards a rationalization of transfer programs for the elderly and for children; in the process, there is increasing use of the tax system to make transfers.

One of the guiding principles of the earlier postwar period was that the state could usefully intervene to correct all kinds of market imperfections in the economy. That belief has faded. Van Loon asked whether the principles that guide policy today are likely to be more enduring. He listed a number, in provocatively stark terms: minimizing interference in markets is the way to maximize economic growth;

social investment is not real investment; public sector jobs are not real jobs; decentralization is a good per se; the nation state is dead or irrelevant; all power should devolve to corporations. His answer was that we must expect such principles – or myths – also to fade with changing circumstances. They would not have fitted with the design of social programs forty years ago. They will not fit in 2030. If we do not think beyond them, we will not get the policies we need for the next generation.

Different though the Battle and Courchene papers on social policy are, they agree on the need for new thrusts in education and training, and both worry about how this will be done if training and unemployment insurance are in different jurisdictions. Both are also concerned to integrate social services and health care. Van Loon suggested that a joint agenda could be drawn. It would involve an attack on child poverty; improved training; further use of the tax-transfer mechanism for income supplementation; and an expanded orbit of integrated health and social service coverage.

Such an agenda involves the entanglement of federal and provincial jurisdictions. It runs counter to the widespread current view that disentanglement is good. But the palmy days of cooperative federalism were days of entanglement. The "Report to Premiers" is implicitly an entanglement document. If the federal government is wise it will, in Van Loon's view, use the provinces' inclination towards national – jointly federal and provincial – conditions and institutions. Social policy requires this, and an incidental but major benefit will be that we will also reengineer federalism for the better. To do so we need to concentrate, as we did before, on what we want to do together. The outcome will not be the same as it was before, but it may be a Canadian policy structure that works as well as anything can.

The spanner in the entanglement works may be Quebec; certainly the current government would be. But by concentrating on substance, not institutional tinkering, the problem may be circumvented. Van Loon ended by suggesting that the nine provinces, and perhaps the federal government, are developing towards the present government of Quebec the attitude: we would love to have you with us; but if you are not with us, we are not about to down tools and collapse.

LARS OSBERG

Lars Osberg began his contribution with the discussion of the public good noted earlier. He went on to agree with Pierre Fortin on almost all points of macroeconomic policy. High unemployment is not only a waste in economic terms, it is socially destructive. It involves greater inequality in income and in insecurity. The combination of years of poor economic growth and the destabilization of the public debt, which has arisen primarily from monetary policy, is forcing drastic cuts in the programs that had mitigated inequality and enabled Canada to deliver some basic economic and social rights.

Though the fashion in economics is to look only at the very long run, the country needs a set of short-run policies consistent with long-run growth. There is no substance to the incantations beloved in political and business circles, and voiced once or twice at the conference, that when we have "got the fundamentals right" good times are just around the corner. Downsizing government and eliminating deficits will not increase employment, and good times will never come if a small easing of unemployment leads the Bank of Canada again to strangle the economy with increased interest rates. Reform of the Bank is crucial.

Osberg then turned to Richard Harris's fairly benign view of our economic growth. Gross domestic product (GDP) per head of population is a misleading measure. The fact is that real hourly wages have been stagnant since the mid-1970s. The GDP per capita figures take no account of the shifts in income distribution resulting from high interest rates and increased inequality of earned incomes, nor of the hours people work and the sense of insecurity they feel. What matters to most people is family income, and family incomes increased until 1989 only because the family as a whole was in paid work for longer hours, sacrificing leisure and housework; and since 1989, average real family incomes have fallen.

Osberg also dissented from Harris's emphasis on "Fordism" and the productivity gains from increasing the scale of production. The manufacturing that can provide a niche in world markets for high-wage countries is, increasingly, flexible manufacturing. And just-in-time techniques require both more high-quality infrastructure and greater cognitive and social skills. These are more important to us than Fordism.

On education, Osberg thought that our postwar performance is not bad. In the 1950s, education in Canada was poorer than in the United States; now it is better. For example, while postsecondary attendance in the United States increased by only 6 percent during the 1980s, in Canada it increased by 33 percent. While Osberg fully accepted the current emphasis on human capital, he put it in the broader context of social capital. By that he meant a social structure that facilitates, through trust and shared norms, coordination and cooperation among individuals, institutions, and enterprises. It is not enough to have skilled people. If people are not motivated to cooperate, at work and in civic society, the benefits of their skills will not be fully realized.

When social capital deteriorates, governments have to spend more on police and penitentiaries at the expense of education and health. It is also particularly inefficient, as well as unfair, that the children of poor families are so handicapped in developing skills and finding a satisfactory place in society.

Osberg emphasized, as Van Loon had done, the intergenerational aspect of human capital development: inequality of incomes in one generation creates inequality of opportunity for the next. He also cited evidence that more equal societies tend to achieve faster economic growth than those with greater inequalities. Not only are more equal societies better at human capital formation; their workforce adjusts more readily to industrial change. Economic globalization does not mean that societies have to be homogenized. Canada can compete in world markets without competing in the extent of inequality and the incidence of poverty.

Until recently, our transfers through social programs have offset tendencies for market incomes to become more unequal. We are now decreasing this redistribution. If we diminish the welfare state and unravel the institutions that have reinforced our sense of community and our social coherence, then, in Osberg's view, it is not only social welfare that will be diminished; rising inequality will also lessen the economic growth that we could have.

PETER NICHOLSON

Peter Nicholson sought to identify what seem to be the overriding challenges now facing Canadian policy makers.

While granting that there are important lessons to be learned from mistakes in the past, we should approach the future mindful of how remarkably successful Canada has been. And continues to be. Many of the country's economic problems – some of which seemed intractable only a year or two ago – are now rapidly on the mend. The cost competitiveness of Canadian industry is today stronger than at any time in the past fifty years. Canada's exports have grown more than 60 percent in volume terms since 1990, proving that we can handle international competition and, more particularly, that Canadian companies can hold their own in free trade with the United States. In 1996, Canada's current account (i.e., the total balance of payments with the rest of the world) was in surplus for the first time since the early 1980s, a turnaround that seemed impossible only a couple of years ago. Governments at both the federal and provincial levels have finally gained fiscal control, averting a crisis in public finance that had seemed inevitable. Now, our national government is projecting the lowest financial requirements (as a percentage of GDP) among the G7 countries. And this has been accomplished without any increase in personal tax rates at the federal level.

These accomplishments, combined with continued discipline on the inflation front, have caused a dramatic decline of Canadian interest rates to the lowest levels since the 1960s. Virtually all of Canada's economic vital signs are finally moving in the right direction. Why, then, do we not feel better about ourselves?

Leaving aside the chronic anxiety associated with the future of Quebec, we fail to see ourselves in a true comparative light. Expectations may therefore be unrealistic. It is also the case that we are forced to view the country through a media lens that dotes on the dismal. Partly too, there is genuine and rational anxiety that our success is threatened. Pessimists have no trouble marshalling evidence. Our unemployment rate – stuck stubbornly around 10 percent – is unacceptably high, and compares very unfavorably with our neighbours to the south, though not with continental Europe. Particularly worrisome is the high rate of youth unemployment since the disappointed hope and alienation of young people have ominous implications for the long-term.

People are also concerned because real incomes, on average, are no longer growing very much. In fact, most wage contracts have lately been negotiated for less than the rate of inflation. Combine this with the facts that personal debt (relative to disposable income) is at an all-time high, and that employment insecurity continues to be widely felt, and one begins to understand why the average consumer is still reluctant to spend. Nicholson was nevertheless confident that falling interest rates will coax consumers off the sidelines and kick-start the self-reinforcing cycle of spending, leading to job creation, leading to more spending, more jobs, and so forth. The problem is that no one can predict the timing of this revival. Until they see it, most people will hedge their bets.

On top of all of this, there is a sense of growing economic inequality in Canadian society which governments are either reluctant, or unable, to counter with increasing transfer payments; in fact, just the opposite. The underlying source of this inequality (the extent of which is still much less in Canada than appears to be the case in the US) is the widening chasm between those who can cope successfully with an increasingly technological and globalized economy, and those who cannot.

So, in spite of a great deal that is right about Canada, we have not dealt with the two central challenges of economics. They are the production problem, how to make the pie absolutely bigger in per capita terms; and the distribution problem, how to share the pie more fairly (which is not necessarily to say more equally). These problems show up in the stagnating growth of average real incomes and a rising rate of core unemployment together with increasing income inequality. We will have to refocus on the twin challenges of production and distribution, but in the new context of public sector fiscal restraint and an economy that is increasingly knowledge-based and global.

The production problem comes down to boosting Canada's rather dismal rate of productivity growth. In basic terms, improved productivity means getting more from less by working smarter. Productivity growth has stagnated in all of the advanced industrial nations since the mid-1970s. However, our expectations as consumers (and our belief in the limitless fiscal capacity of the public sector) were formed in the first three postwar decades. Perhaps, as Sylvia Ostry has speculated, the extraordinary productivity growth of that era was the exception in historical terms. Perhaps we have since simply returned to a more normal state of affairs. Perhaps. But Nicholson doubted that most people are prepared to settle just yet for permanently stagnant per capita growth. In part at least, this is because the distributional problem is far more difficult to deal with in a slow growth economy.

We can take some comfort that the distributional problem, in global terms, has ameliorated significantly since the days when Allan MacEachen was bravely championing the cause of greater openness to the exports of developing countries. Today, ironically, the very success of some of those countries is often, but mistakenly, interpreted in the industrialized world as a key cause of our own job and income problems. But when we look closely at the numbers, we see that the average rate of unemployment in all of the developed countries has been on an increasing trend since the mid-1970s, well before the recent surge in Third World hypercompetitiveness. The main exception to the trend of increased joblessness has been the United States. The US has been able to reduce its unemployment rate, without igniting inflation, to a level not seen since the 1960s. And it has been able to accomplish this despite increased openness to imports from Asia and Latin America.

The price, some might say, has been dramatically increased income inequality as the wages of less-skilled US workers have been squeezed toward Third World levels. But again, careful studies seem to show that low-wage competition from developing countries has been at most a minor contributor. The real dividing line in today's job market is determined by skill and adaptability in coping with sophisticated and constantly changing technology.

What does all of this imply for those who wish to promote the public economic good in the early years of the third millennium? There are three overriding challenges: What should government do to promote higher productivity growth? What public policies are needed to lower the core rate of unemployment? And what policies are needed to produce an education system that is both relevant and effective, including both workplace training and early childhood development?

There is a fourth challenge, at least as important but for now eclipsed by our more immediate economic concerns. That challenge is to ensure a healthy environment given the ambition of much of the world's population to achieve "western" levels of consumption. The good news is that the energy and material resource content of a unit of economic output continues to diminish. The unsettling news is that the total number of units of economic output is growing even more rapidly, thus increasing the overall strain on global environmental systems. Good news perhaps for Canadian resource industries, but a huge institutional challenge for humanity since we lack effective transnational political means to deal with the global collective challenge of environmental sustainability.

All four are challenges to the imagination of governments and other social and economic institutions, including those in the private and voluntary sectors. They are challenges to the imagination because we still do not have any widespread consensus as to how we can restore productivity growth to postwar levels; or how we can reduce the core rate of unemployment and, more particularly, solve the dilemma of youth unemployment; or how to produce an education system that works in Canada's multicultural, federal context; or how to build the transnational mechanisms for environmental sustainability.

There is no shortage of contending ideas and theories as to how these challenges can and should be met, but leadership is required to set a course of action that most Canadians are prepared to follow. For much of the past forty years, governments in Canada, and in virtually all industrialized countries, came to rely less on policy imagination and more on massive public spending programs to meet society's challenges. That approach led us to the brink of fiscal crisis which thankfully has been averted in the nick of time. But in Canada we now face years of spending austerity at levels (relative to GDP) not experienced since the early 1950s. The central question in this strange new world of semipermanent fiscal austerity is: What will be the new locus of activity in politics?

The answer to this question will define how Canadians address the public good in the third millennium. The encouraging thought is that the nonspending roles of government – those that affect the regulatory and policy framework of our economic and social life – appear to be the most appropriate and effective. For example, better systems for health care and education depend on institutional design and on getting the incentives and policies right, not on spending more money. Canada already spends relatively more on health and education than virtually any other country. Getting the economy right, and thereby boosting our productivity and entrepreneurial initiative, will depend far more on continued fiscal prudence, on a sound monetary policy, and on an appropriate tax policy, than on massive spending on make-work projects or business subsidies. Wise regulation, not spending, is the way to ensure a healthier environment. Similarly, many of our leading-edge industries, such as telecommunications, do not need government financial help, but they do need enlightened "framework" policies in respect of competition, export financing, and the research and development environment.

We can be confident, therefore, that politicians and bureaucrats will have plenty of ways to promote the public good within the constraint of fiscal prudence. The challenge is that government, no less than individuals and businesses, must learn to behave smarter, relying in future on policy brains, not fiscal brawn. Invoking a nautical metaphor, the pursuit of the public good in the third millennium will require a government fashioned after the tiller of a sailboat, not the propeller of a steam ship.

OTHERS

The presentations on social and economic policy – the essays of Battle, Courchene, Fortin, and Harris, and the comments of Banting, Van Loon, Osberg, and Nicholson summarized in this chapter – provoked at the conference vigorous discussion for all the time available. The dominant voices were those expressing unhappiness with Canada's retreat from full employment and social security. Warren Allmand gave eloquent voice to this concern. The purposes of social security had been defined as security, redistribution, and social integration, but what we have seen since the 1980s is more insecurity, less redistribution, and less social integration. The gap between rich and poor was narrowing but is now widening again. We have more poverty, more polarization, more social unrest, fewer good jobs. Even if we could train everyone for good jobs, most would not get them; there are too few. Of the new jobs that are available, many are part-time, low-wage, nonunion, with no benefits and promising no future. Young people cannot establish homes and families on such jobs.

There is something wrong, Allmand continued, with a society where we are encouraged to spend more and more on cars and boats, on backyard swimming pools, cosmetics, all kinds of luxuries. We are even encouraged to borrow money for these things, yet we do not have enough money for proper health care, for effective help to people in poverty. We should not accept rationalizations about why this situation has to be accepted as inevitable. We should be able to look for creative solutions.

Charles Cuccia said that the public good requires good social policy as the foundation for good economics. Even conservatively inclined business people want lower crime rates, good roads, clean air and water, high health and education standards. Why should we adopt the "Asian dragon" model rather than the European model? Canada, Caccia observed, is among the lesser-taxed of the wealthy, OECD countries. If international economic forces are as strong as they are represented, it is all the more necessary to balance them by the social role of the state.

But, in the Canadian federation, what state? Herb Breau took issue with the Courchene decentralist prescription. Can we leave social policy to a series of arrangements among the provinces? That is not how it evolved. Comprehensive social security was the product of political alliances and arrangements at the national level. It would be naïve to expect that a social policy effective for redistribution and social cohesion can be achieved and maintained without a strong federal government. An era of provincial accommodations may enable us to deal with the fiscal problem, with the debt, but we are only dreaming about an effective social policy if it is divorced from the federal role. This does not necessarily require a rich federal government, but it does need strategic political alliances at the federal level. And those are based on attitudes. In the postwar era to the 1970s, there was in Canada a combination of the optimism of the intellect and the optimism of the will, not only in the Liberal party but in the Conservative party as well. We should focus on how to restore such attitudes and political alliances for the future.

Paul Hellyer supported Pierre Fortin's views on monetary policy as the cause of high unemployment and went rather further in criticizing the Bank of Canada. In addition to its concentration on repressing inflation, the Bank, in the 1970s, abandoned the traditional control of the commercial banking system through the ratio of cash reserves to deposit liabilities. Instead of the so-called open market operations of a central bank – buying and selling government bonds according to the economy's monetary requirements – the Bank greatly reduced its holding of bonds. The effect was to increase the cost to taxpayers of the national debt, because interest on bonds held by the Bank is returned to the exchequer as income from the Bank. Moreover, the Bank has, by high interest rates, bribed foreigners to buy the bonds it no longer holds. The consequences will plague us for a long time to come.

Hellyer also commented that if Peter Nicholson read the newspapers of the 1930s he would find, almost word for word, what he is saying now. For example, President Hoover claimed in 1932 that "we got the fundamentals right" and so pretty soon things would come out all right. What has happened over the last twenty years is that we have, in effect, reverted to the policies of the 1930s; Nicholson is prescribing for us years of silent depression before we get the promised benefits of such policies.

In Hellyer's view, the monetarists went wrong in the 1990s by assuming that all inflation is monetary, when what was happening was cost-push inflation. With the exception of real estate in a few cities, we have not had classic inflation – too much money chasing too few goods – since the end of the Korean war. Retail stores are going bankrupt every day because they cannot sell the goods they have. Monetary policy has created massive unemployment, and there is no orthodox escape. We have to have another war: a war against poverty, against inadequate housing, against ill health, against illiteracy. That is possible if we stimulate the economy. Debt has to be capped, but with sharply increased production we could both balance budgets and do the things we need to do. Without radical change, however, we will have all the disillusionment that is being forecast.

David Dodge dismissed Hellyer's views as simplistic. The Bank of Canada cannot go on expanding its balance sheet by printing money without putting us in a situation, after some period of time, that Argentina, or Chile, or Brazil found themselves in, and that, in fact, held them back. It is only now that people have some confidence in the exchange value of money that those countries are growing.

Pierre Fortin's view was exempted from this criticism. While we cannot "go on printing money indefinitely and having higher and higher inflation rates," Dodge conceded that there could be "a legitimate argument" for an inflation target of three to five percent instead of one to three percent. But in 1975 "the confidence Canadians had in their monetary system had disappeared." The situation had become "unhinged" and confidence had to be restored. "I think that largely we have succeeded."

Dodge saw "an enormous role" for social policy in fostering a climate for economic growth. He agreed with Harris on the need to increase the savings rate, which means "we have to try to balance a little bit more toward the individual's responsibility to save for his or her old age." We need further investment in human capital infrastructure, which includes health as well as education. In health, social policy has given Canada an international comparative advantage. But, Dodge concluded, "we are going to go through a difficult period where we move our social policy from being transfers to providing real goods and services for Canadians, so that individuals have equal opportunity to move from being given a hand out to a hand up."

JOHN STEWART

The conference moved from social and economic issues to the political party system. A panel of politicians and one academic responded to Kenneth Carty's stimulating paper.

Senator Stewart began by pointing out that in the eighteenth century the public good was thought of chiefly in terms of international relations. Was the nation state powerful enough, and rich enough, to perform its international role: to defend itself; to help maintain the balance of power; and, increasingly, to promote its trade. Significantly, Adam Smith wrote about the wealth of nations. The apostle of laissez faire did not call his book *"The Wealth of Private Persons, Natural and Artificial."*

At the end of the twentieth century we ask what we mean by the public good. In other words, what goals are public goals and how are they to be achieved? Specifically, which of those goals can be left, perhaps in a global economy must be left, to the invisible hand, the market? Within a political system such as Canada's, we rely on political parties to answer these questions, to define the public good, and to provide for its achievement.

Stewart expressed two concerns. For roughly ninety years, beginning in 1896, the Liberal party was Canada's "government party." Ordinarily, it won the elections. The Liberals were lucky. They lost in 1911; thus they did not have to deal with the problem of military recruitment, the great public-good problem of the First World War. They lost in 1930; consequently, they did not have to try to solve the problems posed by the Great Depression. Then Mr King managed to get them through the conscription crisis of the Second World War without the party being shattered.

The key to Liberal success at the polls, the factor which made the Liberal party the government party for almost a century, was the support the party enjoyed in Quebec. Begin with sixty or so seats in Quebec, add solid support in the Atlantic region, then do reasonably well in parts of Ontario and the West, and the government party wins again.

Given Liberal strength in Quebec, the Conservatives had the tough task of trying to draw together groups who often were more hostile to each other than they were to the Liberals; for example, the protectionist Tories of Ontario and the natural resource producers of the West. But all this changed in 1983: the Progressive Conservatives selected a leader from Quebec. Mr Mulroney undertook to destroy the Liberal power base in that province. He enlisted support from the remnants of the old Union Nationale by promising them the fruits of victory. He enlisted support from the left-leaning nationalists by promising them happiness in an entirely new order. The result has been that since 1984 the Liberals no longer can count on Quebec. This starts a question: Does Canada still have a government party? Assuming that the Bloc does not vanish, can either the Liberals or the Conservatives regularly achieve a majority in a country as large and diverse as Canada? If not, who will be able to define, to protect, and to advance the public good of Canadians?

Stewart's second concern was about the very nature of "the Canadian public."

As Professor Carty tells us, our system of government – the Westminster model – exerts a strong pressure on politicians to gather into two parties: those who support the government of the day, and those who want to supplant it. Like baseball, it is a two-team game. Our system has little room for other teams, teams which speak for special interests or areas. Other teams, "third parties," have come on the field. But, in the past, almost all have had their origin west of Lake Superior, in provinces heavily reliant on natural resources. And given the strength of the Liberals in Quebec, the presence of such parties did not make it impossible for the Liberals usually to govern.

The prospect now before us is different. In the early days, one of the causes of Canadian unity from coast to coast, as the saying then was, was the fact that we were not Americans. In more recent times, since the Second World War, one of the main causes has been our transfer-payments system: equalization payments and shared-cost programs. But, given the Free Trade Agreement, and given increasing globalization, will the people in the "have" provinces be prepared to pay the taxes that enable Ottawa to finance the transfer-payments system? Now that Ontario manufacturers no longer enjoy a fairly high level of protection against American competition, can they pay those taxes?

We must ask whether the people of Nova Scotia, for example, can expect to have it both ways; that is, to be able to buy on the North American market and to receive transfer payments from certain other parts of Canada. The economies of Alberta and British Columbia produce largely for the international market. Increasingly they look south and west. How much positive interest will they have in the Ottawa Parliament and government? There is nothing new about western discontent with the Westminster model. What is new is the new economic strength and the increasing population of Alberta and British Columbia.

The premise of Quebec separatism is that the separatist is not a member of the Canadian public. How long will it be before we will be confronted by serious separatism in Alberta and British Columbia? Senator Stewart concluded by posing the question: What can we do to reshape our institutions and thus to redefine the Canadian public good so as to prevent a new separatism in western Canada?

LOWELL MURRAY

Senator Murray took up Professor Carty's points about the present weakness of partisan loyalties, the ambivalence of partisans, and their lack of commitment. He added that relatively few Canadians consider partisan activity worthwhile. People who seek to influence political decisions, whether of local or national significance, are now more likely to join an advocacy group than to work within a political party.

Political parties are indispensable to our democratic parliamentary system. Unfortunately, our national political parties are now not much more than election day machines and fund-raising organizations. Even in these roles, some of the traditional activities of party members – canvassing, organizing, collecting money, and getting out the vote – have been overtaken in importance by modern polling, marketing and communications campaigns run by outside professionals and party staff. The technology is sophisticated enough to target "personalized" messages to subsets of voters, addressing their issue concerns. Local poll chairmen and canvassers whose activities were once vital to political intelligence gathering and campaign strategy are now deployed, where they still exist, to supplement the work of the pollsters and political consultants.

As a result, the number of volunteers actively involved, even at election time, is small. Of the almost 14 million Canadians who voted in the 1993 federal election, Murray guessed that fewer than 200,000 took part in the campaign, working in their constituencies for a party and its candidate.

At the local level, political parties in recent times are seen to have far less influence than in earlier days over federal government policy and decisions that affect the constituency. A constant and legitimate complaint of MPs is that they have less information and less influence than regionally based bureaucrats in, say, the Department of Fisheries and Oceans, the Department of Transport or Parks Canada. These complaints come not only from rural MPs and their constituency associations; a recurrent protest of Toronto-area MPs in recent times has been Ottawa's lack of understanding of Toronto and its failure to consult or communicate at all adequately with them on matters affecting their region.

When, as in this volume, the great issues of economic and social policy are discussed, a political practitioner can only be embarrassed and troubled to reflect on the woeful inadequacy of the policy process in our national political parties. At the national headquarters of any of the parties, you will find staff assigned to programs in communications, finance, organization, youth activity, and so on. What you will not find is a comparable effort to organize and stimulate continuing discussion of current issues and future policy from the constituency level up to the national level.

There are, of course, occasional national policy conferences, sometimes preceded by regional conferences. Sometimes there are debates, leading to resolutions. But the agenda is usually so broad that most of the issues are given hasty and superficial treatment. Little if any sense of a party's priorities can be gleaned from such an exercise. Policy advisory committees, comprising people with expertise in various subjects, exist. But they seem to be for the purpose of briefing and advising the leader and caucus, rather than helping to clarify issues for the party rank and file. An election platform eventually materializes, but any resemblance between this document and the party policy process is purely coincidental. All in all, when it comes to what used to be called political education, our national political parties are seriously remiss.

The policy process in our national parties provides completely inadequate preparation for party candidates who become cabinet ministers and for their parliamentary supporters and opponents. Compared to the senior bureaucracy, to think tanks, to single interest groups, and to the media, our political parties are not seen as important contributors to the development of policy.

As a nation we are paying an increasingly heavy price for this dysfunction in our democratic and parliamentary systems. Professor Fortin points to the threat posed to our sense of national community by some current economic and social problems. Economic insecurity is rife, and the grievances of insecure people are sometimes visited upon people who are even less secure. We need national political parties able to help resolve conflicts among Canadians in different circumstances and walks of life, to help create consensus and strengthen the fabric of society. There is no other forum that can do the job that political parties were intended to do. Our parties have historically played a major role in nation-building. Now more than ever they are needed in this role, to help bridge the differences of language, region, and culture that threaten to break up the country. To do so they will have to articulate a national vision and help Canadians relearn the value of honourable compromise in achieving our common interest.

Neither the Conservatives nor the other established national parties, the Liberals and NDP, were able, after 1990, to provide a satisfactory response to the grievances caused in Quebec by the failure of the Meech Lake Accord, in the West by our failure to achieve our deficit-reduction targets, and everywhere by the GST, the economic recession, and the painful adjustment by the private sector to global competition. But Murray did not conclude from this, as Senator Stewart seems to do, that common cause cannot be made among Canadians in different regions and that it cannot be brokered in national political parties. Before the roof fell in, the Conservatives had won two majority victories, with support in all regions.

Professor Carty believes that a relaxation of caucus discipline would allow for better expression of regional differences in Parliament. Murray agreed that our party leaders and whips are far too up-tight about maintaining total caucus solidarity on virtually every vote in the Commons and Senate. Discipline is much less rigid in the UK Parliament. Still, it has to be said that the issues that traditionally divide Canadians along lines of region, economic interest, and language will not be satisfactorily resolved by a straight majority vote, even if it is across party lines. The grievances of the outvoted minority will not be long assuaged by the knowledge that its MPs defied the party whips in order to uphold their constituents' interests.

National parties have to work things out. The process of honourable compromise, sanctioned by caucus solidarity, may be stressful and untidy, and the outcome not completely satisfactory to anybody; but it is the only way to proceed in a country like this one.

Those of us, Murray said, who have had responsibility for the affairs of our parties would support Professor Carty's proposal to subject political parties to greater public regulation and accountability. However, he was much less enthusiastic about the current trend to create some kind of US primary system for party leadership contests. These US-style primaries are as open to abuse and manipulation as any delegated convention, perhaps more so. It is simply a different kind of manipulation, focusing on the front end of the process; that is, signing up

new party members. There is no guarantee that these "instant" partisans will either continue to participate or, more importantly, participate
in a meaningful way in the operations and deliberations of the party.
There is no guarantee that this process would broaden the base of the
party, or even increase the participation of current party members.

The experience of both the Ontario PCs and the Nova Scotia Liberals suggests that less than half of party members actually voted.
When the Alberta PCs chose their present leader, anybody could walk
in off the street, buy a membership card, and vote. One could even
join up between the first and second ballots, for the sole purpose of
casting a vote for party leader. In Nova Scotia, hundreds of people,
displeased with the Liberal government, rushed to buy membership
in the Liberal party for the purpose of deposing its leader. A debacle
was prevented only when the party executive took its responsibility
seriously and called off the confrontation.

This more "open" process of leadership selection and review is superficially more democratic and stimulates an increased, if passing,
interest in the party. But it does not at all increase the power and responsibility of the committed rank and file members and of constituency associations, which is what we need to foster in order to
revitalize our parties and our democratic system. The Reform party's
panaceas of instant polling of constituents, national referendums, and
recall of MPs are even less likely to strengthen our democratic and
parliamentary systems and promote national unity.

The need, Senator Murray concluded, is to redesign the policy-
making capacities of our parties. We need to reinforce the role of our
parties in brokering the national interest. We need to increase the
opportunities for party members to come together between elections,
to meet and broaden their own and their party's perspectives on important issues.

JAMES BICKERTON

James Bickerton pointed out that, in contemplating the future of
national political parties, we would be mistaken to think that until
now such parties have continuously existed. Perhaps it could be said
that before 1958, there was always one national political party, the
Liberals. The Conservatives certainly could not be considered as such
between 1935 and 1957, nor could the western protest parties, the CCF
and Social Credit. Between 1962 and 1984, the period referred to in
the literature on parties and elections as the "third-party system," no
party could claim to be truly national, if the criteria for such a desig-
nation are having adequate representation from, and a viable political

organization in, all regions of the country, sufficient to provide the party with an ongoing, systematic presentation of the demands, concerns, and opinions of all parts of the country and sufficient to allow the party to be competitive in national elections.

While both the Conservatives and the NDP expanded their reach during the era of the third-party system, compared with the previous period of party competition, the former had no significant presence in Quebec and the latter none east of the Ottawa River. The Liberals, on the other hand, for much of this period, governed on a narrowed geographic base that had shrunk to eastern Canada, with a virtual monopoly position in Quebec. The Liberal electoral base during this period has been called the party's "Catholic Canada" core. No truly national parties and no national party system existed. In fact, there were three party systems that coexisted during this period: the Conservatives and NDP were the primary competitors in western Canada; the Liberals and Conservatives in eastern English-speaking Canada (outside Quebec); and in Quebec, the Liberals were virtually without serious competitors at the federal level.

On the surface, the 1984 to 1993 period marked a return to national party politics. In 1988, free trade polarized the national electorate around a policy issue. But even in those propitious circumstances for generating a truly national debate and common national choice for Canadians, antifree trade voters in the West strategically chose the NDP, while in the east they moved to the Liberals, denying both the claim to speak with a strong national voice. The Conservatives clearly benefitted from not having to split the free trade vote with another party. Even so, they won a majority of seats in only two provinces (Quebec and Alberta), an unusually tepid mandate for the national electorate to confer on a majority government.

Now 1993 has shattered even this dubious and half-hearted return to national party competition. Though the Liberals won seats in every province, they suffer from a very weak presence in Alberta, British Columbia, and francophone Quebec. More tellingly, the only other party that has ever been able to assert a realistic claim to national party status throughout our history as a country was totally decimated, replaced by two regional parties that represent diametrically opposite points of view on most public policy questions. The New Democrats, who briefly threatened in the 1988 election to displace the Liberals as the second party in Canada, and thereby fulfil the prophecy that Canada would sooner or later track European history and move toward a more ideological, left-right polarization of its party policies, were similarly devastated by the 1993 results. Their heretofore resilient and slowly growing group of social democratic voters was reduced to a pathetic rump that discouraged even the most die-hard believers in the inevitability of their party's goal of attaining truly national party status and contesting for power.

In the wake of 1993, there are still at least three party systems in Canada. English-speaking Canada is divided along an east-west gradient between a Liberal-Conservative and a Liberal-Reform-NDP system, while Quebec again stands apart but is now itself divided into two one-party dominant systems according to language and ethnicity.

One conclusion that can be drawn from this review of our party system's history is that there are no national parties in Canada, or at least that their existence has been at best sporadic and precarious over the past thirty-five years, before which we experienced a one-party dominant system for over two decades. Furthermore, there is no indication that their future presence on the national scene is likely to be any more secure. The two-party vote – the combined share of Liberals and Conservatives – has declined steadily through each period of party competition in our history.

The Westminster system of one-party government was designed for a two-party system, at least for an official opposition party that could contemplate the possibility of governing. This is no longer the case in Canada. Even if the Liberals superficially benefit by being the only party in a position to govern, the more significant result is likely to be increasing voter alienation with a political system that does not offer them real choices. Even more electoral volatility and insecurity for all political parties may be in store.

That is certainly one popular reading of 1993: that a cranky electorate now has no allegiances to party. But there is no good evidence to support this. A better case can be made that the situation in which Canadian parties find themselves is more a product of our political institutions than it is the result of an increasingly fragmented and unruly electorate. It can be argued that, like Europe, we have evolved a party system that features parties grouped into ideological families that draw sustenance from relatively stable electorates; electoral change occurs within these families rather than across family boundaries.

This description appears to typify the third-party system and, despite its chaotic result, the 1993 election as well. In a recent paper that presents some preliminary results from the 1993 national election study, Richard Johnston and his coinvestigators find that outside Quebec no major dealignment or realignment of voters, in terms of party identification, took place; there was merely a vote shift within ideological families. The reputed flow of western New Democrats to Reform was not large, and tended to be persons impatient with Canada's ethno-linguistic agenda.

Only in Quebec, with the emergence of the Bloc, is there evidence of a fundamental realignment of voters in terms of party identification. The Bloc sucked up Tory and NDP voters; even more significantly, it mobilized those francophone Quebecers who had previously abstained from voting in federal elections as well as new voters entering the electorate; these two categories constituted roughly 40 percent of the Bloc vote.

While the Canadian party system has some characteristics akin to European party systems, it does differ in one key facet. Canada has not developed institutions for accommodating a degree of cooperation and power-sharing between like-minded parties; our electoral system and parliamentary practices work against this rather than facilitate it. Yet any future stability for national parties in Canada, or more appropriately the national party system, requires institutions that will support more interparty cooperation. Our institutional deficiencies need to be addressed.

Future institutional reform or not, does a fragmented Right and weak Left guarantee the Liberals another long period as the governing party? Some elements of that situation seem to be in place, but a key component – an unassailable Quebec base for the Liberals – is missing and seems unlikely to be recovered. Still, as long as it is the Bloc that attracts the allegiance of francophone voters, not a party contesting seats in the rest of Canada, continued Liberal dominance may not be difficult. In these circumstances, a unified and resurgent Right would seem a more likely source of electoral threat. Yet, even if the many obstacles to this development are overcome, the Liberals' current predilection to govern from the Right undercuts its conservative critics. The main threat to continued Liberal predominance may, therefore, originate from the Left: should the NDP be revived, the draining away of left of centre support from the Liberals would force the party to move in that direction and open space for the conservatives to make an appeal to their traditional supporters. A revival of national party competition encompassing a wider-ranging and enriched political debate would ensue. Therefore, we should all hope for a revival of the NDP, the sooner the better.

Finally, there is a lesson for all the parties provided by the Tory debacle of 1993. It is that no party can ignore the need to maintain its base of core supporters; no party can secure its long- term electoral position by attempting to simultaneously appeal to fundamentally different social and political bases, as the Mulroney Tories did. Brokering a national consensus may indeed be the most heroic function our parties can perform, but if done as the centrepiece of a political strategy for winning and holding power, parties can become victims to a form of imperial overstretch, torn asunder while attempting to span deep divisions within Canadian society. Viewed from this perspective, Bickerton concluded, the rise of the Bloc may be the saving grace for the Liberals, displacing the arena for brokerage of the French-English divide from within the governing party to an intergovernmental forum.

AFTERTHOUGHTS

The MacEachen conference was designed to stimulate and clarify thinking about future policies for the public good, not to arrive at agreed conclusions. My comments are therefore necessarily subjective, more a personal postscript to the conference than a conclusion from it.

People and Hand-ups

If one main theme emerged, it was that socio-economic policies should be directed, above all, to the development of people, the enrichment of our human capital. What was surprising was the extent to which this was presented as it if were a great new thought, therefore calling for a revolution in social policy. It has surely been a commonplace at least since the Soviet Union shook North American complacency by putting its first Sputnik into space in 1957. True, it was military competition that first drove the effort to be smarter, but economic considerations were not far behind. I was only summarizing what many others were thinking when I wrote, in a paper for the 1960 Kingston conference: "It needs no saying that modern society must be a more skilful society. The demands that scientific progress imposes on us – the skills demanded by its complexities, and the emotional stability required to cope with its upheavals – cannot be met unless we are less wasteful of the human talent available to society ... [W]hat we have as yet done in public education is surely only a little of what we are going to do. The need to move further is urgent."

These were not just words. It is a complete misrepresentation to identify the social programs of the 1960s with what David Dodge called hand-outs rather than hand-ups. The agenda was not limited to income supplements. Medicare was surely a human capital program. There were massive increases in secondary and technical schooling; a transformation of postsecondary facilities, in colleges as well as universities; the extension of family allowances for those who stayed at school beyond age sixteen; student loans; the building of employment services – job information, counselling, training and training allowances, mobility assistance. All these were components of 1960s social policy, responding to the obvious need to develop our human capital.

The benefits have not been as great as was hoped. In part, that is because the hand-ups were not as well coordinated with the hand-outs as they should have been. In our federal system, programs have to be negotiated and implemented piecemeal. Good coordination can be established only with time, and it may be frustrated because, also with time, vested interests in organizations and sense of entitlements in recipients become politically powerful.

The new enthusiasts for human capital will not escape such problems, but they are minor reasons why the benefit-cost ratio from most hand-up programs has been disappointing. The deeper reason is that they went into full flight only as the economy moved into the rising unemployment that has characterized the past twenty-five years. Retraining is in any case difficult for older workers whose disappearing jobs in mining or fishing or whatever are the only work they have known after leaving school at grade nine or less. And however competent they learn to be as, say, carpenters, little good is done if there are already more carpenters than there are jobs for them.

Keith Banting is clearly right in saying that, in the contemporary economy, security in employment depends on adjustment to change rather than protection from change. It is also true that higher skills will strengthen entrepreneurship and raise productivity. But it is simply an evasion of our economic problem to pretend, as politicians in office like to do, that enhancing the capacity to change is, in itself, a way to reduce unemployment. It will do so only if the new jobs that can be learned are more plentiful than the old jobs that are disappearing. The first thing to do about human resources is to use them instead of wasting them.

Meritocracy or Equal Opportunity

The public good requires that the individual has a place in society, a basis for belonging, for self-esteem and self-support. It requires that the opportunity to earn a living, in a way that gives some expression to the individual's talents, is almost always available to everyone who wishes and is able to work.

The "almost always" recognizes that such full employment is not fully achievable. There are bound to be round pegs that can find, at least for a time, only square holes, as well as a few people who are unable to become competent enough for any job that justifies a living wage; there will always be seasonal variations as well as frictions in adjusting to the changing nature and location of jobs. In the golden age, we thought that an average unemployment rate of around 3 percent was a realistic measure of the full employment goal. The nature and pace of technological change, the globalization of industry, the greater participation of women in the workforce have since combined to make the minimum somewhat higher. But, as Pierre Fortin argues, such factors do not account for the slump of our economy. To expect that the present minimum unemployment rate may be somewhat higher than in the 1960s – we cannot be sure, since we certainly have not been near it for so long – is in no way to resign ourselves to the heavy, persistent, long-term unemployment of our present days.

Resignation has, nevertheless, become the real, if generally unadmitted, attitude of very many politicians, opinion leaders, and policy makers. It is a failure of adjustment at the top, a failure of will and imagination to find new methods for changed circumstances. It is a resignation that has become the worst enemy of the public good. If it persists, a new policy emphasis on human capital, necessary though it is, will become an elitist prescription. It will lead to more good jobs, enjoyed by people who are in varying degrees smarter or luckier than the pack. For the less smart and the less lucky, there will be bad jobs or none. We will create an increasingly privileged meritocracy instead of a broadening democracy.

It will be increasingly privileged because of the intergenerational transfer of opportunity to which Richard Van Loon and Lars Osberg draw attention. The children of the well-to-do start with luck and opportunity, the children of the disadvantaged do not. The social significance of rapidly advancing technology is that most people can cope with it if they start in the mainstream of the affluent society; but for people once outside that stream, particularly at birth, getting into it becomes far harder than it was in quieter times. If we should fail to combat this trend to polarization, the middle class that has grown so much in the twentieth century would shrink in the twenty-first. Canada would become in a new sense a nation of two distinct societies, the advantaged and the disadvantaged. That would not be a stable situation, but there is no point in speculating about what would follow.

What is constructive is to determine how public policies as a whole can better serve the purpose of social cohesion. We cannot reject the prescription given by Tom Courchene and others: social policy will fit the contemporary economy only if it gives new emphasis to the enrichment of our human capital. But emphasis is not isolation. More investment in human capital will advance the public good provided, but only provided, that it is combined with more employment and more equality of opportunity for children.

The employment requirement has long been obvious. Our under-standing of childhood needs is more recent. There are, of course, talents that emerge despite deprivation in early life. But the cases are conspicuous precisely because they are exceptional. Even very bright children learn less well than they could if they go to school hungry, if medical needs go unattended, if their homes lack conversational stimulus, books, games, and other facilities that spark interest and feed curiosity. In such circumstances, "normal" children are all too likely to be underachievers. It is hypocrisy to leave many of our children to grow up in poverty while we preach that they cannot expect to have jobs unless they can adjust to intensely competitive, rapidly changing industrial complexity.

The public good in contemporary society requires, in short, more equality of opportunity in childhood and fuller employment in adult-hood. Our present policies are not providing the employment; they are taking us backward in equality of opportunity.

There are two main barriers to reform. One is the condition of our public finances. The other is the politics of our federalism.

Expansion with Taxes

We cannot go on piling up public debt. As Pierre Fortin demon-strates, the massive budgetary deficits of the 1980s were largely in-duced by ill-judged monetary policy. But the consequence – the accumulated debt – cannot be quickly dissolved even if monetary policy is changed as fast and as far as it should be. For some years, something like a third of the revenue that the federal government raises will be needed to pay interest to bondholders, many of them outside Canada. That revenue is not available to provide public services, which is a large part of the reason for the widespread feeling that our taxes do not give us value for money. (There are subsidiary reasons, conspicuously the spread into the higher reaches of govern-ment of perquisites copied from corporate managements.)

Besides releasing some revenue for program expenditures, lower interest rates – with an accompanying acceptance of a relatively low exchange rate – will stimulate the economy, increasing employment and incomes, and therefore raising government revenues at existing tax rates. The effects are cumulative, but whether they are fast or slow is, as Peter Nicholson notes, unpredictable. In any event, that route alone will not yield all the resources needed to ensure that many more children soon have the start in life that work in their world will require. Additional resources are needed.

We cannot revert at this time to budget deficits. And while there are still some government expenditures sustained by inertia, political advantage, or indulgence, it is unrealistic to count on significant change soon. We will do what we should for Canada's children only if we pay more taxes. That is widely dismissed as impossible. It was barely broached at Antigonish.

Peter Nicholson asserts that for forty years we had too little policy imagination. Others may think that we had too much. Perhaps it is from such lack of imagination today that we continually tinker with the tax system instead of fundamentally reconsidering it.

It was indeed reconsidered thirty and more years ago, by the Carter Royal Commission. Of all the inquiry recommendations that governments have shuffled aside, the shelving of the Carter report most served the public ill. The direction it pointed was and is the public good. Essentially, that direction is to broaden the base of taxation. Fundamental reform means ending the artificial distinction between income and additions to wealth, however they originate, a distinction that is at the root of most tax avoidance and evasion and that greatly impairs the progressiveness of the system. If taxes are levied on such a broadened base, the same rates will yield substantially more revenue. Incentives to work would not be weakened. Not only would taxation be more equitable; a revised system could be structured to strengthen, not weaken, the efficiency and entrepreneurship of the economy.

The details of such reform, and how fast it could be implemented, are beyond the scope of this commentary. (I have made suggestions elsewhere.) The point that is clear, in my view, is twofold. On one hand, we do not have to unbalance the budget in order to undertake a major new thrust in social development. On the other hand, tax reform is not a panacea. Together with some resumption of economic growth, it can promptly justify increased spending for one or two priority purposes, but not the long wish list that good will calls for. There will continue to be harder choices for the public good than there were in the golden era.

The nurturing of children – their health, confidence, socialization, mental stimulation, education – is one need. So is improvement in further education and training (which should be more workplace-based). So is income support for the disabled. So is more assistance to the families of the working poor. So are social housing, pollution clean-up and prevention, improvements in urban and transport infrastructure. The list could go on. The danger in returning to an expansionist mode is that politicians are pressured to do something about all these things. They can end up either by spreading resources too thin, and thereby doing little about anything; or they may try to do too much too soon and overextend either the country's resources or its political will. The second may seen an unlikely danger today, but political cycles are sometimes short.

Concern for the public good requires determination to set priorities. And it seems clear that today the first priority, where the main strands of our economic and social requirements come together, is the well-being and development of our emerging human resources, of our children.

It should be noted that, in addition to its primary purpose, such a program will reinforce other measures to increase employment. The principal costs will be the employment of more people in child care and related health and social services. Admittedly, the gain will be partly offset, as in any tax-financed program, by reduced spending and employment in other sectors. However, the program spending will be labour-intensive, whereas much of the private spending forgone will be capital-intensive and will have a considerable import content. Some, indeed, may not be spending at all, but a reduction in saving. To some economists, that is undesirable. Richard Harris makes the case that we should provide more encouragement for savings as a requisite for economic growth. I hope we will come again to a time when he is right, when the economy is operating at capacity and growth means raising the productivity of resources already in use. But to bring into use resources that are now idle, we need spending, not saving.

Who Does What?

If the needs of children are the agreed first priority, the perennial Canadian question becomes how federal and provincial responsibilities can be melded in a program that operates efficiently and fairly across the country.

So far, the retreat of government in Canada has been primarily the retreat of Ottawa. It has been driven chiefly by the desire to cut spending in the way least painful to itself, by greatly reducing its contribution to the financing of provincial social programs. In their turn, provincial governments, also under financial pressure, have economized in the programs. The variation is chiefly in the extent to which they claim ideological virtue for the cuts.

Tom Courchene, unlike many policy analysts, offers a clear and coherent response to this situation. He accepts the federal downsizing as unavoidable. He likes decentralization. He favours some program economies. On these assumptions, he makes a constructive proposal for a new national policy that would maintain a degree of social union across the country through interprovincial agreement. His views have been strongly criticized by the governments of some of the smaller provinces, still looking to Ottawa for salvation, as well as by social advocates, desperate at least to hold on to the programs they know and that have done so much good. Alternatives are rarer than criticisms. In my view, it has to be recognized that Courchene's way could well be the way that we go. If his assumptions are correct, it is the only proposal on the table that could save us, at least in some degree, from the fragmentation of social Canada that is otherwise in prospect.

But should the assumptions be accepted? The question can be answered only in the context of history, of how the Canadian welfare state was created. It was built, from sea to sea, despite the Constitution's assignment of almost all social responsibilities to the provinces. Ken Battle's paper provides a very valuable, relatively detailed analysis of the process. In summary, three instruments were used.

First, there was unanimous agreement to three constitutional amendments: making the federal Parliament responsible for unemployment insurance; admitting it to concurrent jurisdiction, though with provincial primacy, for old-age pensions; and later extending this to related survivor and disability benefits.

Second, the federal government used its taxing and spending power to provide some benefits directly to individuals. Most notable were family allowances and, later, refundable tax credits; the guaranteed income supplement; training allowances; and courses of training, provided mostly in provincial institutions but purchased from them on behalf of individuals selected through federal programs.

This last is the major example of "procurement federalism," as opposed to the fiscal federalism that was the third, and for a time the most important, instrument. The federal spending power was used to reimburse the provinces for part, generally half, of their costs of providing medicare, social assistance, postsecondary education, and various lesser programs.

In retrospect, all this is widely represented as a power-hungry federal government riding roughshod over provincial jurisdiction. The myth has slight relation to reality. People across the country wanted the programs, wanted them as national programs. In the mood of the times, provincial governments were not opposed to the feds doing good and bearing money. But the recipients looked the gift horse in the mouth. The programs were not dreamed up in an isolated Ottawa. They were widely discussed and then negotiated. In many cases, the original federal proposals were substantially changed. Quebec, in some cases, secured, for virtually identical programs, distinctive administrative arrangements which the other provinces did not want.

Admittedly, there were some battles that one or two provinces lost.
The Manning government of Alberta, alone, objected to medicare in
principle; it regarded health as a personal responsibility, not to be
taken over by any level of government. In 1966, the governments of
the richer provinces wanted training to remain under its original cost-
sharing arrangements, which had proved especially beneficial to
them. They, or at least the departmental officials concerned, bitterly
resented Ottawa's switch to procurement, designed to be fairer to the
provinces where training was most needed but also shifting control
from provincial to federal officials.

It should also be recognized that the federal government was by no
means always as considerate of particular provincial needs and views
as it could have been.

All these are, however, minor qualifications: the Canadian welfare
state was built, brick by brick, through cooperative federalism, not
through the unilateralism that is often alleged and denounced.

What is true is that there now is unilateralism; but it is in the dismantling of social programs, not in building them. Understandably,
politicians are not enthusiasts for levying taxes so that other politicians can spend the money. The federal cabinets of the 1950s and
1960s were exceptional in their willingness to cost-share provincial
programs. They were exceptional because the financial spaciousness
of the period was exceptional. As soon as finances tightened, with declining economic performance and rising debt, the generosity of spirit
faded. The Trudeau government reneged on the commitments to full
cost-sharing for medicare and postsecondary education. The process
began with a small step in the Established Program Financing legislation of 1977 and, extended to social assistance, was continued in increasing steps by subsequent governments. The Chrétien-Martin
government has brought it to its bitter conclusion. There is now no
federal sharing of expenses for the programs that the provinces were
induced to undertake by the promise of sharing. The feeble substitute, the Canada Health and Social Transfer, is merely a small block
grant unrelated to provincial costs. The dismantling has indeed been
unilateral, not cooperative, federalism.

The Canadian welfare state cannot again be as it was. For the fore-
seeable future, the federal spending power will not be used to initiate
provincial programs. No one will put trust in it. Medicare is popular
enough to continue for a time on the same basic principles across the
country. But the service is being eroded by financial stringency; the
erosion is bound to result in widening differences from place to place;
Ottawa now has no financial clout to maintain anything near a consistent national service.

The consequences of federal retreat are not limited to the formerly cost-shared programs. The structure has become disjointed. For example, when more people are shifted to social assistance, as a result of one of the federal government's periodic retrenchments in unemployment insurance, at least it used to be that half of the extra assistance cost fell on the federal treasury; now it is all another burden for the provinces. Further, as the federal government retreats from employment services and training, as a way to placate Quebec without offending all of the other provinces, its role in the related sphere of unemployment insurance becomes highly questionable.

Courchene's preferred solution to all this confusion is in effect that, apart from income supplementation through the tax system, the federal government should stop its whimpering retreat and instead get out of social programs with a bang. The field would then be clear for the provinces to create a new social union by firm agreement among them. My fear is that he underestimates the parochialism of provincial governments. They will sign on to broad agreements in the national interest, but their constituencies are not national. When it comes to detailed implementation, to differences among the provinces, to any enforcement of the agreements, it is their provincial electorates, and particularly the views and interests of their own supporters within those electorates, that will dominate. I doubt that the outcome would be much of a social union for Canada.

A Federal Initiative

There is an alternative, if the federal government is capable of overcoming its psychology of retreat and lethargy. Of the three original instruments of Canada-wide social policy, constitutional amendment is in abeyance and cost-sharing is dead. But the third instrument remains: the federal government can initiate programs that it pays for fully, that benefit individuals directly. To bring this instrument more fully into play, in place of cost-sharing, is the sure way to re-strengthen the social union.

In one area, income support for poorer retired people, the federal government is already proposing to improve its role through the new seniors benefit. My proposal would be that it also target the critically formative age of men and women: childhood.

The measures to this end now widely considered are an enlarged tax credit (of the "refundable" kind) for parents with low- and middle-incomes, together with more provision of subsidized child-care places. While those would be beneficial measures, I think it would be better to be more direct.

The proposal that follows is not intended to be more than an illustration. The motive for it is that generalizations about the public good do not take us far unless they are given life in possible specifics. We will arrive at action for the public good only if – again picking up the Nicholson phrase – we exercise our policy imagination for the constructive exploration of definite possibilities. In that spirit, I suggest three programs for children. They are joint programs to be negotiated between Ottawa and the provinces. But their costs would not be shared; they would be 100 percent federal.

First, the federal government would issue, for all preschool children after, say, their first birthday, vouchers for child care. The vouchers would be usable at centres established or licensed by the province to provide care at quality standards agreed with the federal government; these standards would include staff qualified, and numerous enough, to introduce the children to the processes of learning. The vouchers would cover the full cost of such care, negotiated with each province, and paid to it by the federal government. The vouchers would be universally available, but parents who used them would become liable to a federal surtax, beginning at an average income for the family size and rising on a sliding scale to full cost recovery, at the average provincial level, from large incomes. Parents who did not wish or were unable to use the vouchers could surrender them in exchange for a supplementary child tax credit, in effect for baby-sitting costs. The scaling of the credit to family income would be equitable in relation to the surtax recovery on the vouchers.

Second, the federal government would reimburse provinces for the full cost of school meal programs; this would compensate them for a little of their loss of Canada Assistance Plan funding for social assistance.

Third, and very important, the federal government would reimburse the provinces for the full cost of medical services provided to minors (that is, up to the age of eighteen). These would include in-school medical check-ups, eye and dental services, and prescribed medicines. In this way, the federal government would again be a genuine participant in the financing of medicare. Its identified role – responsibility for children – would be important enough to restore its right to a full voice in defining and maintaining national principles for medicare.

This comprehensive child-care policy would address two of our most important concerns: how most effectively to enrich our human and social capital and so provide for future economic strength; and, at the same time, how to make opportunities more equal and thereby outweigh the market trend to an increasingly polarized society. Further, it is a program that could be brought into being only as a national program rooted in genuinely full cooperation of federal and provincial governments. We may hope that it would express a new relationship superseding the damaging divisiveness that has been recurring.

All too obviously, I have given no more than a preliminary first sketch of a possible policy. The main purpose is to explore, by illustration, the direction in which we may look for the future public good by strengthening the social union joining Canadians.

The Politics of the Good

No such exploration will lead on to action, however, unless our political structure is in reasonably good shape. We do not yet suffer in Canada the degree of cynicism about government that James Schlesinger diagnoses in the United States. Nevertheless, Kenneth Carty's convincing analysis of the tension of our party system rules out complacency, particularly as neither he nor the respondents to his paper prescribe solutions that seem fully adequate for the problem.

Carty is probably right in thinking that a fundamental reform in the European direction – that is, some variety of proportional representation for elections to the House of Commons – would in itself yield little net benefit. In my view, however, it could produce a major advance in political health provided, but only provided, that it is combined with a Senate as a genuine second chamber, with lesser power than the Commons, but elected from single-member constituencies. An elected Senate would better serve its main function, to offset the centralization of political power in the bit of Canadian territory that extends from Montreal to Windsor. As well, senators would not be dominated, as MPs necessarily are, by their primary responsibility to support or oppose the government. That responsibility often now conflicts with the MPs supposed role as representative of his or her constituency's interests, a role that would virtually disappear with proportional representation. An elected Senate could take it over. Since the government would not stand or fall according to their votes, senators elected from single-member constituencies could give more effective voice to the concerns and views of their localities than is possible for MPs.

Such major reform would require, however, a constitutional amendment and is, therefore, not on any present agenda. Some good could be done meantime by the lesser electoral change of the alternative vote. That is, ballot papers would be marked not with a single cross, but with an order of preference. If no candidate received more than 50 percent of the first-preference votes, the bottom candidate would be eliminated and his or her votes redistributed according to the second-preferences marked on the ballots. This process would continue, if necessary, until one candidate's combined vote (in original first-preferences and transferred lower preferences) was more than 50 percent of the total of valid votes cast. The MP thus elected would represent the majority opinion of the constituency, in the sense that more than half the electors preferred him or her to the alternative next in favour.

Such an electoral change would probably make little difference to party strengths in the Commons. But each MP would come with a majority vote, at least on a lesser-evil basis, behind him or her; the government that the Commons sustained would thereby have somewhat more popular legitimacy than is now the case, when 40 percent of the popular vote can give a government a large, tame majority and no one knows for sure whether another 10 percent of voters in their polling booths would have been less unhappy with it than with the opposition.

Lowell Murray goes to the root of the problem in his characterization of contemporary parties as little more than election-day machines and fund raising organizations. The funds are used for polling, marketing, and communications campaigns run by "professionals" – the mechanics of politics. So dominated, the parties make little more than token provision for policy discussion and development within their ranks. Caucuses therefore come ill-prepared for government. The consequences are bad enough now. They will become worse. Globalization is inevitably reducing the extent to which the public good can be served by nation states acting independently. Further surrender to private interests (spear-headed by the frenetic operators of international money-changing) will be avoided only if governments cooperate more effectively through international institutions and transnational arrangements. Good policy making will thereby be even more dependent on good sense in assessing complex considerations. It will be even more important that politicians come to office well prepared by prior thinking and discussion.

Reform of political parties will not come from internal conversion. It will have to be compelled by legislated reform of political financing, by requiring parties to become, in Carty's language, the public utilities of electoral democracy, with more public structuring and regulation of their electoral activities. Much of the necessary reform has been proposed by the Lortie Royal Commission; we may hope that Carty is right in saying that a party that ignores the recommendations will do so at its peril.

The signs, however, are not encouraging. Previous crashes of a national two-party system resulted in minority governments, usually the most open to reform. The 1993 crash did not. And politicians comfortable in office do not rush to change the system by which they have got where they are. Reform is unlikely to come unless it is pressured by public opinion, unless their polls tell the politicians that a party convincingly committed to political reform will thereby gain a great many votes. And that will come only through dedicated work by a citizens' organization for democratically accountable politics.

The building of such an organization might seem remote from the immediate needs of most Canadians, but it could be one of the most constructive of actions to serve the public good for the twenty-first century.

Notes

KEN BATTLE

1 Tom Kent, *Social Policy for Canada: Towards a Philosophy of Social Security* (Ottawa: Policy Press, 1962) (paper for the 1960 Kingston conference, republished in 1962).
2 Caledon Institute of Social Policy, *The Measurement of Social Spending* (Ottawa, 1995).
3 Leonard Marsh, *Report on Social Security for Canada* (Toronto: University of Toronto Press 1975) (originally published by the King's Printer in 1943).
4 Department of Reconstruction, *Employment and Income with Special Reference to the Initial Period of Reconstruction* (Ottawa: Queen's Printer, 1945).
5 Robert Campbell, *The Full-Employment Objective in Canada, 1945–85: Historical, Conceptual, and Comparative Perspectives* (Ottawa: Minister of Supply and Services Canada, 1991).
6 Ken Battle, *Government Fights Growing Gap Between Rich and Poor* (Ottawa: Caledon Institute of Social Policy, 1995).
7 Ken Battle, (Grattan Gray) "Social Policy by Stealth," *Policy Options* (March 1990); Ken Battle and Sherri Torjman, *Federal Social Programs: Setting the Record Straight* (Ottawa: Caledon Institute of Social Policy, 1993); James Rice and Michael Prince, "Lowering the Safety Net and Weakening the Bonds of Nationhood: Social Policy in the Mulroney Years," *How Ottawa Spends 1993–1994: A More Democratic Canada ...?*, ed. Susan D. Phillips (Ottawa: Carleton University Press, 1993); Ken Battle and Sherri Torjman, *How Finance Re-formed Social Policy* (Ottawa: Caledon Institute of Social Policy, 1995).
8 Leon Muszynski, *UI to EI: Brief on Bill C-12 to the Standing Committee on Human Resources Development* (Ottawa: Caledon Institute of Social Policy, 1996).

9 Government of Canada, *The Seniors Benefit*: *Securing the Future* (Ottawa: Her Majesty the Queen in Right of Canada, 1996).

10 Gallup Poll, "Percentage Who Are Confident They Will Receive Old Age Security and Canada/Quebec Pension Plans," October 1994.

11 Federal, Provincial, and Territorial Governments of Canada, *An Information Paper for Consultations on the Canada Pension Plan* (Ottawa: Department of Finance, 1996).

12 Keith Banting, "Who R Us?," in *The Federal Budget*: *Retrospect and Prospect*, eds., Thomas Courchene and Thomas Wilson (Kingston: Queen's University, 1995). Canadian Union of Postal Employees Research Department, *Undoing Health Care*: *The Canada Health and Social Transfer and How the 1995 Budget Will Affect Medicare* (Ottawa: CUPE, 1995); Michael Mendelson, *Looking for Mr Good-Transfer*: *A Guide to the CHST Negotiations* (Ottawa: Caledon Institute of Social Policy, 1995); National Council of Welfare, *The 1995 Budget and Block-funding* (Ottawa: Minister of Supply and Services Canada, 1995); Dr Paul Steinhauer, *The Canada Health and Social Transfer*: *A Threat to the Health, Development and Future Productivity of Canada's Children and Youth* (Ottawa: Caledon Institute of Social Policy, 1995); Sherri Torjman, *CHST Spells COST for Disabled* (Ottawa: Caledon Institute of Social Policy, 1995); Sherri Torjman, *The Let-Them-Eat-Cake Law* (Ottawa: Caledon Institute of Social Policy, 1995); Sherri Torjman, *Milestone or Millstone? The Legacy of the Social Security Review* (Ottawa: Caledon Institute of Social Policy, 1995); Sherri Torjman and Ken Battle, *The Dangers of Block Funding* (Ottawa: Caledon Institute of Social Policy, 1995); Sherri Torjman and Ken Battle, *Can We Have National Standards?* (Ottawa: Caledon Institute of Social Policy, 1995).

13 Thomas Courchene, *Redistributing Money and Power*: *A Guide to the Canada Health and Social Transfer* (Toronto: C.D. Howe Institute, 1995).

14 Torjman, *Milestone or Millstone?*

15 Michael Mendelson, *Is There Life After Death of Federal Transfers?* (Ottawa: Caledon Institute of Social Policy, 1996).

16 Ibid.

17 Battle, "Social Policy by Stealth."

18 Statistics Canada, *Canada's Retirement Income Programs*: *A Statistical Overview* (Ottawa: Minister of Industry, 1996).

19 Statistics Canada, *Income After Tax, Distributions by Size in Canada 1994* (Ottawa: Minister of Industry, 1996).

20 Ibid.

21 Ken Battle, *Thinking the Unthinkable*: *A Targeted, Not Universal, Old Age Pension* (Ottawa: Caledon Institute of Social Policy, 1993).

22 Ken Battle and Sherri Torjman, *The Welfare Wall*: *Reforming the Welfare and Tax Systems* (Ottawa: Caledon Institute of Social Policy, 1993); Nancy

Naylor, Ruth Abbott, and Elizabeth Hewner, *The Design of the Ontario Child Income Program* (Ottawa: Caledon Institute of Social Policy, 1994); Ken Battle and Leon Muszynski, *One Way to Fight Child Poverty* (Ottawa: Caledon Institute of Social Policy, 1995); Caledon Institute of Social Policy, *The Comprehensive Reform of Social Programs* (Ottawa, 1995); Tom Kent, "How to Strengthen the Welfare State," *Policy Options* (June 1996); Ministerial Council on Social Policy Reform and Renewal, *Report to Premiers*, December 1995; Michael Mendelson, *Social Policy After the Referendum* (Ottawa: Caledon Institute of Social Policy, 1995); Michael Mendelson, *Social Policy Before the Next Referendum* (Ottawa: Caledon Institute of Social Policy, 1995).

23 Sherri Torjman, "The Canada Pension Plan Disability Benefit and the Disability Income System," in *Experts' Forum on Canada Pension Plan Reform* (Ottawa: Caledon Institute of Social Policy, 1996).

24 Ibid.

25 Battle and Torjman, *The Welfare Wall*; National Council of Welfare, *Testing Tax Reform: A Brief to the Standing Committee on Finance and Economic Affairs* (Ottawa: Minister of Supply and Services Canada, 1987).

26 National Council of Welfare, *Medicare: The Public Good and Private Practice* (Ottawa: Minister of Supply and Services Canada, 1982).

27 Ministerial Council, *Report*.

THOMAS J. COURCHENE

1 Lester Thurow, *Toronto Star*, 28 January 1992, A21.

2 Thomas J. Courchene, *Social Canada in the Millennium: Reform Imperatives and Restructuring Principles* (Toronto: C.D. Howe Institute, 1994), 339.

3 Hugh Heclo, "Towards a New Welfare State," in *The Development of Welfare States In Europe and America*, eds. Peter Flora and H.J. Heidenheimer (London: Transaction Books, 1984), 383–406.

4 Ibid.

5 Keith Banting, "Universality and the Development of the Welfare State," in *Report on the Forum on Universality and Social Policies in the 1990s*, eds. Alan Green and Nancy Olewiler (Kingston: Queen's University, John Deutsch Institute for the Study of Economic Policy, 1985), 9.

6 Heclo, "Towards a New Welfare State," 391.

7 Scott Gordon, *The Demand and Supply of Government: What We Want and What We Get*, Economic Council of Canada, Discussion Paper no. 79 (Ottawa: Economic Council of Canada, 1974), 43–4.

8 Banting, "Development of the Welfare State," 10–11.

9 Heclo, "Towards a New Welfare State," 399.

10 Daniel Bell, "The Public Household or 'Fiscal Sociology' and the Liberal Society," *The Public Interest* 37 (1974), 39.

11 Thomas J. Courchene, "Towards a Protected Society: The Politicization of Economic Life," *Canadian Journal of Economics* (November 1980), 556–77.

12 Keith Banting, "The Welfare State as Statescraft: Territorial Politics and Canadian Social Policy," in *European Social Policy: Between Fragmentation and Integration*, eds. S. Liebfried and P. Pierson (Washington, D.C.: Brookings Institute, 1995), 269–300.

13 Heclo, "Towards a New Welfare State," 397.

14 Thomas J. Courchene, "Zero Means Almost Nothing: Towards a Preferable Inflation and Macroeconomic Policy," *Queen's Quarterly* 97 (Winter 1990), 543–61; Thomas J. Courchene, "International Dimensions of Macroeconomic Policies; Canada," in *A Handbook on Macroeconomic Policies in Open Economies*, eds. Michele Fratianni, Dominick Salvatore, and Jurgen von Hagen (forthcoming); Pierre Fortin, "The Great Canadian Slump," Presidential Address to the Canadian Economics Association, *Canadian Journal of Economics* (November 1996).

15 Fortin, *The Great Canadian Slump*.

16 Heclo, "Towards a New Welfare State," 400.

17 Banting, "Development of the Welfare State," 11.

18 Thomas J. Courchene, *Social Canada in the 1990s: Agenda For Reform* (Toronto: C.D. Howe Institute, 1987).

19 Thomas J. Courchene, "Revitalizing and Rebalancing Canadian Federalism: In Quest for a New National Policy," in *Quebec Canada: New Challenges and Opportunities*, ed. John Trent, Guy Lachapelle, and Robert Young (Ottawa: University of Ottawa Press, 1996).

20 Thomas J. Courchene, *Celebrating Flexibility: An Interpretive Essay on the Evolution of Canadian Federalism*, The 1995 Benefactors Lecture (Toronto: C.D. Howe Institute, 1995).

21 Courchene, *Social Canada in the Millennium*, Tables 38–41.

22 Kenneth J. Boessenkool, *The Illusion of Equality: Provincial Distribution of the Canada Health and Social Transfer* (Toronto: C.D. Howe Institute, 1996).

23 Thomas J. Courchene, *Redistributing Money and Power: A Guide to the Canada Health and Social Transfer* (Toronto: C.D. Howe Institute, 1995).

24 Thomas J. Courchene, "Chaste and Chastened: Canada's New Social Contract" (Paper prepared for the conference, "The Welfare State in Canada: Past, Present and Future," Mount Allison University, Centre for Canadian Studies, 1996).

25 Timothy C. Sargent, "An Index of Unemployment Insurance Disincentives," Working Paper 95–10 (Ottawa: Department of Finance, 1995).

26 Ministerial Council on Social Policy Reform and Renewal, *Report To Premiers*, mimeographed (1995).

27 Group of 22, *Making Canada Work Better*, mimeographed (1996).

28 André Burelle, "A Renewed Canada To Which Quebec Could Say 'Yes,'" *Canada Opinion* vol. 4, no. 1 (Ottawa: The Council for Canadian Unity, 1996).

29 Thomas J. Courchene, "ACCESS: *A* Convention on the Canadian *Economic* and *Social Systems*," mimeographed (1996).

PIERRE FORTIN

1 This essay overlaps in part with the author's 1996 Presidential Address to the Canadian Economics Association, published under the title "The Great Canadian Slump" in the November 1996 issue of *The Canadian Journal of Economics*, from which it is adapted, with permission.

2 The 2.8 percent estimate is the sum of the 1.6 percent annual growth rate of the working-age population observed in the 1990s, and a moderate assumption of 1.2 percent for the potential growth rate of output per capita (down from 1.9 percent in 1981–9).

3 Together with the strong immigration boom in British Columbia, this readily explains why the western provinces have done much better than the rest of the country since 1991.

4 The retort is sometimes that, while the two economies have had to face the same technological shocks, they have reacted very differently because employment adjustment costs (such as hiring and severance costs, union distortions, etc.) are higher, and real wages more rigid in Canada. But this matter of course assertion has been strongly questioned by recent comparative studies of labour market adjustment. They generally find that labour markets are just as dynamic in Canada as in the United States, and that adjustment costs and the degree of real wage flexibility are very similar in the two countries. John Baldwin, Timothy Dunne, and John Haltiwanger, "A Comparison of Job Creation and Job Destruction in Canada and the United States," Working Paper no. 4726 (Cambridge: National Bureau of Economic Research, 1994); David Card, Francis Kramarz, and Thomas Lemieux, "Changes in the Relative Structure of Wages and Employment: A Comparison of the United States, Canada, and France," Working Paper no. 355 (Princeton University: Industrial Relations Section, 1995); Robert Amano and Tiff Macklem, "Unemployment Persistence and Costly Adjustment of Labour: A Canada-US Comparison" (Paper presented at the Conference on the Canada-US Unemployment Rate Gap, Ottawa, February 1996); Pierre-Yves Crémieux and Marc Van Audenrode, "Is the US/Canada Unemployment Gap Truly Large? A labor flow analysis," in *The Flow Approach to Labor Market Analysis*, ed. R. Shettcat (London: Rutledge, 1996); Stephen R.G. Jones and W. Craig Riddell, "Gross Flows of Labour in Canada and the United States," Working paper (McMaster University and the University of British Columbia, January 1996).

5 Ron Parker, "Aspects of Economic Restructuring in Canada," *Bank of Canada Review* (Summer 1995).

6 This, incidentally, takes care of one of the most enduring popular fallacies of recent years: the "jobless recovery." The idea is that, owing to accelerating technological change and productivity, output has been able to recover from recession without generating new employment. The problem is not that we have had no job creation *despite* the recovery, but rather than we have had no job creation *because* there has been no recovery. Output per capita has actually fallen by 2 percent since 1990.

7 I measure the job offer rate as the ratio between Statistics Canada's help-wanted index and the aggregate labour force.

8 Indirect evidence that the slump has not resulted from accelerating technological change is also obtained from the fact that in the 1990s the employment performance of mature workers with a high school degree or less has *not* deteriorated faster, relative to the performance of those having more than high school education, than projected from past trend and cyclical behaviour.

9 The UI amendments of 1990 to 1994 have led to a 35 percent decline in the proportion of unemployed workers who receive regular UI benefits. The 1996 amendments will likely push that proportion down further. Between 1986 and 1994, real SA benefits increased by 25 percent in Ontario and 16 percent in British Columbia, and decreased by 30 percent in Alberta (National Council on Welfare, 1995). The increases were rolled back entirely in Ontario in October 1995, and partially in British Columbia in January 1996. Average real SA benefits per household have remained stable in Quebec since 1988, and have fallen moderately in other provinces.

10 Pierre Fortin, "The Future of Social Assistance in Canada" (The Timlin Lecture in Economics, University of Saskatchewan, Saskatoon, October 1995).

11 Olivier J. Blanchard and Peter Diamond, "The Beveridge Curve," *Brookings Papers on Economic Activity* 1 (1989): 1–67.

12 Recall that the employment ratio (e), the participation rate (a), and the unemployment rate (u) satisfy the identity $e = (1 - u)a$.

13 A decline of about 1 point in the NAIRU would be entirely consistent with the median estimate that can be extracted from the vast empirical literature on the labour market consequences of the UI reform of the early 1970s. See especially Miles Corak, "Unemployment Insurance, Work Disincentives and the Canadian Labour Market: An Overview," in *Unemployment Insurance: How to Make It Work*, ed. C. Green, F. Lazar, M. Corak, and D. Gross (Toronto: C.D. Howe Institute, 1994).

14 Pierre Fortin, Manfred W. Keil, and James V.S. Symons, "The Sources of Unemployment in Canada, 1967–1991: Evidence from a Panel of Regions and Demographic Groups," Working Paper no. 45 (Toronto: Program in Economic Growth and Policy, Canadian Institute for Advanced Research, 1995).

15 The ratio of supplementary income to wages and salaries rose from 10.6 to 14.8 percent. The labour-force-weighted average of provincial minimum

wages increased from $4.70 to $6.19, and the fixed-weight (1986 = 100) index of all-industry average hourly earnings from 113.6 to 138.4.

16 Bev Dahlby, "Taxation and Social Insurance," in *Taxation to 2000 and Beyond*, Canadian Tax Paper no. 93, ed. R.M. Bird and J.M. Mintz (Toronto: Canadian Tax Foundation, 1992); Daniel Hamermesh, *Labor Demand* (Princeton: Princeton University Press, 1993).

17 Stephen Nickell and Brian Bell, "The Collapse in Demand for the Unskilled and Unemployment across the OECD," *Oxford Review of Economic Policy* 11 (1995).

18 Parker, "Aspects of Economic Restructuring."

19 Ibid., Michael Baker, Dwayne Benjamin, and Shuchita Stranger, "The Highs and Lows of the Minimum Wage Effect: A Time Series-Cross Section Study of the Canadian Law," Working Paper no. 9501 (Toronto: Department of Economics, University of Toronto, 1995); Fortin, Keil, and Symons, "The Sources of Unemployment."

20 David Card and Alan B. Krueger, *Myth and Measurement: The New Economics of the Minimum Wage* (Princeton: Princeton University Press, 1995).

21 A welcome exception has been the strong recent growth in real spending on machinery and equipment (most notably, computers), which can be understood by the continued rapid fall in their real price.

22 The cyclically-adjusted operating balance as a percentage of GDP drawn in Figure 2 is equal to the global effective tax rate (ratio of actual tax revenue to actual GDP), minus cyclically-adjusted program spending (which excludes debt service costs) as a percentage of cyclically-adjusted GDP. The cyclical adjustment to program spending adjusts federal unemployment insurance and provincial social assistance payments to a constant 7.5 percent unemployment rate. Cyclically-adjusted GDP is obtained by interpolating real GDP log-linearly between 1981 and 1989 (two years of 7.5 percent unemployment), and assuming a 2.8 percent potential growth rate for real GDP from 1990 to 1995. These assumptions are retained for their simplicity, since a rising operating balance follows from any reasonable method of cyclical adjustment.

23 Pierre Fortin and Lars Osberg, *Unnecessary Debts* (Toronto: Lorimer, 1996).

24 John Murray and Rita Khemani, "International Interest Linkages and Monetary Policy: A Canadian Perspective," Technical Report no. 52 (Ottawa: Bank of Canada, 1989); David Laider and William Robson, *The Great Canadian Disinflation: The Economics and Politics of Monetary Policy in Canada* (Toronto: C.D. Howe Institute, 1993).

25 David Johnson and Darren McIlwraith, "Opinion Polls and Canadian Bond Yields During the 1995 Quebec Referendum Campaign," Working paper (Department of Economics, Wilfrid Laurier University, June 1996).

26 Pierre Duguay, "Empirical Evidence on the Strength of the Monetary Transmission Mechanism in Canada," *Journal of Monetary Economics* 33 (1994); Fortin, Keil, and Symons, "The Sources of Unemployment";

Christina Romer and David Romer, "What Ends Recessions?" in NBER
Macroeconomics Annual 1994, ed. S. Fischer and J. Rotemberg (Cam-
bridge: MIT Press, 1994); John B. Taylor, *Macroeconomic Policy in a World
Economy: From Econometric Design to Practical Operation* (New York:
Norton, 1993).

27 Frederic S. Mishkin, "Symposium on the Monetary Transmission Mechanism," *Journal of Economic Perspectives* 9 (1995).

28 Duguay, "Empirical Evidence," has estimated that a 1 percentage point increase in the Canadian real short-term interest rate eventually reduces real
GDP by about 1.5 percent, taking into account the impact of the associated
exchange rate appreciation on net foreign demand. The Romers, "What
Ends Recessions," have estimated a real GDP multiplier of the same magnitude as Duguay's for the United States. Fortin, Keil, and Symons, *The
Sources of Unemployment*, have found that an increase of 1 point in the interest rate eventually raises unemployment 0.6 point. Through Okun's Law,
this estimate is consistent with those of Duguay and the Romers.

29 Gordon Thiessen, "Uncertainty and the Transmission of Monetary Policy
in Canada," *Bank of Canada Review* (Summer 1995).

30 Tim Noël, "Bank of Canada Operations in Financial Markets," *Bank of
Canada Review* (Winter 1995–6).

31 Bank of Canada, "Targets for Reducing Inflation: Announcements and
Background Material," *Bank of Canada Review* (March 1991).

32 Bank of Canada, "Record of Press Releases," *Bank of Canada Review* (Winter 1993–4).

33 Jack Selody, "The Goal of Price Stability: A Review of the Issues," Technical Report no. 54 (Bank of Canada, 1990).

34 Bank of Canada, *Annual Report 1990* (Ottawa: 1991).

35 Milton Friedman, "The Role of Monetary Policy," *American Economic Review* 58 (1968).

36 Robert E. Lucas, "Some International Evidence on Output-Inflation
Tradeoffs," *American Economic Review* 63 (1973).

37 Stanley Fischer, "Modern Central Banking," in *The Future of Central Banking*, ed. F. Capie, C. Goodhart, S. Fischer, and N. Schadt (Cambridge, UK:
Cambridge University Press, 1994).

38 David Laidler and William Robson, "Don't Break the Bank! The Role of
Monetary Policy in Deficit Reduction" (C.D. Howe Institute Commentary
no. 66, February 1995); Guy Debelle, "The Ends of Three Small Inflations:
Australia, New Zealand, and Canada," *Canadian Public Policy* 22 (1996).

39 Guy Debelle and Stanley Fischer, "How Independent Should a Central
Bank Be?" in *Goals, Guidelines, and Constraints Facing Monetary Policymak-
ers*, ed. J.C. Fuhrer (Boston: Federal Reserve Bank of Boston, 1994).

40 Daniel Racette and Jacques Raynauld, "Canadian Monetary Policy 1989–
1993: What were the Bank of Canada's True Actions in the Determination

of Monetary Condition?" *Canadian Public Policy* 20 (1994); Kenneth Boessenkool, David Laidler, and William Robson, "Devils in the Details: Improving the Tactics of Recent Canadian Monetary Policy" (C.D. Howe Institute Commentary no. 79, April 1996); Peter Howitt, *Monetary Policy in Transition: A Study of Bank of Canada Policy, 1982–1985* (Toronto: C.D. Howe Institute, 1996); The more recent comments echo Howitt's earlier criticism of similar Bank behaviour in 1984. He was concerned that the Bank's smoothing and delaying tactics in exchange markets were, in fact, destabilizing because they were giving speculators one-way-bet opportunities. He also attacked the recurring fallacy that changing market expectations impose serious limitations on the Bank's ability to stimulate aggregate demand. The Bank's *willingness* to expand is, of course, determined by the degree of exchange rate flexibility it is ready to allow.

41 Bank of Canada, *Monetary Policy Report* (May 1995).

42 Pierre Fortin, "How 'Natural' is Canada's High Unemployment Rate?" *European Economic Review* 33 (1989); Barry Cozier and Gordon Wilkinson, "Some Evidence on Hysteresis and the Costs of Disinflation in Canada," Technical Report no. 55 (Ottawa: Bank of Canada, 1991).

43 Stephen R.G. Jones, *The Persistence of Unemployment: Hysteresis in Canadian Labour Markets* (Montreal and Kingston: McGill-Queen's University Press, 1995).

44 James Tobin, "Inflation and Unemployment," *American Economic Review* 62 (1972).

45 Pierre Fortin, "Tobin's Wage Floor Hypothesis: Evidence from Canadian Wage Settlements, and Implications for Inflation Policy" (Paper presented at the annual meeting of the Atlantic Canada Economics Association, Fredericton, October 1995); George A. Akerlof, William T. Dickens, and George L. Perry, "The Macroeconomics of Low Inflation," *Brookings Papers on Economic Activity* 1 (1996).

46 Akerlof, Dickens, and Perry, "Low Inflation."

47 Fischer, "Modern Central Banking."

48 House of Commons, *The Mandate and Governance of the Bank of Canada*, First Report of the Sub-Committee on the Bank of Canada, Standing Committee on Finance (Ottawa, 1992).

49 A very important further question for the future is whether Canada should peg its currency to the US dollar once the country has recovered from the current slump and has achieved much the same inflation rate as the United States.

RICHARD G. HARRIS

1 This section is derived from R.G. Harris, "Trade, Money, and Wealth in the Canadian Economy" (C.D. Howe Institute Benefactors Lecture, 1993).

2 R. Nelson and G. Wright, "The Rise and Fall of American Technological Leadership," *Journal of Economic Literature* (December 1992).

3 J.R. Baldwin and P. Gorecki, *The Role of Scale in Canada/US Productivity Differences in the Manufacturing Sector, 1970–9*, Research Studies of the Royal Commission on the Economic Union and Development Prospects for Canada, vol. 16 (Toronto: University of Toronto Press, 1986).

4 P. Wonnacott and R.J. Wonnacott, *Free Trade Between Canada and the United States: The Potential Economic Effects* (Cambridge: Harvard University Press, 1967).

5 The basic arguments on globalization and wages are discussed in R.G. Harris "Globalization, Trade and Income," *Canadian Journal of Economics* XXVI (1993).

6 That is, the stock of buildings, machinery, transportation and communications infrastructure which constitutes the productive capacity of the nation given the availability of other inputs.

7 The debate was ignited with the controversial paper of J.B. De Long and L.H. Summers, "Equipment Investment and Economic Growth," *Quarterly Journal of Economics* 106 (1991).

8 See for example R.J. Barre, "Economic Growth in a Cross Section of Countries," *Quarterly Journal of Economics* 106 (1991).

9 R. Lipsey and C. Bekar, "A Structuralist View of Technical Change and Economic Growth," Working Paper no. 45 (Toronto: Canadian Institute for Advanced Research, Program in Economic Growth and Policy, 1995).

10 D. Cox and R. Harris, *International Trade and the Service Sector in the Canadian Economy: An Input-Output Analysis* (Vancouver: Fraser Institute, 1991).

R. KENNETH CARTY

1 For the most sophisticated analyses to date of electoral flows in 1993 see Richard Johnston et al., "The 1993 Canadian General Election: Realignment, Dealignment, or Something Else?" (Paper presented to the 1996 annual meeting of the Canadian Political Science Association, St Catharines, Ontario). See particularly the estimations of vote exchanges reported in Tables 3–5.

2 Royal Commission on Electoral Reform and Party Financing, *Reforming Electoral Democracy* (Ottawa, 1991), 207.

3 The language of Canadian politics can be misleading here for the term "third party" has traditionally been applied to any number of parties seeking to challenge existing patterns of party competition. The most successful third party, the NDP, could not really be called one once (no longer new) it had become part of the institutionalized party system, even though it remained very much in third place behind the two old-line parties. To

add to the confusion, the term is now increasingly used to refer to nonpo-
litical party (interest) groups who seek to inject themselves into election
campaigns.

4 The Reform party's leader suspended several members of "his" caucus in
the spring of 1996 for comments they made about policy issues or other
party members. This is hardly what Reform voters might have expected
given the party's claims on behalf of a politics that would feature more
freedom and autonomy for elected representatives.

5 For evidence on the residential mobility rates in federal constituencies see
Munroe Eagles et al., *The Almanac of Canadian Politics*, 2nd ed. (Toronto:
Oxford University Press, 1995). There is a good deal of variation across
the country: in the 1986–91 census period it ranged from a high of 68.8%
in Vancouver Centre to a low of 18.7% in Bonavista-Trinity-Conception.

6 Modern democratic political parties were invented in the 1820s. In America, Andrew Jackson's supporters spawned a distinctive set of political
parties, disparate uneasy alliances that were almost perfectly designed to
reflect and represent the diversity of American society. Across the Atlantic, Ireland's Daniel O'Connell was building the prototypical, disciplined
mass membership party organization geared to capturing and controlling
European parliamentary institutions. Both those party types satisfied the
demands of their respective societies and governing institutions. Not surprisingly, they did not look much alike.

7 On the beginnings of federal-provincial party organizational separation
see J. Wearing, *The L-Shaped Party: The Liberal Party of Canada 1958–1980*
(Toronto: McGraw-Hill Ryerson, 1981), 108, 112.

8 See Johnston et al., "The 1993 Canadian General Election."

9 D.E. Blake, "Party Competition and Electoral Volatility: Canada in Comparative Perspective," in *Representation, Integration and Political Parties in
Canada*, ed. H. Bakvis (Toronto: Dundurn Press, 1991).

10 For an account of party membership patterns, and their cyclical and volatile character, see R.K. Carty, *Canadian Political Parties in the Constituencies*
(Toronto: Dundurn Press, 1991).

11 These estimates come from delegate surveys of the seven Liberal and
Conservative national leadership conventions from 1967 through 1993. I
thank George Perlin of Queen's University for making them available to
me.

12 D.E. Blake and R.K. Carty, "The BC Liberal Televote," a study available
on-line through the UBC data library.

13 This figure is taken from an unpublished study of candidate recruitment
in the 1993 general election by Lynda Erickson of Simon Fraser University.
I am grateful to her for providing access to the data.

14 There are accounts of the politics of previous Canadian party systems in
R.K. Carty, "On the Road Again: 'The Stalled Omnibus' Revisited," in

Canada's Century: Governance in a Maturing Society, eds. C.E.S. Franks et al. (Montreal: McGill-Queen's University Press, 1995). For more focused looks at the governance, organizational, and electoral faces of earlier Canadian party systems see the first three essays by David Smith, R.K. Carty, and Richard Johnston et al. respectively in part four, *Canadian Political Party Systems*, ed. R.K. Carty (Peterborough: Broadview Press, 1992), 531–623.

15 For an analysis of the impact of the growth as well as changes to the character and geographic distribution of the Canadian electorate see R.K. Carty, "The Electorate and the Evolution of Canadian Electoral Politics," *American Review of Canadian Studies* (Spring 1996).

16 See J.C. Courtney, "The Recognition of Canadian Political Parties in Parliament and in Law," *Canadian Journal of Political Science* 11, 1 (1978).

17 The Bloc Quebecois may stick to its separatist agenda, but that commitment must make it difficult to sustain enthusiasm for opposition politics in Ottawa, especially when partisan colleagues are busy running a government in Quebec City.

18 Royal Commission, *Reforming Electoral Democracy.* See especially the discussion in chapters 5, 6, and 7 of volume 1.

19 For an account of the Alberta Conservative leadership selection process see David K. Stewart, "Electing the Premier: An Examination of the 1992 Alberta Progressive Conservative Leadership Election" (Paper prepared for the 1994 Annual Meeting of the Canadian Political Science Association, Calgary, Alberta).

Contributors

KEN BATTLE is President of the Caledon Institute of Social Policy, a "think tank" based in Ottawa. Before founding Caledon in 1992, he was Director of the National Council of Welfare and has also worked at the Department of Manpower and Immigration, Secretary of State, and Queen's University. Educated at Queen's and Oxford, he has researched in many areas of social policy. He is a media commentator, conference speaker, lecturer, and adviser to government, serving on the Task Force on Social Security Reform in 1994 and as policy adviser on child benefits reform to the minister of Human Resources Development in 1996 and 1997.

MICHAEL BLISS is a Professor of History at the University of Toronto and a senior fellow of Massey College. He teaches a variety of undergraduate and graduate courses and is active in the History of Medicine Program. His ten books have received numerous honours. He also writes regular columns in Canadian periodicals, comments frequently about public affairs on national radio and television, and lectures on a wide variety of topics. He is a fellow of the Royal Society of Canada, which has awarded him its Tyrrell Medal "for outstanding work in the history of Canada." He is currently writing a biography of Sir William Osler.

R. KENNETH CARTY is Professor of Political Science and a senior fellow of Green College at the University of British Columbia where he also chairs the publications board of UBC Press. Educated at the University of New Brunswick, Oxford, and Queen's, his primary research and teaching have been concerned with the structure and organization of democratic competition. He is the author of books on party politics in Ireland, Canada, and British Columbia and has edited several volumes on various aspects of Canadian politics.

THOMAS J. COURCHENE is the Jarislowsky-Deutsch Professor of Economic and Financial Policy at Queen's University, Director of the John Deutsch Institute for the Study of Economic Policy, and a member of Queen's School of Policy Studies, of which he was the first Director. He previously taught economics at the University of Western Ontario and has been a visiting Professor at Ecole national d'administration publique in Montreal and at York University. He is a fellow of the Royal Society of Canada, a senior fellow of the C.D. Howe Institute, former chair of the Ontario Economic Council, a former member of the Economic Council of Canada, and a past president of the Canadian Economics Association. His books and articles on policy issues total some two hundred, and consultations also contribute to his influence on the consideration of many areas of public policy.

PIERRE FORTIN is a Professor of Economics at the Université du Québec à Montréal and a research associate with the Canadian Institute for Advanced Research. He is a past president of the Canadian Economics Association and a fellow of the Royal Society of Canada. In the last twenty years, he has authored some 110 scholarly publications in Canada and abroad, mostly in the areas of wage-price determination, unemployment, and fiscal and monetary policies. The Association des économistes québécois recently selected him as the most influential Quebec economist of the last decade. In addition to his university duties, he is active as an adviser to government, business, and community organizations.

RICHARD G. HARRIS is the BC Telephone Professor of Economics at Simon Fraser University and the Canadian Pacific fellow of the Canadian Institute for Advanced Research. Before 1990, he spent most of his professional career at Queen's University, with visiting appointments at Berkeley, MIT, and the University of New South Wales. His area of specialization is international economics. In addition to a number of technical articles, he has published policy-oriented books and articles on Canada-US free trade, international macroeconomics, economic growth, and Canadian public policy.

TOM KENT served in Ottawa as deputy minister of two departments and, as Policy Secretary to Prime Minister Pearson, was deeply involved in the social and economic programs and federal- provincial relations of the 1960s. He has also been president of two crown corporations, Chairman of the Royal Commission on Newspapers, Assistant Editor of *The Economist*, Editor of the *Winnipeg Free Press* and of *Policy Options*, and Dean of Administrative Studies at Dalhousie University. Author of four books and many papers on public policy, he is now a visiting fellow in the School of Policy Studies of Queen's University.

JAMES SCHLESINGER has had a close association with Canada, both in and out of government. He has served in the US government as Secretary of Defense and formed the US Department of Energy, then serving as its first Secretary. Most relevant for this essay, he earlier served as Deputy Director of the Bureau of Budget and as a professor of economics. He has, over the years, been a friend to Allan MacEachen and to Canada. All his degrees are from Harvard.